Women as Learners

Elisabeth Hayes
and Daniele D. Flannery

with Ann K. Brooks, Elizabeth J. Tisdell,
and Jane M. Hugo

Women as Learners

The Significance of Gender in Adult Learning

Jossey-Bass Publishers
San Francisco

Jossey-Bass books and products are available through most bookstores. To contact
Jossey-Bass directly, call (888) 378-2537, fax to (800) 605-2665, or visit our website at
www.josseybass.com.

Substantial discounts on bulk quantities of Jossey-Bass books are available to corpora-
tions, professional associations, and other organizations. For details and discount information, contact the special sales department at Jossey-Bass.

 Manufactured in the United States of America on Lyons Falls Turin Book.
This paper is acid-free and 100 percent totally chlorine-free.

Excerpts in Chapter Three from *Through the Flower* by Judy Chicago, Introduction by
Anaïs Nin, copyright © 1975 by Anaïs Nin. Used by permission of Viking Penguin, a
division of Penguin Putnam, Inc.

Excerpt in Chapter Six reprinted with permission from "The Transformation of Silence
into Language and Action" in *Sister Outsider: Essays and Speeches* by Audre Lorde. © 1984.
Published by The Crossing Press, Freedom, CA.

Library of Congress Cataloging-in-Publication Data

Hayes, Elisabeth.
     Women as learners: the significance of gender in adult learning /
by Elisabeth Hayes and Daniele D. Flannery; with chapters by
Ann K. Brooks, Jane Hugo, and Elizabeth Tisdell.—1st ed.
         p. cm.—(The Jossey-Bass higher and adult education series)
     Includes bibliographical references (p.) and index.
     ISBN 0-7879-0920-3 (alk. paper)
     1. Adult learning. 2. Women—Education. 3. Feminism and education. I. Flannery,
Daniele D., 1942– II. Title. III. Series.
LC5225.L42 H39 2000
374'.0082—dc21   99-042960

HB Printing   10 9 8 7 6 5 4 3 2   FIRST EDITION

The Jossey-Bass
Higher and Adult Education Series

Contents

Preface

This book is intended to address the prevailing lack of information and understanding about adult women's learning and education. The impetus for the book arose from our own concern, and from that of many other adult educators, that women's learning either is not addressed in most of the literature on adult learning and adult education or is treated superficially. Because a prevailing philosophical stance has assumed the universality of learning theories, learning settings, and learning participants, women's learning has been all but ignored. When it is mentioned, it is typically in a "postscript" to a general discussion of adult learning. Furthermore, adult women's learning is frequently not considered even in literature specifically about women and education in general. This literature tends to focus primarily on the learning of girls in schools and on that of young women who are students of traditional age in higher education.

A limited understanding of women's learning is also reflected in the practices of adult and continuing education. Changing social and economic factors have led to a tremendous growth in the number of women who are participating in formal and informal learning activities. Nevertheless, the typical scenario is either that little is actually done to meet their needs or that efforts to do so are based on outdated information and perspectives. Clearly, there is a demand for a comprehensive resource that can summarize current information and perspectives on women as learners and serve as a guide to practice.

Feminism is an area of scholarship with important implications for our understanding of women's learning. This book uses a feminist perspective as the organizing framework for the book's contents and as a standpoint from which to assess the current understanding of women's learning. Several key assumptions drawn from feminist scholarship underlie this perspective:

1. Women's learning must be understood and valued in its own right.

2. Women's learning must be understood within a broader social context that should encompass the social determinants of gender roles and norms.

3. The diversity of women's lives and learning should be recognized as much as the similarities.

4. Efforts are needed to overcome the limitations that continue to be placed on women's learning opportunities and outcomes.

Purposes of This Volume

In view of our key assumptions, it is our intention that this volume serve several purposes. The first of its purposes is to assemble, in one place, knowledge about women and their learning. The relevant information about adult women's learning that does exist is scattered across a wide variety of sources and professional literatures; for example, one book on women in higher education may include a single chapter on adult women as learners, whereas another volume in the field of social work may describe programs in special education for adult women. There are a growing number of journal articles, monographs, and research reports that offer new perspectives on women as adult learners, but few people may have the time or inclination to seek out these varied sources. Further, much of this material does not appear in mainstream journals devoted to adult and continuing education or in conference proceedings, and so even scholars in the area of adult education may not be able to find this work and incorporate its perspectives into their own scholarship.

A second purpose of this volume is to place women's learning experiences in the contexts where women live— namely, the prevailing interactive and dynamic social structures (economic, political, social, and cultural) and institutions that influence women's learning and their participation in educational activities. We consider women to be active agents who are both challenging and conforming to these social structures and institutions.

A third purpose is to promote an understanding of women's diversity. We attempt to identify the significance of such factors as race, class, and culture in shaping women's learning experiences. Nevertheless, our attainment of this purpose will depend on how explicitly such factors have been examined in the literature.

A fourth purpose of this volume is to make recommendations, on the basis of our critical appraisal of the existing literature, for future research and practice. We hope that these recommendations will promote an understanding of women's learning as an important area of study, spur the development of comfortable learning environments that excite and empower women, and inspire the development of strategies for changing the politics of making and exchanging knowledge so that women will have freedom of choice in learning and control over their learning.

Who Are We and What Are Our Beliefs?

Before continuing to introduce you to the book, we feel that it is important to introduce ourselves and to say a bit about three values: knowing, re-searching, and changing, which reveal how we view the world and how we view women's learning.

We believe that there are many kinds of knowing and that each is important for learning. Among these kinds of knowing we believe are artistic, religious, and scientific knowing. We revere indigenous knowledge, the knowledge people and cultures take from their life experiences. We try to respect and understand the cultural knowledge of different peoples and understand the ways in which learning is viewed by cultures different from our own. We respect both oral traditions of passing on knowledge and traditions that emphasize the written word. As academics, we come from a tradition that places a hierarchy of values on different kinds of knowledge. We acknowledge that we are steeped in a world where scientific knowledge is most valued, but we are trying to remove that hierarchy from our own way of thinking. Our efforts have been inspired and supported by others, such as Marlo Morgan's (1994) work on aboriginal learning, Cherrie Moraga and Gloria Anzaldúa's (1983) collection of feminist writings by women of Color, Nancy Goldberger's (1996) explorations of cultural diversity in ways of knowing, and Carol Witherell and Nel Noddings's (1991) stories of how women's lives have given shape to their classroom teaching and research.

Our changing notions of research parallel our attempts to value different knowledges. For us, research is more appropriately thought of as "re-searching"; it continually attends to and notices life, a perspective in which seeing things in different ways through different lenses is encouraged. We believe that all of us, not just formally designated researchers, engage in re-searching. We cannot assign the making of meaning or the building of theory to any one institution or group. For example, the birth of a child is captured in a mother's words as they are spoken or written in a journal, in the needlework and weavings of Judy Chicago's Childbirth Quilt Project (1982–1985), and by academics who record parents' responses immediately after the birth of their child. Each medium of making meaning gives us insights into the phenomenon of birth. For us this is re-searching in life. Such re-search includes the contributions of women's insights, conversations with their neighbors, stories, autobiographies, diaries, and the like. bell hooks (1994) suggests that all people are re-searchers with different lenses and issues who have the power to speak, to find reciprocity in exchange, and thus to practice freedom.

We accept life as a work in progress where roles and the meanings of roles change over time, where we are continually developing, where learning, unlearning, and relearning are constantly going on. We recognize that all learning is interwoven with our lives. As Carolyn Heilbrun in *Writing a Woman's Life* (1989) says, "We live our lives through texts. They may be read, chanted, or experienced electronically or come to us like the murmurings of our mothers, telling us what conventions demand. Whatever their form or medium, these stories have formed us all; they are what we must use to make new fictions, new narratives" (p. 128).

A Different Kind of Book

This book is an anomaly. It has a clear unity of themes drawn from the extensive literature searches that we have conducted over two years. However, besides the two of us, three other authors have contributed chapters to the book. We are all White middle-class women with high levels of academic training and experience. We share similar feminist perspectives, informed in particular by poststructural feminist theories. Thus the perspectives reflected in the book are influenced by our backgrounds and our feminism. We allow for our individual voices and experiences to emerge in different places through the use of *I* and explicit references to our own personal histories.

We believe that in this book we offer valuable perspectives on women's learning, ones that have been neglected in previous literature on adult learning and education. We acknowledge wholeheartedly that our perspectives are not the only way to view women's learning. We cannot claim to speak for all women. To some extent, we have tried to let women speak for themselves by incorporating narratives from qualitative studies of women's lives. Yet even such narratives have been selected and interpreted through the lens of our own perspectives. Our purpose in this book was not to juxtapose radically different viewpoints on women's learning or feminist theories, although they certainly can and do exist. Instead we aspire to be clear about the point of view that we bring to this project, recognizing that any point of view is always partial and incomplete.

One obvious way that our own perspectives affected the book was the inclusion and exclusion of topics. While our identification of the broader themes and more specific information was largely based on the most frequently discussed topics in the literature, there were certainly biases in what we chose to select. For example, we gave limited attention to research on sex differences in cognitive processing, such as current brain research. This decision was partly based on our own preferences for more sociologically oriented perspectives on gender and gender differences, as well as the currently limited practical application of findings from such research. There is other source material that might have been incorporated as well, particularly in terms of the nonacademic sources we have included. We chose what "spoke" to us most vividly and thus are biased by our own values and experiences. Others could make different meaning of the same source material.

We also recognize how many areas we could not deal with in a way we would have liked. For example, diversity among women as it relates to learning is not often addressed fully in our discussion. Our ability to address such diversity was limited by the conceptual tools available to us in the literature.* Another example is our decision to exclude literature about women's learning in other societies and nations, which was important from a more practical stance— to keep the issues and topics we dealt with to a size appropriate for one book. However, this literature undoubtedly has important implications for broadening and enhancing our understanding of women's learning in different social contexts, and in particular for

---

* We do wish to note that such tools are not completely lacking. The work of a few authors, such as Patricia Hill Collins (1991), has greatly enriched our thinking about diversity among women.

extending our knowledge of diversity among women. Chapter Nine provides a more detailed discussion of these limitations and suggestions for future research.

Overview of the Chapters

This book consists of nine chapters, with Chapter One setting the scene, Chapters Two through Six explicating the major themes associated with women's learning that we found in the literature, Chapter Seven discussing feminist pedagogies, Chapter Eight considering the implications of the previous chapters for educational practice, and Chapter Nine addressing the implications for future research and scholarship on women's learning. The book concludes with a brief "postscript" intended to speak to all women about the importance of knowing and believing in their own learning as women.

In Chapter Two, Social Contexts, Elisabeth (Betty) Hayes locates women's learning in a variety of academic and nonacademic settings. These include formal educational institutions, the workplace, the home, the family, and the community. The author explores how these contexts serve as locations for learning about gender-related identities and social roles, and she describes how the existing literature portrays women as both resisting and conforming to these expectations. The chapter concludes with a consideration of how women negotiate the often conflicting demands of learning across these institutional, family, and community contexts.

In Chapter Three, Identity and Self-Esteem, Daniele Flannery examines the interrelationships of women's identity, self-esteem, and learning. Women's identity formation is described from three different perspectives: the achievement of increased autonomy, the centrality of relationships, and the influence of social and historical factors. The author briefly describes how girls learn gender roles, and she discusses the significance of those roles for women's learning in adulthood. Finally, she examines how women's learning experiences in adulthood can shape their self-esteem and identity.

In Chapter Four, Voice, Betty Hayes develops voice as a common and powerful metaphor in the literature on women's learning. The author describes three metaphorical meanings of voice—as talk, identity, and power—and discusses their implications for our understanding of women's learning.

In Chapter Five, Connection, Daniele Flannery examines the issues of connectedness, connected knowing, and connected learning, issues that appear in so much of the literature. The author, noting the frequent use of the concept of connection in terms of women's learning, as well as the variance in this concept's meaning, organizes these different meanings under the categories of connection with the self (cognitive processing linked to experience, subjective knowing, and intuition) and connection with others (affiliation or bonding, connected knowing, and related concepts).

In Chapter Six, Transformation, Annie Brooks discusses transformative learning in terms of its specific nature and significance for women. She describes how transformative learning can be understood as a process of rewriting identity, whereby women learn, with groups of other women, to give voice to and transform their own life stories, a process that can contribute to social change.

In Chapter Seven, Feminist Pedagogies, Elizabeth (Libby) Tisdell discusses teaching approaches that are intended specifically to address the learning needs of women. She lays out three major models of feminist pedagogy—the psychological, structural, and poststructural models—and identifies the assumptions about women's characteristics and needs that underlie these models. She then shows what each model looks like in learning settings and discusses the strengths and weaknesses of the practices associated with each model.

In Chapter Eight, Perspectives on Practice, Jane Hugo, a practitioner of adult education, explores the implications of knowledge about women's learning for adult education practice in all kinds of settings. These include literacy programs, the workplace, formal institutions of education, churches, and counseling groups.

In Chapter Nine, Creating Knowledge About Women's Learning, Betty Hayes discusses the kinds of knowledge and approaches to building knowledge that are needed in furthering our understanding of women's learning.

In the postscript, Re-searching for Women's Learning, Daniele Flannery asks what the material in the preceding chapters means for women themselves as learners and is intended to guide women in celebrating their own learning, reflecting on their own personal learning stories, and learning from the learning stories of other women.

We ask you now to begin the journey of *Women as Learners*. Take your life experiences and join them with those of all the women in this book who have helped us to begin to understand women's learning.

December 1999   Elisabeth Hayes
                                                  Daniele D. Flannery

The Authors

Elisabeth Hayes is professor of curriculum and instruction and a faculty member in the Graduate Program in Continuing and Vocational Education at the University of Wisconsin–Madison. She received her Ph.D. degree in adult education from Rutgers University in 1987. She has been a consultant to local, state, and national organizations and government agencies on projects associated with adult education.

Hayes's research interests have focused on women's learning, feminist issues in adult education, and teaching/learning issues in adult literacy education. A current research project is a study of what and how low-income women learn about work in the intersecting contexts of family, home, workplace, and school.

Hayes is the author of *Effective Teaching Styles* and editor of *Confronting Racism and Sexism* (with Scipio Colin) and *Handbook 2000: Adult and Continuing Education* (with Arthur Wilson), a compendium of adult education scholarship and practice sponsored every decade by the American Association of Adult and Continuing Education. She also serves on the editorial review boards of *Adult Education Quarterly* and *Adult Basic Education*. She is a 1990 recipient of the Teachers of English as a Second Language Association's Distinguished Research Award and of the 1995 Leadership in Adult Education award from the Wisconsin Association for Adult and Continuing Education.

Daniele D. Flannery is assistant professor of adult education and faculty member in the Graduate Program in Adult Education at The Pennsylvania State University, Harrisburg. She also teaches in the Women's Studies Program. Her consulting and service activities focus primarily on issues concerning the education of women and girls and the development and assessment of learning in diverse settings.

Flannery's research interests are in the area of adult learning, particularly cognition, the sociology of learning, and postmodern critique of adult learning theory. Her recent work includes articles and chapters focusing on gender, race, and class in adult learning. She is editor of *Applying Cognitive Learning Theory to Adult Learning* and serves on the editorial boards of the *Adult Education Quarterly*, the *Canadian Journal for the Study of Adult Education*, and the *Pennsylvania Journal of Adult, Continuing and Community Education*.

Ann K. Brooks is associate professor of adult education and codirector of the Human Resource Development Leadership Program at the University of Texas at Austin. She has also taught at the School for International Training, at Xi'an Foreign Languages Institute in the People's Republic of China, and at the Language Institute of Japan.

She earned her B.A. degree in English at the University of Nebraska–Lincoln in 1973, her Master of Arts in Teaching (M.A.T.) degree in Teaching English as a Second Language from the School for International Training, and her Ph.D. degree in adult and higher education from Teachers College of Columbia University in 1989.

Brooks's research interests have focused on transformative learning, team learning, and organizational learning. Her current research is on the development of bicultural and multicultural women and on women's sexual development across the life span.

Brooks is coauthor (with Judith Ottoson) of the *Management Development Bibliography*, sponsored by the American Society for Training and Development, and is coeditor (with Karen Watkins) of *The Emerging Power of Action Learning Technology*. She serves as associate editor of the *International Journal of Qualitative Research in*

Education, is qualitative editor for the *Human Resource Development Quarterly*, and is a review editor for the *Adult Education Quarterly*. She is a 1990 recipient of the Research of the Year Award from the International Society for Performance and Instruction and Arthur Anderson for her work on organizational learning and has been honored for her research on team learning by the National University Continuing Education Association.

Jane M. Hugo is employed by Laubach Literacy in Syracuse, New York, as a member of its national field service staff. She is also an adjunct instructor in adult education at Elmira College. She earned her Ph.D. degree (1996) in adult education at Syracuse University. Since 1979 she has been certified as a teacher of English as a second language. Hugo's research interests are in the education of women, educational access in general, teaching strategies, the design of effective learning opportunities, staff development, education as a tool for community change, and intersections among race, class, and gender in the lives of middle-class women seeking to create and maintain their own learning communities. She has published articles on the history of adult education and the value of feminist theory to adult education.

Elizabeth J. Tisdell is an associate professor in the Department of Adult and Continuing Education at National–Louis University, in Chicago. She completed her Ed.D. in adult education (1992) at the University of Georgia with an emphasis in women's studies and multicultural adult education. Her research interests are in diversity and equity issues, and in the connection between spirituality and social justice among women adult educators. She is the author of numerous publications on feminist pedagogy and adult education, including *Creating Inclusive Adult Learning Environments: Insights from Multicultural and Feminist Pedagogy*.

Women's Learning: A Kaleidoscope

Daniele D. Flannery, Elisabeth Hayes

Women's learning, and our search to begin to understand it, are like kaleidoscopes: an endless variety of patterns.

This book had its origins in our personal experiences as learners as well as in our professional interests as adult educators. Perhaps one of the earliest experiences that drew us into the study of women's learning was our first encounter with *Women's Ways of Knowing* by Mary Belenky, Blythe Clinchy, Nancy Goldberger, and Jill Tarule (1986). We both read the book when it was first published, more than a decade ago, and we each found it both moving and intellectually exciting, telling stories of women's learning in a way both familiar and new to us. Many of our students, friends, and other women still identify with *Women's Ways of Knowing*. Some of them say, "This book is talking about me," "This is how I know," or "I can't believe there is finally someplace where my story is told." Others, who question the portrayal of women's learning in the book, still find the book powerful simply because the authors give central importance to women's learning in particular.

In our professional lives, as professors of adult education, we each began some years ago to focus much of our research and reflection on women. We found it surprising and troubling that so few scholars in our field made women's learning a central focus (recently this has begun to change somewhat as more new scholars enter the field who have embraced feminist perspectives). In higher education, the ideas from *Women's Ways of Knowing* created considerable discussion among educators and, along with other feminist writings, formed the basis for women-friendly instructional approaches and even curricular reform in some institutions (Goldberger, Tarule, Clinchy, and Belenky, 1996). However, most of this work has taken place in the context of formal postsecondary education, which represents only a small aspect of adult education. Adult education as a field of scholarship and practice is concerned with the learning and education of adults in multiple settings, such as adult literacy education, vocational education, continuing education for professionals, training in business and industry, religious education, and labor education. Our field is also concerned with how adults learn in settings not specifically designated for education, such as in the home and in community groups. We found that much of the mainstream literature on adult education in these contexts continued to offer limited attention to women's learning.

To compensate for this lack, we pulled relevant literature from other sources for our own teaching and scholarship. For example, from education scholarship we used literature on the learning and education of girls and adolescent young women. In this relatively random and haphazard way, we gained some valuable insights but were left with quite a few unanswered questions; certainly, we gleaned only fragments of knowledge, some bright pieces for our kaleidoscope, but not enough to create meaningful patterns. Finally, about five years ago, we decided to work together in an effort to locate, synthesize, and critique literature on women as learners from a wide variety of source material. We hoped to make existing scholarship more accessible to our students, to other adult educators, and to anyone else who might have an interest in the learning of adult women. This book represents the results of that effort.

The rest of this chapter provides a foundation for the book. We provide a rationale for the particular focus on women's learning and address the question "What about men?" We explain our basic assumptions about women and learning and describe how these assumptions relate to our personal histories, as well as how these assumptions reflect particular feminist perspectives. We describe the process we used to gather information for the book, as well as issues that arose in this process. We conclude by acknowledging both what we have been able to accomplish and what remains to be done.

Why Women's Learning?

Changing social norms and roles for women, combined with other social and economic factors, have led to a tremendous growth in the number of adult women who are participating in formal educational programs and informal learning activities. Over the last decade, it has become increasingly important to educators in almost all adult and continuing education settings to improve learning opportunities for women, and yet actual practice in adult and continuing education shows a limited understanding of women's learning, or it is based on outdated information and perspectives. For example, it is common to find women described simplistically as "collaborative" learners, a characterization that seems to reinforce dominant stereotypes about women's orientation toward others rather than providing more nuanced insights that give attention to diversity among women and to the particular kinds of relationships that might be beneficial.

More specifically, the significance of gender has been given little attention in adult learning theory, and yet women and men are products of social and cultural beliefs about what it means to be a gendered being. As authors, we share the perspective that "gender is not a natural fact, rooted in anatomical sex differences" (Baber and Allen, 1992, p. 10), nor does gender represent the opposition of male to female (Baber and Allen, 1992; Flax, 1987). Judith Solsken (1993, p. 123) writes, "The analysis of how gender (or any other social category) figures in learning does not depend upon identifying consistent patterns of differences between groups of males and females but rather upon tracing the patterns in [individuals'] learning biographies back to sources in the system of gender relations." We view gender as a type of social relation that is constantly changing, created and recreated in daily interactions as well as on a broader scale through such institutions as school, work, and the family. As gendered persons, we learn who we are as girls and women; we learn how to act, how to interact with others, how we are valued because of our gender, and what place and power we have as women in various groups and societies.

Sandra Harding (1996) writes about the effects that gender, as a system of social relationships, has on knowledge and learning. She describes the existence, within the broader cultures of society, of "gender cultures," such as the "masculine" cultures of the military or sports and the "feminine" cultures of the fashion world or elementary schools. Women and men can be found in both cultures, but these cultures shape women's and men's experiences in different ways, giving them the opportunity to acquire different sorts of knowledge and abilities. As stereotypical examples, Harding notes that women may have more opportunities to interact with babies, whereas men have more opportunities to interact with car motors; and, moreover, the system of gender relations can give women and men different interests and concerns even when they are in similar situations, and so the knowledge they have about similar situations may be different. To use another stereotypical example, when a woman who has primary responsibility for childrearing is seeking a job, she may gather detailed information about potential employers' policies with respect to maternity leave and provision of childcare; by contrast, a man who has primary responsibility for financial support of his wife and his family may seek more knowledge about employers' healthcare plans and life insurance policies. The system of gender relations may also lead women and men to develop different ways of creating and sharing knowledge, and Harding provides examples of how women scientists seem to use skills, resources, and forms of interaction that are different from those used by men.

These gendered knowledge systems, like gender relations, may differ by society, culture, ethnic group, locality, and so on, and so may produce different knowledge systems within the cohort of all women as well as between women and men. For example, women of Color's knowledge about racism will be different from that of White women. One of the coauthors (Elisabeth Hayes) became quite aware of this kind of difference after shopping in a women's clothing store with a Black woman friend: her friend was ignored, whereas the coauthor was repeatedly approached by saleswomen offering assistance. Her friend was quite familiar with this type of racism, but the experience of observing it gave the coauthor a completely new insight.

Inattention to gender is linked to a broader philosophical stance in adult learning theory that assumes the universal relevance and applicability of dominant learning theories to all adult learning settings and participants in adult education. Although diversity among learners (including differences between women and men) has often been acknowledged, it is frequently characterized in terms of learning styles, personal experience or background, and self-concept or is otherwise put in very individualistic, psychologized terms. Until quite recently, the fundamental assumptions on which theories of learning and teaching have been based remained largely unquestioned. Such theories have significant biases toward certain values and cultural norms, which are often inconsistent with the experiences of women and many men alike. For example, a dominant theory of self-directed learning posits that the "development of self-directed individuals," that is, "people who exhibit the qualities of moral, emotional and intellectual autonomy," is the "long term goal of most, if not all, education endeavours" (Candy, 1991, p. 19). However, as Nell Keddie (1980, p. 54) has argued, "the notion of individuality as a desirable personality goal is not universal, but is culturally specific and tends to be found in those cultures (such as ours) where high status is obtained by competitive individual achievement." Self-direction and autonomy as learning goals are "elitist by nature" (Cunningham, 1988, p. 133) and reinforce a Western, middle-class, White masculinist value system.

In fact, self-direction is neither valued nor practiced even by all people in our own society (Flannery, 1994, 1995). Generalizations about groups must be interpreted with caution, to avoid stereotyping, but the example of culture is nevertheless instructive. In Navajo culture, commitment to family can be considered more important than individual achievement. This kind of commitment is particularly important for Navajo women because traditional Navajo culture is matriarchical, and women play a particularly key role in ensuring the continuity and strength of families. These values lead some Navajo young women to leave school because the orientation of the dominant educational programs toward individual success is at odds with these young women's own orientation toward the future and an emphasis on contributing to the common good of their kin (Deyhle and Margonis, 1995). It is important to acknowledge not only that such differences do exist but also that these values are not inferior to the values of the dominant culture, as reflected in theories and assumptions about adult learning.

Our commitment to write a book specifically about women as learners is a commitment to political and social justice. As Harding (1996, p. 437) and many others have stressed, "gender relations are always power relations." Women make up more than half the population of the world, more than half the learners in formal and informal learning institutions and settings. Women, women's thoughts, women's writings, and research specifically about women's lives and learning have been absent, subsumed, ignored, and misrepresented. We work to include, distinguish, attend to, and more accurately represent women's lives and women's learning. This goal includes the goal of acknowledging the contributions of other women scholars to our own work. In each chapter of this book, we introduce authors of different sources by their first and last names, in an effort to make more visible the role of women as producers of knowledge. We support the assertion of other scholars that "feminist scholarship is for women, not about women" (Baber and Allen, 1992, p. 18). Scholarship for women is not simply an issue of pursuing scientific "truths"; it is a question of challenging the inequitable relationships of power and authority that continue to pervade educational scholarship and practice.

We would be remiss if we didn't acknowledge our own personal interest in seeking greater understanding of women as learners. We each wanted to look for our own learning stories and those of our relatives and friends, sisters and mothers, grandmothers and nieces. Where were they? Could we find them reflected in the literature we might be able to identify? Where is Aunt Margaret's learning story of struggling to manage with a husband who drank too much, and of coping with the death of a teenaged son? Where is her story of learning to live with the frailties of age and continuing to be a Scrabble champion and a volunteer at the local historical society, of returning to swimming at the age of seventy-eight, and finally of learning how to adapt, as an intellectually bright woman, to an acute-care nursing home where most of the people around her are no longer intellectually flexible? Where is the story of Miz Johnson, who taught herself to read by using soup cans, and who, as the wife of a minister, learned to preach from the pulpit, be the "other mother" for a host of children, organize church affairs, and manage a church congregation, and who ultimately, at the age of sixty-five, enrolled in an adult education program to earn her high school diploma? We asked ourselves whether we could discover ways of better understanding and celebrating their experiences while at the same time gaining more insight, perhaps, into ourselves, beyond the often limiting images from dominant adult education literature, such as the images of so-called reentry women—"reentering" from where? from someplace beyond the known world?—and the images of barriers to women's participation: in other words, beyond perspectives that, in general, show women as deficient, marginalized, or simply invisible (Hayes and Smith, 1994).

What About Men?

When we tell people we are writing a book on adult women's learning, some ask, "Is it true that men and women learn differently?" We reiterate as clearly as possible that our purpose in writing this book is to center our inquiry on women, to fill a void where data and synthesis are lacking. We do not imply comparison and contrast by what we write; when we describe women's learning, readers should not assume that men's learning is necessarily different or characterized by the opposite of what we say applies to women. One problem with this orientation toward difference, all too often, is an assumption embedded in such comparisons: that one way of learning is better than another. We do believe that women can be different from men. Our previous discussion of gender relations suggests that women and men are quite likely to have different opportunities for learning, different learning experiences, and different approaches to learning. Nevertheless, such differences do not mean that women's learning is inferior to men's learning, nor does it mean that women's learning is superior to men's.

We also do not believe in making generalizations about all women or all men. Understanding the significance of gender in relation to learning is more complex than saying, "Women are like this, and men are like that." Such generalizations may represent the preferences and values of a particular group while marginalizing and making invisible all people (women and men) who do not fit the generic description. Assumptions of universality box all men into stereotypes as well. For us, there is a kaleidoscope of ways of learning, which overlap at times but are unique because people are of different races and genders and because people's histories, cultures, and life circumstances also differ. We place value on appreciating the nuances of learning by making diversity more visible. We believe that an understanding of women's learning, with particular attention to how, more recently, feminists have struggled with issues of diversity, will provide new ways of thinking about the learning of both women and men. In this way, we hope that both women and men will benefit from our discussion. Furthermore, we believe that our long-term goal of contributing to positive social change for women will improve the lives of men as well.

Multiple Feminisms and Women's Learning

We are feminists, and our feminist perspective will be used throughout the book as a lens through which we view women's learning. Feminism can mean many things to many people. For some, the mere hearing of the term creates a negative reaction, prompting images of hostile, militant women burning bras and rejecting all men as oppressors. For others, the term *feminist* means nothing. For yet others, feminism is sweet music to the ears—not just a comfort but also a strong identifying image of beliefs and values and commitment. Our purpose here is not to proselytize but rather to explain concepts so that, first, our readers can understand what we are saying and the context for our own perspective and, second, so that we can be clear about how and why we analyzed and selected the material for this book. For now, we want to note the following aspects of feminism that have been important to us in our lives and in writing this book.

As feminists we make women the focal point of our discussion, in order to understand and value women's learning in its own right rather than in relationship to men's learning. We recognize that to be women is to be gendered, that is, to be products of social and cultural beliefs and practices that surround our daily lives. Therefore, we place gender at the center of our analysis, choosing to understand women's learning within a broader social context, which includes attention to the social determinants of gender roles and norms.

We believe in the need to acknowledge the diversity of women's lives and learning—to recognize the multiple realities of women's learning across race, culture, and class, as well as the similarities that exist. We acknowledge that racial and economic oppression may have greater impacts than gender oppression, but we also believe that they are not separate from gender oppression.

We have social and political goals for our work. We assume that many women lack voice, visibility, and power. We seek to identify and challenge the limitations constantly placed on women's learning, learning opportunities, and learning outcomes.

We have, as women, some historical experiences in common, but our individual experiences as females are not identical to those of any other women. We acknowledge the differences that accompany differences in race, class, ethnic group, religion, nationality, culture, age-graded expectations, and combinations of these and other circumstances. We try, with and in spite of our backgrounds, to portray women's learning with all the similarities and diversity that exist.

In addition to identifying the broad feminist principles that guide our own work, we must locate these beliefs more specifically within the current range of feminist theoretical perspectives. It is beyond the scope of this chapter to discuss feminist theories in detail, but we identify here some key ideas associated with different feminisms. We have found the three broad frameworks described by the feminist adult educator Elizabeth J. (Libby) Tisdell (1995), author of Chapter Seven of this volume, to be useful as a starting point for representing similarities and differences among feminist theories (she elaborates on these frameworks in her chapter, with respect to feminist pedagogies). Like any other approach to categorization, this representation imposes somewhat artificially neat and static distinctions among feminisms that in reality are interrelated and continually evolving. Nevertheless, these three frameworks provide a means of understanding the different perspectives that inform the literature on which we drew for our review, and they further clarify our own beliefs and viewpoints.

Psychological Feminist Theories

Feminist scholars who draw on this type of feminist perspective tend to emphasize an understanding of the differences between women and men, using such constructs as gender-role socialization. *Women's*

Ways of Knowing (Belenky, Clinchy, Goldberger, and Tarule, 1986) is a prominent example of research associated with this framework. The goal of that work was to develop a theory based on women's experience and, in doing so, to establish women's ways of knowing as legitimate and as valuable as those of men. These authors explain women's orientation to knowing primarily in terms of relationships with male authority figures and patterns of family interaction in childhood. The authors ultimately use their findings to argue for an approach to education that they call "connected teaching," which they claim would benefit men as well. Underlying this kind of feminist perspective is a liberal political perspective that seeks to achieve equality for women and men within the existing social order. In terms of education, the emphasis is more on achieving equal educational opportunities for women than on developing a critique of the educational and social structures that oppress women.

What do feminist theories that focus on the individual contribute to our understanding of women's learning? Perhaps their most important contribution is that they challenge the invisibility and marginalization of women's experience in the knowledge-building process. They show us how it is possible to look at women's learning from a new perspective, one that treats women's ways of being and knowing as valuable in their own right.

This framework also has its limitations. In earlier work, women were viewed as a generic and unitary category; and, typically, the experience of White middle-class women became the basis for generalizations about women. Race- and class-based differences among women have been recognized more recently by theorists working within this framework, but these differences usually are not analyzed in any depth. Studies associated with this framework have also been criticized for not discussing women's behavior and experiences with respect to structural causes of women's oppression. For example, Belenky, Clinchy, Goldberger, and Tarule (1986) might also have explained women's orientation toward what they call "connected learning" in terms of women's subordinate position in society, which requires them to be dependent on meeting the needs of others, rather than explaining it as a reflection of women's "natural" preferences. Further, there is the danger that the liberal goal of achieving equity for women within existing arrangements can still foster the perception that women are individually deficient and that they need remedial support in order to become, ultimately, more like men. Theory informed by this framework seeks to change women's status in society, but it does not question the nature of the social order.

Structural Feminist Theories

Feminist theorists working within this framework have focused on understanding the social structures that contribute to women's oppression. They have attempted to explain how patriarchy (which leads to gender-based oppression) and capitalism (which leads to class-based oppression) affect women's status and experiences. More recently, other forms of oppression (such as racial oppression) have become objects of concern within this framework. A key issue, frequently unresolved, is the question of how to understand the relationships among different forms of structural oppression. The goal of work undertaken within this framework tends to be change in social structures rather than individual change. On a more individual or interpersonal level, this framework draws our attention to the reproduction of power relationships in settings like the classroom, the family, and the workplace.

An example of a study related to women's learning within this framework is Wendy Luttrell's (1989) analysis of the influence of gender, race, and class on the way in which a group of working-class women defined and claimed knowledge. Luttrell uses an analysis of class differences to explain the women's distinction between "common sense" or "real intelligence," which affirms the value of working-class abilities, and the "schoolwise intelligence" that is associated with schooling and that may often be in conflict with working-class culture. Luttrell uses structural gender oppression to explain the women's conceptions of their knowledge as affective and intuitive rather than cognitive and learned—a reflection of society's devaluation of women's intellectual abilities. Finally, she points out how race made a difference in the women's views of their knowledge: Black women tended to place more value on the intelligence that they themselves demonstrated in their ability to provide for their families and deal with racism, whereas White women tended to place value primarily on the intelligence demonstrated by men in their ability to perform skilled manual labor (but women's labor in the home was not equated with "real intelligence").

The structural feminist framework helps us locate women's learning in light of social structures. It draws our attention to the concept of power as central to an understanding of women's learning experiences. This framework also helps us begin to understand how groups of women may have different experiences, given the additional effects of class- and race-based oppression. Through social explanations for gender-related differences, it challenges assumptions about women's natural or essential attributes.

Typically, however, this framework offers only limited explanations of how multiple oppressions intersect and are experienced differently in the lives of individual women. In addition, there is a danger within this framework of viewing women as passive victims of oppressive social forces.

Poststructural Feminist Theories

Theorists working within this framework attempt to recognize and understand how each of us is at once oppressed and privileged and how this experience continually changes according to the contexts in which we find ourselves. Rather than focusing on the effects of one or two forms of oppression, poststructural feminist theories place emphasis on understanding the intersections of multiple systems of oppression and privilege. There is also attention to individual resistance and agency in the face of oppressive social forces; there is more stress on understanding how individual women respond to their unique and particular experiences of oppression than on developing theories about how broad types of oppression affect

groups of women. Attention to language as a means of constructing reality is another hallmark of poststructuralist feminist theories. (Libby Tisdell includes in this framework those feminist theories
that are influenced by postmodern thought. There are certain differences in the origins and assumptions of poststructuralism and
postmodernism, but we will follow her lead by combining them in
this way.)

An example of work within this framework is that of Elizabeth
Debold, Deborah Tolman, and Lyn Mikel Brown (1996). These authors
provide a new reading of *Women's Ways of Knowing* (Belenky, Clinchy,
Goldberger, and Tarule, 1986), in which they highlight how individual women have varied experiences of voice and self that are not
fixed and that do not develop along a predictable continuum. They
use their research on adolescent girls of different class and cultural
backgrounds to illustrate how these young women both struggled
against and learned to conform to oppressive cultural notions of
women's idealized behavior. The diversity of these girls' experience
is noted, for example, in the working-class girls' more open hostil-
ity and resistance to the authority of their middle-class female
teachers. Using several case studies, the authors illustrate how the
girls encounter and come to internalize society's dualism of mind
and body, thought and feeling, and how they may accept, in the
process, an oppressive rationality that divorces them from their
bodies and emotions—their full range of experience—as a legitimate source of knowing.

This framework helps us connect individual experience and
social structures in new ways. For example, it can show us how our
ways of naming our experiences are not neutral but are instead
based on assumptions that can reinforce privilege and oppression.
Its attention to individual agency helps us see the possibility of resistance and change, even though the social forces that affect women's
lives are powerful. Poststructural feminist thought gives legitimacy
to the particularity of each woman's experience, helping us recog-

nize the complexity of our identities and our differences as well as our similarities.

Nevertheless, the focus on diversity and particularity of experience can leave women with no apparent basis for either common knowledge about their experience or unified action. The concern with language and thought as representations of experience can also become excessively abstract and theoretical, and this can make it difficult to draw concrete implications for women's everyday lives and learning. It can be difficult to articulate a political agenda—what sort of individual and social change is needed to overcome oppression—on the basis of the poststructural feminist framework.

Use of Feminism in *Women as Learners*

As already noted, we believe that all types of feminist theories have made contributions to our understanding of women's learning. Throughout this book we have incorporated the findings and perspectives of authors using diverse feminist perspectives; the development of our own thinking has been influenced by all of these frameworks. Nevertheless, our current thinking is most closely aligned with the poststructural feminist framework. This perspective is reflected in how we conceptualize gender as a system of social relations that are continually renegotiated, both at the level of daily interactions and at the level of the broader social structures. It is also reflected in our attention to the sociocultural context of women's lives, our attempts to make the social forces that influence women's lives more visible, and our emphasis on understanding how women are active agents in resisting oppressive forces and shaping their own lives and learning. It has informed our desire to recognize not only similarities among women but also differences related to such factors as age, race, class, and sexual orientation. In turn, these beliefs have influenced how we approached our discussion of the topics and literature in each chapter.

Locating Sources of Information

Gathering source material was not an easy task; it was certainly more difficult than we anticipated at the outset of our project. We began with what we intended to be a rigorous and systematic search of academic literature on adult women's learning. Our initial intent was to focus primarily on literature that described research or theory about the actual process of women's learning, women's attributes as learners, or the outcomes of their learning experiences. It is important to note that we did not want learning, for our purposes, to be confined to traditional settings of formal education because most learning for adults takes place in many other settings of everyday life. We sought out information about learning that ranged from the pursuit of formal education to such experiences as learning to be a mom, recovering from alcoholism, and becoming a business executive.

Defining learning for so-called adult women was not a clear-cut task. Following the normal practices of adult education scholarship, we excluded most of the literature on young women (those between the ages of eighteen and twenty-one) in traditional postsecondary undergraduate degree programs (this is typically considered to be a continuation of preparatory education rather than adult education). Nevertheless, such a distinction is to some extent arbitrary, and we have drawn selectively on certain influential studies of this age group and setting.

Our search encompassed a wide variety of literature (for more details about searches, see Hayes and Flannery, 1995, 1997; Flannery and Hayes, 1996). Our source material was primarily academic, consisting of books and articles in professional education journals as well as scholarly journals in such disciplines as psychology, sociology, and women's studies. With a few exceptions, we confined ourselves to research and theory about women's learning and education in the context of North America. Our dissatisfaction with the source material that we identified in this way led us also to search in doctoral dissertations, which, although frequently difficult to obtain, yielded some useful material. We even flirted with the idea of reviewing more popular kinds of books, biographies, autobiographies, and even fiction, to gain more insight into women's learning beyond formal education, the focus of most academic work. We quickly realized, however, that this would have meant a completely different type of analysis (and probably a lifetime project), and so we kept largely to our original conception of a book based on a more academic body of literature. We did make some selective use of other literature, both fiction and nonfiction, as well as our own personal narratives, to overcome some of the limitations of the academic literature. In the next section, we briefly describe, from a more academic perspective, some of these limitations.

Issues in the Literature on Women's Learning

At least initially, we were quite disappointed in what we found—or didn't find—in the literature. Perhaps our major disappointment was that, in terms of sheer quantity, there turned out to be a relatively limited amount of scholarship specifically focused on women's learning in adulthood. At the outset, when we searched the databases with such conventional descriptors as *learning* and *women,* we identified what seemed to be a vast body of literature. Unfortunately, we quickly found that *learning* is such a broad term that it was almost useless in helping us locate appropriate material. In many instances, we found that journal articles identified by the descriptor *learning* are actually descriptions of educational programs designed for women, teaching methods advocated for women learners, strategies to increase women's participation in formal education, and so forth. Moreover, much of this literature is based on assumptions about how women learn that do not have any obvious support. We were also disturbed to find that a number of authors make unsubstantiated statements about women's learning.

Even when authors do provide some kind of support for their assertions, that support is often questionable. Some authors make assertions about adult women's learning that are based on research with schoolchildren; apparently these authors assume that women's characteristics as learners do not change from childhood to adulthood. There were instances of overgeneralization and of other types of sexism, both in research designs and in interpretations (Eichler, 1988). For example, many discussions of leadership in adult education and other settings make generalizations about women leaders as caring and men leaders as firm and aggressive. Such discussions create a simplistic dichotomy that reinforces traditional stereotypes about women and men, and they gloss over any diversity in leadership styles. (Chapter Nine, by Elisabeth Hayes, describes some weaknesses of the literature in more detail.)

Our old inspiration, *Women's Ways of Knowing* (Belenky, Clinchy, Goldberger, and Tarule, 1986), was cited time and again in support of various educational approaches for women; unfortunately, we found that those four authors' ideas were commonly misinterpreted or misapplied. For example, some of these approaches seemed to equate a "way of knowing" (or an epistemological stance, as described in that work) with a learning style, such as a preference for "concrete experience." We were surprised to find that few researchers had sought to pursue further research that might elaborate on, confirm, or challenge *Women's Ways of Knowing* (see Goldberger, Tarule, Clinchy, and Belenky, 1996, for further discussion of such issues and examples of scholarship that addresses this lack).

For us, a key concern that emerged is researchers' frequent failure to move beyond mere descriptions of women's learning, and toward a more theoretical or conceptual level of analysis. Related to this concern is the fact that there is scant research informed by feminist theories, and what little there is tends to draw primarily on psychologically oriented feminisms. Sociological perspectives are neglected, and so there is an obscuring of issues related to the social construction of knowledge, learning, and learning situations and to the social determinants of gender roles and gender norms. For the most part, then, researchers have failed to look at issues of sexism in the power

relationships involved in learning, and they have neglected to conduct wider social, economic, and political analyses of the constraints
under which the process of learning actually takes place for women.

There is also a notable lack of racial, cultural, and economic
diversity among the women who have been studied for much of this
literature. Issues related to sexual orientation and to mental or physical disabilities are rarely addressed. Generalizations about groups are
sometimes made on the basis of the experiences of a mere handful
of women, with little attention to differences within such groups.
We found enough literature for us to feel justified in suggesting that
it is important to consider, for example, how culture intersects with
gender to affect women's learning experiences, but we did not find
enough to allow us to draw many conclusions about particular groups
or influences.

Emerging Themes

From a scholarly perspective, much of what we found was problematic, but our concerns prompted us to move in new directions
with our own work. In retrospect, we see that as we began our original search, we were using a masculine model of science that mirrored our formal training as researchers. We assumed that we could
gather a body of evidence, evaluate it with traditional forms of academic analysis and critique, and draw conclusions about women's
learning that could be applied by other researchers and educators.
To put the matter simply, however, that model didn't work for us.
There is a dearth of literature, and what does exist frequently offers
very limited insights. Moreover, some of the more academically rigorous work is in fact the least helpful because it reduces learning to
a set of seemingly isolated experiences or attributes. Often it seems
as if researchers are more concerned with the interests of educational institutions than with women learners themselves (Edwards,
1993). Much of the literature fails to go deeply into what women
as women are saying about their learning.

Despite these limitations, we ultimately did gather a body of literature that began to offer us more useful insights. In particular, we concentrated on studies that emphasize the use of women's narratives and personal stories of learning. We were inspired and intrigued by selected stories of women's learning in formal educational settings but even more so by isolated studies conducted in settings other than formal education. These hint at the richness of women's learning in other contexts and often challenge the dominant portrayals of women in more formal academic situations. For example, there were studies of the learning of working-class Appalachian women active in community organizations, of Latina women's learning in study circles, of working-class White women's learning as trade apprentices, of women in a religious order learning to change as their church changed, of older widowed women learning to make significant life decisions, of learning in connection with life events (marriage, separation and divorce, childbirth), and of women's learning through play. Women's learning began to reveal itself in myriad ways and settings, and among women with varied backgrounds and characteristics (although these were not as diverse as we would eventually like to see).

Our focus on women's narratives allowed us to see that women's stories were not just about learning to do something, such as selling a home or mastering algebra. These stories were more fundamentally about women trying to learn new gender roles at the age of sixty-five or older, about women trying to figure out who they were, because they had been taught that girls and women were to obtain their identities from their relationships with others. The stories were about women learning together in ways that joined their spirits as well as their minds. Women learned and were empowered in caring study circles; they learned at play and while singing; they learned through meditation. Affective and emotional components of learning; intuition; learning in and throughout life; connections between personal and social influences on learning; contexts of learning; historical, social, ethnic, and economic influences on the learner—all these multiple, interconnected themes were vital to these women's learning and could not be separated from their lives.

As researchers and authors, we learned we were too structured in our own conceptualizations. We needed to move away from our linear approach to gathering information and go in multiple directions at once. We needed to think differently, to be more creative in our reflections, to look at what we were learning upside down and sideways, to allow ourselves to see as we hadn't seen before. We threw out our initial outline, which had been based on traditional topics associated with adult learning (such as "cognition and learning" and "why women participate in learning"). We sat down together with large sheets of paper and drew maps of important ideas about women's learning that were emerging from the women's narratives as well as more formal scholarship. These maps helped us conceptualize the connections among the ideas, and this exercise led to the inductive creation of the themes that became the chapters of the book. In this way, the significance for women's learning of social contexts, self-esteem and identity, voice, connection, and transformation became key themes and chapters, to which we added chapters on feminist pedagogies, perspectives on practice, and the creation of future knowledge.

Once we identified the chapter themes, it became apparent to us that several of our colleagues had expertise in themes we did not. We shared with them our overall vision for the book, as well as the particular literature and ideas we had found in the area of their expertise, and asked them each to write a chapter, drawing on their own knowledge but fitting it into the overall framework of the book.

With the themes as our guide, we set out to pull together whatever disparate sources would help us understand the depth of women's learning. We went wherever we were led by our sources, our ideas, our intuitions, and our desire to understand. We went back to the scholarly literature with new lenses, looking for new patterns and ideas. We also drew on other sources, some not overtly concerned with learning, such as books about communication patterns between men and women, autobiographies, and poems that helped us understand what it was to be, for example, a woman in Alaskan Inuit culture. Both of us developed and taught university-level courses on women's learning, and with our students we explored women's learning through art, popular culture, meditation and yoga, and more formal avenues of study. We learned to allow the coexistence of links among women's learning, social contexts, identity, self-esteem, voice, connectedness, and transformation, as if our explorations were a weaving in progress. For us, this meant learning to learn in a completely new way.

We adopted the kaleidoscope as a visual image for our work, and each of us kept one on her desk while working on this book. We saw the kaleidoscope as a metaphor for this writing. The kaleidoscope's collection of items, such as bits of glass or beads held loosely at the end of a rotating tube, continually change forms as they are reflected in mirrors set at angles to each other—interacting, complex, teeming, varied. Our attempts to articulate the themes in this book may appear as symmetrical as the discrete forms seen in a kaleidoscope, but in reality these themes are never completely discrete from one another, and they vary for different women in different circumstances. Moreover, as the transition from one visual design to another is often cloudy and indistinct in a kaleidoscope, so are the interconnections among the themes of women's learning. Some images are distorted in the process of turning the scope as are some of the aspects we found. In this book, we have tried to understand, as well as we can, these themes and their subtle nuances. We hope that this work provides a beginning from which others will continue to seek an understanding of adult women's learning, to keep rotating the kaleidoscope's images, looking upside down and sideways, through indistinct and distorted pieces in order to better present an understanding of adult women's learning and our learning.

2

Social Contexts

Elisabeth Hayes

W omen's learning takes place in a wide variety of social contexts: in community groups, in the home, in the workplace,
in religious associations, in leisure activities, and in more formal
educational settings—in literally every context of life. Unfortunately, formal scholarship on women's learning paints only a partial
picture of these diverse environments. Women's learning in formal
education, higher education in particular, has received primary
attention, and we have only sketches punctuated by an occasional
vivid snapshot of women's learning in other contexts. The imbal-
ance of this focus may be a consequence of how learning and learning situations have been conceptualized by researchers and
professionals, with greater value given to formal education. In the
past, for example, educators seemed to assume that the home was
not an environment for significant learning, as reflected in the belief
that women's learning abilities might be deficient after a period of
full-time homemaking. In describing the social contexts of women's
learning, it is possible to say much more about formal education
than about other settings, but I stress the significance of all social
contexts in understanding women's learning.

Marilyn's Story

As an illustration, I'd like to begin this discussion with the story of
Marilyn, one of several Black women whose lives are described by

Kesho Yvonne Scott (1991). Although her story is one of hardship and struggle, Marilyn showed great courage and determination in confronting the challenges that life offered her as a Black woman born in the 1940s. Her story includes learning experiences as an adult student in higher education, but it also suggests how Marilyn learned in the contexts of home, workplace, and community.

Marilyn's passage into adulthood was marked by her pregnancy and marriage at the age of seventeen. The focus of her learning shifted dramatically, from being in high school to learning to be a wife and mother. Her story captures the fear and helplessness she felt in the face of what appeared to be an immense learning task.

Marilyn quickly overcame her intimidation about household tasks and began to feel stifled by traditional female roles in the home. She enrolled in college to study English and writing but was forced to quit when her husband began to see her education as a threat. She began studying the Bible and became involved in door-to-door ministry. She traveled and learned about international affairs through contact with ministry members from around the world. When her husband again became threatened by her activities, she divorced him and now had three children to support.

Marilyn's learning underwent a major shift when she entered the world of work and found a job as a technician for the phone company. In addition to acquiring technical skills, she learned about racism in the workplace. She observed that White women were more often promoted to management, whereas Black women remained in the lower technical positions. When Marilyn finally was promoted to supervisor, she learned that she had no power as a Black woman because she was expected to carry out the decisions of her White boss.

Marilyn also became more aware of racism, as well as of sexism, in her church. She observed segregation between poor Black church members and well-to-do White professionals, as well as inequities between the positions of the men who were church leaders and the women who continued to do the lowest-level tasks.

Marilyn's growing dissatisfaction and unrest culminated in her attempted suicide. In her continued search for fulfillment, she began again to take college classes in poetry and literature. As she learned about Black women authors, she developed her own identity as a writer and began a novel. The story ends with Marilyn at the age of forty-six. She has quit her job and left her home in Detroit to study writing at the University of Iowa; her final comments reflect the deeply personal significance of higher education at this point in her life. I'll refer to Marilyn's story periodically throughout this chapter, to provide some specific examples of learning across social contexts.

The Gendered Nature of Learning Across Contexts

Marilyn's life story highlights how formal education, family, workplace, and community each have been sites of significant learning on her part. Her story also suggests how gender has played a role in the opportunities she had for learning in these environments, in what she learned, and in the consequences of her learning. Of particular importance from a feminist perspective is how these environments served as sites for learning, or relearning, gender-related identities and roles.

We commonly think only of written materials as "texts" for learning, and yet every social setting is a text from which people learn important lessons about themselves and relationships with others. In formal education, the term *hidden curriculum* has been used to describe the implicit messages (such as the need to obey authority) conveyed by the organization and practices of schooling. Other social settings convey a similar hidden curriculum through the organization of social relationships, the value placed on certain kinds of knowledge, and so on. For example, the structure of Marilyn's work environment conveyed the implicit message that Black women do not have the ability to be administrators, a message that she resisted by seeing the racism inherent in Black women's difficulty in achieving promotions. The overt and hidden curriculum can also be more liberating, however. When Marilyn took a class on Black women writers, a class taught by a Black woman, she learned that women like herself could be real writers and that their experience was a valid source of artistic expression and knowledge.

To understand women's learning in these settings, we must understand how they respond to the "texts" they encounter in relation to gender, race, class, and other social structures. Whereas scholarship in the past has often assumed that women experience oppression uniformly across social contexts, more recent feminist theories suggest that the complexity of individual situations and the intersection of multiple social factors lead to great diversity in women's experience of and response to dominant social structures. People are not totally free agents; social structures shape both our external circumstances and our internal consciousness. Nevertheless, we have the capacity to become aware of these social forces and to choose to act in opposition to them.

Women's resistance to dominant social structures is most obvious in overt actions, such as Marilyn's divorcing her husband or questioning gender roles in her church. But it may also consist of more covert, less directly oppositional behavior and may be what informs a woman's decision *not* to act. For example, Marilyn did not openly confront the racism she encountered on her job; she kept quiet because the money she was earning was important in supporting her family. When such acts of resistance are so identified, this identification can serve to challenge the pervasive portrayal, in the adult education literature, of women learners as passive victims of social forces, unaware of oppression or helpless in the face of it (Hayes and Smith, 1994).

In the following sections, I describe in more detail the social contexts of women's learning, starting with formal education and moving on to a discussion of women's learning in the workplace, the home and family, and the community. My discussion devotes particular attention to how gender shapes women's opportunities for learning in each of these contexts. I point out the significance not only of the more overt subject matter but also of the hidden curriculum of these contexts, as well as how women actively respond to these "texts." I conclude the chapter with a discussion of the contradictions women may experience in their learning across social contexts and of how these contradictions themselves can be important sources of learning.

Women's Learning in Formal Education

When we think of learning, we often think first of learning that occurs in formal educational settings. Such settings range from adult basic education to vocational training programs to postsecondary education in colleges and universities.

Women's learning is shaped in part simply by their access to formal education. In the past, women tended to be excluded from participation in many types of formal education, but in more recent times women have constituted the largest proportion and most rapidly growing cohort of participants in many educational settings, particularly higher education. According to Teresita Kopka and Roslyn Korb (1996), between 1970 and 1993 the number of women enrolled in higher education rose from 3.5 million to 7.9 million. The increase in women's participation has exceeded the increase in men's participation, and there are currently more women than men receiving bachelor's and master's degrees. Men still earn more doctoral degrees, but women's proportion of all doctoral degrees awarded has risen considerably, to 38 percent in 1992–1993. Women of Color lag behind White women in their overall participation rates, although they, too, have made notable strides. For example, the number of Hispanic women earning bachelor's degrees rose from 8,425 in 1977 to 25,511 in 1993, moving from 44 percent to 55 percent of bachelor's degrees awarded to all Hispanics. Nevertheless, such gains have not been consistent across racial and ethnic groups and degree levels. For example, 13,256 Black women received master's degrees in 1977, but that number dropped to a low of 8,720 in 1987, although it increased to 12,959 in 1993. Still, Black women outnumber Black men in earning master's degrees by almost two to one.

Although women constitute the majority of students in higher education, there continues to be considerable variation in women's participation in different areas of study. The concentration of women in traditionally female fields is particularly evident in graduate study. For example, in 1992–1993, women received 59 percent of the doctoral degrees awarded in education, but only 11 percent of doctoral degrees in engineering were awarded to women (Kopka and Korb, 1996). During the same period, women received only one-quarter of the doctoral degrees awarded in math. Therefore, the types of subject matter and knowledge gained from formal education can be significantly different for women and men. One obvious concern is that women still tend to be clustered in areas that lead to employment with lower status and lower financial rewards. Moreover, within certain areas, women's specializations may differ from men's. For example, 45 percent of medical students are now women, but many more women study pediatrics than study surgery (Steinhauer, 1999). Such choices are affected by a complex range of factors, which include persistent social norms and beliefs regarding women's abilities (women are "good with children" or "less able to handle stress"). Women may also deliberately choose to opt out of studies and careers that require total commitment of time and energy, particularly when these are perceived to interfere with marriage- and family-related goals (whereas such combinations may be less problematic for men). Furthermore, women may be influenced by the hidden curriculum of formal education itself, which can reinforce gender-based stereotypes about women's abilities as learners.

In the following sections, I discuss three influential aspects of formal educational contexts: curricula, interpersonal interactions, and institutional culture. Most of the examples I use come from higher education, but these factors have an impact on women's (and men's) learning in all types of formal educational settings.

Curricula

Textbooks, instructional materials, and teachers' lectures are not simply sources of knowledge about subject matter; they are also influential sources of learning about gender. Studies of curricula in K–12 and higher education (see Sadker, Sadker, and Klein, 1991) have demonstrated how texts and curricula reinforce stereotypical roles and images of women and men—for example, by portraying only men in leadership roles, whereas women are portrayed as passive and subordinate or are not represented at all. The predominance of male authors has been cited as contributing to a focus on "male" issues and to a neglect of concerns more specific to women's experiences. Despite widespread awareness of and attempts to redress these biases, they continue, if in more subtle forms.

There have been few studies of curricula in adult education specifically, but the existing research suggests that such biases persist there as well. For example, B. Allan Quigley and Ella Holsinger (1993) found evidence of sexism as well as racism and classism in three series of adult literacy instructional materials: women were represented as characters less frequently than men; fewer than half the women characters had stated occupations, and of those who did, almost one-third were in domestic roles, with the others in highly stereotypical occupations (such as secretary or librarian). Women in these materials were commonly depicted as engaged in domestic roles, whereas men had domestic roles in only two of the stories. In another study, Elizabeth Tisdell (1993) found that both the overt and the hidden curricula in two higher education classes favored the experiences of White males. This bias was especially apparent in these curricula's failure to represent racial and ethnic minorities, but there was also greater emphasis on male than on female experience. For example, one instructor's stories and examples focused almost exclusively on males, and the curricular materials for the other class generally portrayed men as more powerful than women. In instructional videos women were also underrepresented, and their speaking roles were more limited. The two instructors in these classes were unaware of these biases, a finding that may indicate just how difficult it is to identify and change a hidden curriculum.

Interpersonal Interactions

In a widely cited report that was published almost two decades ago, Roberta Hall and Bernice Sandler (1982) identified a number of ways in which faculty in higher education may interact differently with women and men in the classroom, thus reflecting and repro-ducing inequitable power relationships linked to gender roles. These types of behavior persist in current classrooms—for example, call-ing directly on men students but not on women, responding more extensively to men's comments than to women's, and interrupting women students more often than men. Men may be given more informal and formal encouragement, may be more involved in men-toring relationships, and may be selected more frequently for grad-uate assistantships. These biases may be linked to faculty members' unconscious or conscious assumptions that men are more talented, more intelligent, or more serious students. Sexual attraction also affects how students and instructors interact with each other: issues of power are inherent in sexual relationships and are magnified by the power differences between instructors and students.

Biases in teacher-student interactions are not solely the result of teachers' perceptions, however. Women and men may act in differ-ent ways, thus evoking different responses from teachers. Some researchers claim that women learn to use language in ways that dif-fer from men's and that reflect women's subordinate roles in society. Women may not find it easy or natural to express their ideas in the forceful, argumentative way that often is necessary if their contri-butions are to be taken seriously in classroom discussions. (In Chap-ter Four, I discuss these patterns of classroom talk in more depth.)

Even subtle biases in classroom and advising interactions can lead women to doubt their abilities and may affect their further par-ticipation in education as well as their career decisions. Not all women experience these biases in the same way, however: faculty members may interact differently with different students of the same sex; therefore, not all male students are given the same kind of recognition and support, nor are all female students ignored. At any rate, faculty-student interactions, like the educational curriculum, serve to reproduce societal power relationships. Gender subordination is one type of power relationship, but we must also take account of power relationships stemming from issues of race, class, and other social identities. Tisdell's study (1993) of adult higher education classes illustrates the complexity of power relationships in classroom interactions: of the three students who were perceived by their peers to have the most influence in class, two were men and one was a woman, and all three were upper-middle-class or upper-class students; the two students whose contributions were least often recognized by their peers were both women, one a working-class White student and the other a Black student. These patterns suggest how race and class, in combination with gender, can determine students' influence and participation in class.

Nevertheless, societal power relationships are not always automatically or perfectly reproduced in formal education. Students and teachers may deliberately and unconsciously resist the reproduction of sexist, racist, and other inequitable power relationships. Many faculty development programs have helped faculty change sexist and racist patterns of classroom interactions. The sex or race of the instructor, in and of itself, may disrupt power relationships. Certainly women faculty can reproduce biased interactions, just as men faculty can, but there is some evidence that women faculty are more likely to create classroom situations that are conducive to greater participation by students of both sexes (Tisdell, 1995). Much of the research documenting overt biases toward women was conducted at a time when women students, particularly adult women, were a distinct minority in higher education. As the number of women students and faculty increases, these overt biases are becoming less prevalent, at least in some institutions, a finding that points to the significance of institutional culture in affecting women's learning.

Institutional Culture

The culture of an educational institution will have both obvious and covert influences on a woman's learning. In this connection, perhaps the most obvious aspect of a supportive institutional culture is the provision of services (such as childcare) that permit adult women to attend classes. Another obvious aspect involves scheduling: Are courses offered at times that accommodate the work and family responsibilities of adult women? The proportion of adult women students in an educational program or institution is another, more obvious aspect of institutional culture that can affect women's learning. In one sense, the proportion of women reflects the extent that other institutional factors support women's participation and learning. What is equally important, however, is that the proportion of women students itself can contribute to women's feelings of belonging as learners, and to their overall comfort with the learning environment. Women of Color are particularly likely to feel like outsiders because their numbers remain relatively small (Johnson-Bailey, 1994).

The presence of women faculty can be an important factor in supporting women's learning. A program with a minority of women students typically has a correspondingly low proportion of female faculty. In 1992, 50 percent of education faculty were women, but only 6 percent of engineering faculty were women (Kopka and Korb, 1996). Women faculty may also serve a critical function as role models and mentors for women students. Debra Schroeder and Clifford Mynatt (1993) report in their study of women graduate students that although women rated female and male faculty members fairly equally on the quality of their advisement, the women still placed considerable importance on female faculty as role models. Joyce Stalker (1994) argues that women faculty mentors, as both "insiders" and "outsiders," can help women learn to succeed in educational institutions and simultaneously learn to challenge oppressive structures.

Even high numbers of women teachers and learners cannot guarantee that the culture of formal educational programs will be supportive of all women's learning. For example, in contrast to many higher education settings, adult literacy education is dominated by female teachers and tutors. In fact, the perception of literacy education as "women's work" has been cited as an explanation for its lack of status and funding. But although the prevalence of women educators would seem to make literacy education a supportive context for women learners, that is not necessarily the case. Many women literacy teachers differ greatly from learners in their racial, cultural, and class backgrounds. As well-intentioned as literacy teachers might be, it is easy to imagine that they could be unresponsive to the needs and cultures of their students. For example, Sheryl Gowen and Carol Bartlett (1997) point out how their ignorance of domestic abuse among their women literacy students led them to use teaching methods that were in conflict with the women's desire for a safe learning environment. Jenny Horsman (1990), in her study of low-literate women in Nova Scotia, found that some literacy tutors misinterpreted women's desire for social interaction in the classroom as evidence that they were not "serious" students and that they lacked motivation to learn; from the women's perspective, however, the classes were an important means of overcoming the isolation that they experienced in their homes.

Another perspective on institutional culture suggests that the intellectual culture in higher education, as in other kinds of formal education, places value on certain kinds of knowledge and ways of knowing that are sexist (as well as racist and classist). Some feminist educators and scholars have argued that women's learning is better supported in environments that are different from those in traditional higher education and from those that support men's learning. The various forms of feminist pedagogy, as described in Chapter Seven, reflect efforts to create approaches to teaching that acknowledge the significance of gender and support women's learning in particular.

Women's Learning in Other Social Contexts

As I indicated by retelling some of Marilyn's story, much of women's learning takes place in contexts other than formal education. As in formal education, however, explicit and implicit "texts" in these settings affect women's opportunities for learning in general, as well as what they learn about themselves as women in these contexts. In the following sections, I examine how the workplace, the home and family, and the community serve as contexts for women's learning.

Learning in the Workplace

Paid employment has always been a part of many women's lives, but in recent decades the number of women working outside the home has increased considerably. Kopka and Korb (1996) report that the proportion of women between the ages of twenty-five and fifty-four who were working or looking for work rose between 1970 and 1993, from 50 percent to 75 percent. The nature of women's paid employment and the context of the workplace affect the skills and knowledge that women need to learn, what they learn, and how they learn these skills and knowledge. The labor force, like higher education, continues to be highly segregated by gender, with most women workers concentrated in traditionally female occupations. The predominant occupational category for women in 1993 was technical, sales, or administrative support, which included 46 percent of women workers, by comparison with 19 percent of men employed in this category. About 19 percent of women worked in service occupations, by comparison with 9 percent of men. Only 2 percent of women were employed in production, precision, craft, and repair occupations, by comparison with 19 percent of men (Kopka and Korb, 1996).

Women's jobs tend to be lower-paying than men's; in 1993, the median annual earnings of women were 71 percent those of men. Even in the same occupation, women tend to be paid less than men. More women than men work part-time, often to accommodate household and childcare responsibilities. Women are often in positions that have limited power and autonomy and are more likely to be secretaries than managers, teachers than school principals, and nurses than physicians.

How does the nature of women's work affect their workplace learning? As part-time workers, women may be given fewer opportunities for formal job training. The devaluation of female-dominated occupations and the perception that these jobs do not require considerable skill can contribute to fewer formal training opportunities. Women may find it difficult to participate in training provided outside normal work hours, given their household and childcare responsibilities. Employers' sponsorship of formal training opportunities is often a result of collective bargaining agreements, and fewer women than men belong to unions. In 1990 only 14.9 percent of female full-time workers belonged to unions, by comparison with 21.4 percent of full-time male workers (1991 U.S. Department of Labor Statistics, cited in Thornborrow and Sheldon, 1995).

The type of job training available to many women may be limiting. For example, much of the training offered to single mothers receiving public assistance has been for jobs (such as clerical assistant or nurse's aide) that are stereotypically female and poorly paid and that have limited opportunities for advancement, and women may simply opt out of such training altogether. Sheryl Gowen (1991) found that Black women resisted a workplace literacy program that was intended to teach them basic skills related to their jobs in housekeeping, food service, and laundry services. The women refused to do assignments, fell asleep in class, or simply dropped out of the program. They were not resistant to education, but they wanted a curriculum oriented toward a high school equivalency diploma—a curriculum that would give them a credential that they believed would improve their ability to get better jobs. The women's resistance to management was an act of self-assertion, but they remained caught nevertheless in their low-paying, menial jobs, with few prospects for advancement. Typical job training programs may not address issues of combining family and work, sexual harassment, or discrimination, which can serve as additional barriers to women's job performance, work satisfaction, and career advancement.

Women's informal, on-the-job learning is also affected by gender. The workplace can reinforce a hidden curriculum similar to those in formal education. For example, in a study of women's "working knowledge" (MacKerarcher and McFarland, 1993/1994) a nurse described how she was sexually harassed by an elderly male patient during her clinical training, and how her supervising professor accused her of creating the problem by flirting with the patient. The implicit message of this incident was that women are powerless in the face of sexual exploitation and in fact are themselves to blame for being objects of sexist practices. From a more positive perspective, another woman described how gender bias in training assignments helped her develop greater technical knowledge. When she was a trainee, she said, she "had the dubious honor" of taking over for a senior teller who was on maternity leave and performing "all the secretarial functions." She added that all the male trainees were posted to positions above the teller level before any of the female trainees, but that the women turned out to be better managers than the men because they "ended up with more technical experience and more human resource experience" (MacKerarcher and McFarland, 1993/1994, p. 55). It also seems that this woman was able to reject the implicit message that women were more suited to secretarial positions than to management.

Women's on-the-job learning may be particularly challenging in occupations that are dominated by men. The types of behavior that make men successful may not work for women because these kinds of behavior conflict with "feminine" behavior. For example,

Diane Horgan (1989) describes how a woman manager may be perceived as "overly aggressive" if she uses the same direct methods of confrontation as a male manager. Male mentors and supervisors may also give women inappropriate guidance that is based on their own experience as men, and the small number of women role models available to women in male-dominated occupations may offer only examples of idiosyncratic behavior. With respect to management positions, Horgan argues that mentors need to develop greater awareness of gender differences in effective managerial behavior and of alternative managerial strategies that will work for women. She seems to assume that women's success depends on learning "effective" behaviors that will enable them to perform their jobs well. Nevertheless, as Stalker (1994) has argued in connection with formal settings for education, workplace mentors might also help women learn ways of challenging structures that perpetuate inequities that are based on gender as well as on race and class.

Career counseling, which is taking on greater importance throughout life, can expand or limit women's learning about work. In the past, there were obvious biases in how counselors steered women toward traditionally female occupations; today the biases are less prevalent, and there have been many efforts to introduce women into nontraditional occupations for women, ranging from such skilled trades as welding and plumbing to professional occupations in math and engineering. Still, subtle biases continue to exist in most of the models of career development and decision making that inform counseling practice. Lawrence Hotchkiss and Henry Brown (1996) point out that much counseling practice is based on a psychological, rational model of career choice that involves matching personal attributes to the functional requirements of jobs. This type of model ignores structural barriers that are particularly likely to affect people of Color's capacity to achieve the positions of greatest status and economic reward. One role for career counselors, a currently underdeveloped one, might be to help women learn about the structural barriers they face in the workplace and about the strategies they might use in confronting these barriers. The career counseling literature seems to offer only weak examples of how counselors can approach this task. There is also limited attention to the integration of work and family roles, the learning context that I will next discuss.

Learning in the Home and Family

Women's learning in the home and family has received relatively little attention from adult education researchers. Past literature might lead one to believe that for adult women the family and home are at best locations of few opportunities for learning, at worst stifling and restrictive environments. Literature from the 1970s and early 1980s on "re-entry women," for example, portrays these women as deficient in self-confidence, communication skills, and thinking skills because of their isolation in the home and their limited contact with other adults (Hayes and Smith, 1994). One could argue, however, that the work of raising children and managing a household requires considerable skill and learning. Why was and is this learning "invisible" to women learners and to educators? A structural feminist perspective suggests that the patriarchal structure of society renders such learning invisible precisely because it is associated with women's work in the private realm of the home, traditionally treated as less significant than work and learning in the "public" world. In her study of working-class women, Wendy Luttrell (1989) found that the women perceived men to be more intelligent than themselves. Luttrell attributes this perception to the fact that many of the women's skills and abilities were learned and used in the home and perceived as intuitive and natural rather than learned.

Some current perspectives on the home and family provide a starting point for a better understanding of women's learning in this context. What is perhaps most obvious is that different family structures provide different opportunities for and constraints on women's learning. As Kristine Baber and Katherine Allen (1992) point out, there is no unitary family experience for women. The traditional nuclear family still serves as a dominant image of the family in the United States, but its existence is relatively scarce. To understand women's learning in the family in a way that is inclusive, we must recognize a plurality of family forms. Such a plurality would include multigenerational family structures and households, extended families that include members who are not blood relatives, and lesbian relationships. Women have different roles and relationships across these diverse family forms, and these lead to different learning experiences. In a more overt sense, a woman who is a single head of household may learn to be more self-reliant than a woman who has other adults in her household who share responsibilities. Nevertheless, the single woman may develop a stronger network of friends, whom she can use as sources of information and learning, than will the woman who has a more immediate (but perhaps also more restricted) source of learning in her immediate family members. Dissatisfaction with existing family structures and roles, and a desire for change, can be motivations for learning. Actual changes in the family's structure (such as a divorce) can also precipitate learning. Many women are faced with the challenge of learning to construct forms of family life that differ from those they experienced as children. For example, it has become more common both for adult women to assume roles as caregivers to their aging parents and older relatives and for young people to remain in their parents' households for longer periods.

Furthermore, families and home life also serve as important sites for learning and questioning gender roles and relationships; there is a hidden curriculum in family life as well as in formal education and the workplace. In families, people construct gendered identities, develop beliefs about the sexual division of labor, and experience the effects of gender hierarchies in personal ways (Baber and Allen, 1992). Feminist analyses have challenged "the myth of the family as a safe and stable haven" (Baber and Allen, 1992, p. 1).

The patriarchal structure of society is replicated in many families, in which women experience oppression and domination. A basic conflict for many women is between serving the needs of others and meeting their own needs. Many women have learned in the home to sacrifice their own interests to those of their families—a choice that, in the long run, can be ruinous to their own growth and identities. Marilyn's story provides obvious examples of these tensions, ranging from her early fears about handling motherhood and household responsibilities to the struggles she experienced with her husband over her right to pursue education and her ministry work.

This experience of oppression is not uniform or pervasive for all women. Some women have relative power and control in family life. Such power may be linked to differences in cultural values and norms. For example, Donna Deyhle and Frank Margonis (1995) point out that Navajo women have considerable authority in the home and are treated with respect for their role in sustaining strong family networks; in other cases, however, as Baber and Allen point out, this power may be in areas relatively unimportant to men. In Marilyn's story, for example, she described how her mother and female in-laws would get their way with the men in their households over such issues as buying a new appliance. But major life decisions, such as the decision that Marilyn should marry the father of her child, were still in male hands, and Marilyn was left with the belief that she should subordinate her own wishes to those of her husband. Women may also oppress other women in the home—for example, in their treatment of domestic help or childcare providers. To make things more contradictory, the very aspects of family life that may oppress women may also offer confirmation and fulfillment. For example, a woman who takes on the role of caregiver to her aging parents may fulfill some of her own interpersonal needs and enhance her sense of connection to her parents through this role. At the same time, she may also resent her brother for not assuming similar responsibility and may feel the stress of constantly trying to anticipate her parents' needs. Accordingly, women's learning in this context can be similarly complex.

Motherhood is one example of a significant and potentially contradictory learning opportunity for women in the context of family
life. From a positive perspective, Mary Belenky, Blythe Clinchy,
Nancy Goldberger, and Jill Tarule (1986) remark that many mothers have described childbirth as the most important learning experience they have ever had. Motherhood has often prompted women,
who previously thought of themselves as dependent and incapable
of learning, to develop new views of themselves as learners and as
teachers of others. Nevertheless, motherhood can pose conflicts
between what women have learned about the "ideal" mother and
what they are learning from their actual experience. Society offers a
romanticized picture of motherhood as a natural, fulfilling, and
important role for women. But mothering does not necessarily come
naturally; it requires considerable learning to be a good mother, and
conceptions of good mothering vary considerably. Motherhood is
experienced by some women as unfulfilling, and they may find themselves feeling guilty for having such feelings. Mary Guerrerea Congo
(1988) describes how she exhausted herself in trying to live up to
culturally determined images of the "good mother" (always ener-
getic, patient, loving, and self-sacrificing). Her feelings of inadequacy, pain, and frustration helped her become aware that these
mothering ideals were in many ways a reflection of an oppressive
and patriarchal society. This realization, bolstered by her sharing of
her experiences with other mothers and a therapist, contributed to
new perspectives on her own self-worth and identity (Congo, 1988,
p. 82): "I have learned to look at the way I have valued myself as a
woman and valued other women. Do other women value themselves (and other women)? Too often we have to say that we have
not valued ourselves very much. Who then benefits from these
romanticized myths about motherhood?" Congo's story illustrates
both how oppression may be hidden in seemingly positive conceptions of women's roles and how women can learn to assert themselves against it.

A particularly powerful way that gendered roles and identities can
be learned in the home is through the media. Women's magazines,

TV shows, newspapers, and, most recently, the Internet can communicate biased and stereotypical messages about women's needs and abilities. For example, feminist scholars have been highly critical of the self-help literature for its construction of various female pathologies that are characterized as individual failures rather than rooted in oppressive patriarchal systems. Women do not blindly accept these images, however. Debra Grodin (1995) has found that women readers did not totally accept or totally reject the cultural images of female identity and the "solutions" to their failures that were presented in self-help books. The women did find validation of their experiences and a sense of connection in reading about other women's stories, but they often rejected the authors' interpretations of these experiences, as well as the models of independence and separation advocated as solutions. Women made comments like "Well, I guess I am a woman who loves too much, but not in the sense that the author seems to be saying" or "I'm more than a woman who loves too much" (p. 131). Nevertheless, although the women rejected oppressive images of women's pathology and failure, they were not necessarily left with any more adequate or helpful conceptions of self and relationships. These examples suggest the blurring of boundaries between resistance and acceptance of dominant beliefs in women's learning.

Learning in the Community

Women's learning in the community encompasses a vast and rich array of contexts in itself. In this section, I confine my discussion to the context of organized community groups, although, obviously, women's learning occurs through a wider range of experiences in the community as a whole. Such groups may include church groups, clubs, or political groups that do not have women's issues as their primary concern. They also include agencies or organizations that are created, sometimes by professionals, with the explicit purpose of serving particular groups of women, such as single mothers, small-business owners, or women with eating disorders. Other relevant groups are those organized by women to address their own particular needs or interests. Many of these community groups have an explicit purpose of educating their members and the public; most are sites of considerable informal learning for participants. Formal studies of women's learning in community groups are few, as is also true with respect to studies of women's learning in the workplace and the family, but the existing studies do offer some insights into the kinds of opportunities offered by different community groups, as well as into the overt and hidden lessons that women learn in these groups.

What is most obvious is that women can acquire skills and knowledge in any kind of community group, usually through actual "doing" but also through more organized learning activities. For example, educator Mary Beth Bingham (1995) found that Appalachian women who became active in local community centers reported a wide range of learning outcomes, which included instrumental skills, increased self-understanding, and enhanced ability to work with other people. Their experiences at the community centers changed their perspectives on what they were capable of doing in their lives and communities. Bingham points out that this learning was not merely incidental but was instead the result of the centers' commitment to leadership development and collaborative teamwork and of other women's continuous support.

Women's learning in such groups is not uniformly positive, however. Community groups are similar to formal education, work, and the family in their potential to replicate oppressive patriarchal structures and ideology. Recall Marilyn's story of the sexism and racism in the organization of her church, as well as the patriarchal belief systems that mandated a woman's subordination to her husband. Even in the purportedly egalitarian civil rights and antiwar activist groups of the 1960s and early 1970s, women were treated like second-class citizens, relegated to typing letters and other support functions while the men assumed intellectual and positional leadership. In Margaret Cain's study (1998) of environmental action groups, women ultimately dropped out of one group because of the overbearing and competitive working style of the male members. Ultimately, such experiences may heighten women's awareness of sexism and of their subordinate status. For example, some women in the activist groups of earlier decades initiated their own radical feminist groups as they became more aware of the oppressive nature of their treatment by their male cohorts (Donovan, 1987).

Some community groups are specifically designed to foster such emancipatory learning among women. Descriptions of these groups tend to emphasize very similar elements that are commonly advocated in popular education more generally (see, for example, Belenky, Bond, and Weinstock, 1997; Schmitt-Boshnick, 1995). These elements include opportunities for women to share their experiences, identify common concerns, and develop an awareness of social structures affecting them as women. Taking action to improve their collective situations is typically an essential part of the learning experience. One such example is the United States Mothers' Center movement, described by Mary Belenky, Lynne Bond, and Jacqueline Weinstock (1997). The Mothers' Centers began with small groups of mothers discussing concerns related to mothering. One concern identified by an initial group was difficulties related to childbirth. Through their conversations, the mothers began to see how their individual experiences were shared by others and were related to hospital practices and policies that did not address their needs. They took action, first by interviewing other women about their experiences and studying hospital policies, and ultimately by presenting their findings publicly. Their efforts were successful in leading to a reform in maternity services in local hospitals.

The self-help groups that were focal points in the movement for the creation and sharing of new health-related knowledge among women offer another example of such emancipatory learning. As described by Mary Zimmerman (1987), these groups tended to be participatory and nonhierarchical, with women learning about their bodies in a firsthand manner and using their personal experience to critique the information they located and the health care they received. The well-known book *Our Bodies, Ourselves* and its updated edition, *The New Our Bodies, Ourselves* (Boston Women's Health Book Collective, 1984) grew out of the research of a group of women who wanted to distinguish between myth and fact in their own experience of female health problems (Beckwith, 1985, cited in Zimmerman, 1987).

These selective examples might suggest that all women's groups lead to individual empowerment and positive change for women in the broader community, but not all such groups are so successful; some may be exclusionary, create power differences among their members, and reproduce oppressive gender norms. A less positive example involves the concern that women of Color have expressed about feminist groups that assume a common female experience based on White middle-class women's perspectives. More specifically, Zimmerman (1987) points out the limitations of women's self-help groups like the Boston Women's Health Book Collective; the extensive research conducted by members, as well as their participatory approach, can be too time-consuming or demanding for women who have urgent health needs or time restrictions. Perhaps because of these factors, such groups have attracted primarily middle-class rather than poor or working-class women. Some recent self-help groups initiated by formal healthcare providers may contribute to women's feelings of powerlessness and lack of self-worth. Zimmerman (1987) uses the examples of groups formed for mastectomy patients and for weight reduction. Such groups have often reinforced preoccupations with physical attractiveness and appearance rather than health and productive activity. Self-help risks the possibility of reinforcing a "blame the victim" mentality, whereby the individual is seen as the source of her own healthcare problems and the problem is not located in the nature of healthcare provision (Kronenfeld, 1979, cited in Zimmerman, 1987).

Continuity and Contradictions Across Contexts

The well-known movie *Educating Rita* provides a popular conception of the potential conflicts between the learning environments of
higher education and family that some women may experience. Rita,
a young British working-class woman, decides to enroll in the Open
University because she wants something more from life than what
she sees in the lives of people around her. The ideas she is exposed
to and the mentoring she receives change her views of herself and
her lifestyle. During her studies, her husband burns her books and
divorces her because she refuses to start a family. Finally, she begins
to feel out of place in her working-class community, even with her
own parents and siblings. Her changing sense of self is reflected
(somewhat humorously) in changes in her hairstyle and dress.

Rita's story illustrates a theme repeated in other women's stories
of formal education (such as Marilyn's), and explored in more scholarly studies of women's learning. I have chosen to discuss various
settings separately, but women actually move continually among
these settings. Sometimes what they learn in one setting will challenge the knowledge, roles, and identities they have learned in
other settings. Furthermore, as the discussion so far has been emphasizing, each setting is itself complex, not clearly either liberating or
oppressive for women; it may be both simultaneously. Edie Black
(1989) describes an example of this complexity and the intersection of contexts in her study of adult women students in an office
skills training program. The women seemed to obediently follow a
tightly teacher-controlled classroom curriculum, oriented to skills
that would make them employable in obviously female-dominated
and low-status positions as office workers. Through interviews,
Black discovered that the women were critical of the curriculum,
aware that some of it was irrelevant to actual job demands, but the
women needed the skills to pass employment tests, and so they did
not openly resist the subject matter. The women saw the opportunity for employment as a means of gaining some personal autonomy

and economic independence, thus "resisting" their former situation as housewives. Nevertheless, although they may have succeeded in obtaining employment and a certain new level of independence, they were still entering positions with limited status or economic rewards, and although they might have been resisting family structures, they were still conforming to oppressive conditions in the labor market.

Accordingly, understanding the intersections among contexts is not simply a matter of contrasting oppression with liberation, or of identifying mutually reinforcing oppressive structures. Instead, such understanding requires an appreciation of how learning in each context may support or complement learning in other contexts, offering similar and different opportunities and constraints.

The Demands of Greedy Institutions

Women's opportunities for learning can be affected by conflicting demands on their time and energy across social contexts. The tensions experienced by women between their family roles and learning in higher education provides a particularly prominent example of the gendered nature of these conflicts. Rosalind Edwards (1993) describes both the family and higher education as "greedy institutions" demanding total commitment of time and energy from women. Women, more so than men, are expected to be constantly available to meet their families' physical and emotional needs. Higher education demands a similar devotion of mental and physical energy, along with the ability to separate oneself from the concerns of daily living for concentrated periods of intellectual activity. To meet the demands of both institutions simultaneously would seem to be impossible, and yet that is the position that many adult women find themselves in.

Doing It All

Women's response to this situation often seems to be an effort to meet all the demands, and to blame themselves for failure. Juanita Johnson-Bailey (1994) describes how Black women in college degree programs "negotiated" with family members and themselves for the freedom to attend school by agreeing to continue bearing primary responsibility for household tasks. As a result, the women sacrificed their free time, their sleep, and often their health to these inordinate demands.

Many women seem to assume that their success depends on their ability to "manage" their time efficiently. Both Edwards (1993), who studied full-time women undergraduates, and researcher Marlene Morrison (1996), who studied part-time women undergraduates, found that the women reported detailed planning of their schedules, and some attributed their lack of ability to "cope" to insufficient organization. Women's problems in the family and in school may also be interpreted by others as a sign of poor time management. Morrison (1996) mentions that a male student in her study contrasted his own construction of a weekly schedule with a "personal organizer" to what he perceived as a lack of organization on the part of some female students. Morrison wryly comments that perhaps the solution would be to equip women with personal organizers. As ludicrous as this sounds, recommendations for time-management workshops, as well as other strategies for educating women in how to better control their time, are not uncommon. Women's stories suggest, however, that their organizational abilities are not the crux of the problem; rather, their difficulties are in the social organization of family and education and in the extent to which women's time is controlled by the demands of others.

Connecting or Separating

As Edwards (1993) explains, women also respond to these institutional conflicts through varied emphases on connecting or separating family and education. Women made connections by discussing what they were learning with partners and children, seeking their partners' support in domestic tasks, bringing school friends home, and so on. They also attempted to bring their personal experiences and knowledge into their academic learning experiences. Some women made separations by ensuring that education affected their family lives as little as possible. They retained primary responsibility for domestic chores, avoided discussing what they were learning with children or partners, and did not mix school friendships with their other relationships. Further, they expressed pleasure at having "separate" identities as students.

Neither connection nor separation is an obviously better response to family and school conflicts, and the women in Edwards's study tended to use a mixture of both connection and separation, but women who placed more emphasis on connection also tended to report more problems with their marital relationships than did women who relied more on separating family and school. Making connections involves more potential change in relationships, both in terms of women's expectations for their partners' domestic roles and in terms of their appreciation of their own new knowledge and, perhaps, their own new self-images. This idea suggests another dimension of potential contradiction in women's learning across contexts: the gendered nature of women's identities and relationships.

Contradictions in Gendered Identities and Relationships

A nineteenth-century feminist argument for the higher education of women was that it would elevate women as equal to their husbands in the home and enhance their relationships with them. Nevertheless, our liberal feminist foremothers did not give sufficient thought, perhaps, to men's reactions to these changes. Rockhill (1987) states that a woman's pursuit of further education can be a deliberate attempt (or can be interpreted as such by men) to gain more independence and, as such, may be a threat to power relationships in the home. The male response can be a subtle (or not so subtle) sabotage of women's educational efforts. Educators and researchers are becoming more aware of how emotional, physical, and sexual abuse in the family pose significant barriers to women's learning and participation in education. Gowen and Bartlett (1997, p. 151) suggest that the effects of abuse are reflected in some women's negative self-images as learners, self-images that include lack of confidence in their learning abilities and a perception of themselves as "voiceless and mindless" (p. 151).

For some women, education is a deliberate attempt to escape from restrictive roles and relationships; others gain new insights through education, which allow them to question previously taken-for-granted roles and self-images. As one woman said, "I think that going back to school has helped me realize that you can be strong, you can be powerful, you can speak out and you can still be a woman, and that is okay, and that feels good, you know that the two can co-exist" (Saltonstall, 1989, p. 274). Such feelings can create conflicts for women if their family situations do not permit them to act out this new sense of self. Stephanie Adams (1996), in a study of adult women undergraduates, found that many women who had redefined their identities as women, wives, and mothers while in school felt unable to fulfill their new expectations for themselves. As one woman said, poignantly, "I have changed but nothing has changed at home. . . . And it hurts more when you have a taste of what things could and should be like" (Adams, 1996, p. 215). Adams suggests that the women blamed themselves for not doing something about the situation, which became another source of guilt about "not doing it right" (p. 215). For some women, the solution is to end a marriage or a relationship altogether, whereas others choose to sacrifice their new identities in favor of maintaining their family situations.

If we shift our lens from formal education to the intersections among women's learning at work, in the family, and in the community, we may find similar issues of connection, separation, and conflict, although not all education, work, and community contexts are the "greedy institutions" that higher education and the family can be. Experiences of conflict and contradiction across contexts can be a source of women's greater awareness of oppressive forces and challenges to them. Women may gain skills and confidence in the workplace or community work, for example, that lead them to question subordinate roles learned and maintained in their family lives. Conversely, the knowledge and abilities that women develop in their family lives may lead them to question their roles and knowledge in the workplace. For some women, these contradictions may lead to a decision to make major life changes.

Conclusion

Women's learning cannot be understood if the social contexts in which it takes place are not taken into account. These contexts offer complex and sometimes conflicting learning opportunities for women. The scholarship on women's learning indicates that we must take account of how broader social structures affect the hidden curriculum of any context and of the more overt subject matter or teaching/learning methods. As Tom Heaney (1995, p. 149) has suggested, learning is not simply an "individual-in-the-head" process; there is a social dimension of learning, in terms of both "the social relations which are reproduced in us and the transformative consequences of our learning [for] society." For adult educators, this implies a need for greater awareness of this social dimension of learning in formal education, as well as in other contexts of learning. In all contexts, women learn much more than subject matter or skills. They learn implicit and explicit lessons about themselves as women and, more specifically, about themselves as women of a particular race, class, and culture. These lessons in turn affect how they see themselves as learners and shape their future learning experiences. (Chapter Three discusses, in more depth, the significance of self and identity in women's learning across contexts.)

An understanding of women's learning also requires an appreciation of how women actively respond to the social contexts of their learning. A key concern for many feminist scholars has been identifying how women learn different ways of responding to oppression—in particular, ways that are self-affirming and growth-enhancing. Scott (1991) observes that Marilyn most often engaged in "private rebellions" against the oppressive aspects of family, work, and educational institutions. She recognized sexism and racism yet kept silent and adapted in order to survive. Her survival skills were admirable, but she was compelled to deny her own needs and desires.

The limitations of such private rebellions have led some feminist theorists and activists to argue that more organized, collective resistance is necessary for women to mount real challenges to social structures that oppress them. Adult education can play a key role as a site for fostering more public, organized forms of resistance. Some examples of this collective resistance are found in the more emancipatory community groups. These groups demonstrate the more positive, growth-enhancing aspects of many contexts of women's learning. Even those environments that may not seem optimal have given women opportunities to create new knowledge, question old beliefs, and engage in personal and social change. Women's learning does not simply lead them to reproduce existing social relations. As the statement by Heaney (1995, p. 149) indicates, such learning can transform the context in which learning itself takes place.

3

Identity and Self-Esteem

Daniele D. Flannery

*When I went to the university to study art I became
more conscious of my situation as a female student.
Continuing hostile comments from men and the
absence of other serious women combined to make me
conclude that some men didn't seem to like women
who had aspirations as artists. . . . As I remember
this period of my life, I realize that there was a knowing and a not-knowing going on within me simultaneously. I was coming to recognize that there was a
serious gap between the way I saw myself and the
way I was seen by the world. . . . By the time I left
school, I had incorporated many of the attitudes that
had been brought to bear on me and my work, both
in school and in the art scene. I had abandoned the
paintings that my graduate advisors disliked so
intensely, leaving them in a garage to be destroyed.
I had begun to compensate for my situation as a
woman by trying to continually prove that I was as
tough as a man, and I had begun to change my work
so that it would be accepted by men.*

Judy Chicago, Through the Flower:
My Struggle as a Woman Artist

M uch of women's learning has to do with women's identity and self-esteem, even though these concepts are not often treated explicitly in discussions of women's learning. *Identity* refers to who women are and how they identify themselves. *Self-esteem* refers to the positive or negative evaluations that women give to their identities. Identity and self-esteem can change. Families, histories, cultures, varying contexts, life situations, and the positions women hold can contribute to changes in identity and self-esteem. Women have choices about whether to change aspects of their identity.

Judy Chicago, author of this chapter's opening epigraph, saw herself as a woman (who she was) who was an artist (what she was) when she started at the university. She was proud of herself as a woman artist (her evaluation of who and what she was). As she began to perceive herself as less of an artist because of her professors' critiques, she threw her own work away and began doing more "male" artwork. In time she tired of doing art the way other people wanted her to. Chicago writes: "After a while, I recovered from my distress and realized that whether my work would be accepted or not, . . . I would have to find a way to affirm myself and my own identity as a woman artist" (Chicago, 1974, p. 53). She did this and became famous for a piece called *The Dinner Party*. Incorporating the traditional women's media of weaving and ceramics, as well as the domestic surroundings of a dinner table with porcelain plates, Chicago portrayed the story of women's history, using women's sex organs "as a reflection of each woman's need to explore her own identity, to assert her sense of her own sexuality" (p. 143).

Learning, unlearning, and relearning occurred for the artist. Her identity as a female artist, her ways of knowing, and her artistic choices were questioned and challenged by professors and other critics in the art world. Women's identities, self-expectations, and self-evaluations can change, as Chicago's did, when and as learning occurs. Women often revisit, unlearn, and recreate their own self-definitions and those others have for them. Mary Catherine Bateson (1990, p. 1) calls this constant learning the "act of creation that engages us all, the composition of our lives." She says that people, for the most part, don't set out with a certain particular self in mind but are in the process of improvising, discovering the "shape of our creation along the way" (p. 1). Women have common themes of searching for self, of being found, of being lost, and of wrestling with the societal expectations of what it is to be women. Women differ in how they experience those common themes because their unlearnings and recreations are unique and singular in that personal histories, cultures, and meanings differ. Women may be White women or women of Color, lesbian or heterosexual; they may work primarily in the home or primarily outside the home. Women are all sorts of combinations of identities.

This chapter deals with the concepts of identity and self-esteem and their interconnections with women's learning. In the following section, I briefly describe different definitions and approaches to understanding identity and self-esteem. Next, I discuss the process of identity formation as an important kind of learning in which women are engaged throughout their lives. In this discussion, I differentiate among several key perspectives on identity formation for women. After this discussion, I give a few examples of how women learn gender identities in particular, and I discuss how race and class are interrelated with gender in shaping women's identities. In the last section, I provide some examples of how women's identities, and more specifically their identities as learners, are affected by their experiences in different contexts.

Identity and Self-Esteem: Definitions and Approaches

"Identity is the interface between the individual and the world, defining as it does what the individual will stand for and be recognized as" (Josselson, 1987, p. 8). Generally, identity develops through internal and external influences. Such externals as family, history, social groups, and so forth, influence the developing identity. Many agree that early identity formation is an important influence through-out people's lives. Opinion varies, however, on the extent to which identity is influenced from within or from without, on whether its formation is a conscious or an unconscious process, and on the extent to which early identity formation remains influential.

A more psychological view sees the development of identity as an unconscious process whereby the focus is on needs, defenses, and maintenance of a sense of internal coherence. From this perspective, identity is a stable, consistent sense of who a person is. There are links between the individual and the world, but the emphasis is on the individual. Comparing themselves to others heightens people's sense of uniqueness and provides people with a reference point for judging their identity in relation to those they choose to imitate.

A sociological view sees the development of identity as a much more conscious process, whereby the focus is on the influences of the social world on identity. In this view, people deliberately choose to define themselves. They may keep their identities intact or change identities. They form implicit or explicit identity goals (Charmaz, 1987). From this perspective, identity is the way people "define, locate, and differentiate themselves from others" (Hewitt, 1992, p. 32).

Self-Esteem

As already mentioned, self-esteem has to do with how people feel about their identities. "Core" self-esteem has to do with people's conviction of "being loved and lovable, valued and valuable as [they] are, regardless of what they do" (Steinem, 1993, p. 66). This is the most fundamental kind of self-esteem. Many believe self-esteem forms early in children's lives.

"Specific" self-esteem is situational. This kind of self-esteem comes more from people's awarenesses of what they can do well, from expectations of others (relatives, teachers, coaches), and from particular contexts in which they find themselves. People may have positive self-esteem and negative self-esteem, which may change as they change or as situations change. For example, if someone who has poor school-related self-esteem from failures in high school returns to school as an adult and does well, her school-related self-esteem changes.

Self-esteems are expressed in all kinds of ways. Gloria Steinem (1993) indirectly expressed her own self-esteem in a book in which she reviewed current thinking on factors affecting self-esteem and combined the current thinking with the experiences of individual women. She sent her book in manuscript form to a friend, who sent it back and said, "I don't know how to tell you this—but I think *you* have a self-esteem problem. You forgot to put yourself in" (Steinem, 1993, p. 5). Steinem rewrote her book, trying to weave her own story into it, and dedicated the book to "everyone whose power has been limited by a lack of self-esteem" (p. 5).

Essentialist and Nonessentialist Views

Views of identity and self-esteem also depend on whether theorists hold essentialist or nonessentialist assumptions about human nature. These assumptions can be found in both psychology and sociology.

An essentialist perspective seeks to delineate the ultimate nature of identity and self-esteem. This perspective looks for what is fundamental and indispensable to identity and self-esteem. In its search for "truth," this approach assumes a common set of identity and self-esteem characteristics that are manifested by all people in particular ways that do not change significantly over time.

A nonessentialist perspective considers many possible expressions of identity and self-esteem and assumes multiple identities and types of self-esteem that change across time, and that may conflict with each other. The nonessentialist position looks at aspects of similarity and difference. These aspects include the issue of how socially constructed realities (such as the realities constructed by gender, class, sexuality, religion, and race) influence identity. The nonessentialist perspective acknowledges that people may have different positions in different settings (this phenomenon is often referred to as the "politics of location").

It is also important that the nonessentialist view stresses agency. Identity can be both constructed and chosen (Moon, 1993). People can choose to change identities. They can lower or raise their identity goals, giving up some identities in favor of retaining others.

Approaches to Identity Formation for Women

Identity formation is a significant learning process for women (and men), although it is not always conceptualized as learning. In this section, I describe various theories of identity formation in women. These theories are important because they provide not only descriptions of but also prescriptions for women's identities. Three literatures represent different conceptualizations of identity formation. These literatures discuss identity formation as directed toward (1) the achievement of autonomy, (2) the achievement of relationship, and (3) the prevailing and interwoven social constructions of identity that are continually reinterpreted by individuals. Rather than offer a complete survey of studies of women's identity formation, I provide examples of each of the prevalent literatures and note their strengths and weaknesses. (An excellent review of studies about the psychosocial development of women can be found in Rosemary Caffarella and Sharon Olson, 1993.)

Identity Formation and Autonomy

Erik Erikson (1968), one of the most influential thinkers in this tradition, saw identity formation as the accomplishment of separation, individuation, and autonomy. Although Erikson extended his theory to include girls and women, his research subjects were boys; therefore, his emphasis on autonomy and individuation was based on typically masculine types of behavior.

James Marcia (1960), continuing Erikson's work, details four possible paths to the negotiation of identity: foreclosure, achievement, moratorium, and diffusion. In foreclosure, the individual bypasses the identity stage, continuing to live out parentally derived standards and goals. Through achievement, the individual tests identity options and commits the self to particular ways of being. In moratorium, the individual tries to resolve identity-related questions but does not. In diffusion, the individual avoids the process of developing a personal identity and drifts along, neither experiencing crisis in identity matters nor forming a commitment to any particular set of values.

Ruth Josselson (1987) asked how women proceed through Erikson's identity stages and Marcia's identity paths. She interviewed sixty senior-year women from four colleges and universities, and twelve years later she reinterviewed thirty-four women from the same group. She found that women's notion of separation was different from men's: women separated from childhood connections to their families but maintained attachment to their families; identity formation was directed toward contact with others, cooperation, and being together. Anchoring is the metaphor that Josselson uses to describe the communion aspect of the separation-individuation process for women. She suggests that girls, as they separate from their mothers, must find someone else to replace that connection. The college-age women who had achieved adult identity were comfortable with themselves. Twelve years later, the women in this group were "in general, more flexible, more open to experience, more firmly rooted in an internal sense of self" (Josselson, 1987, p. 72). The college-age women who had foreclosed were also comfortable with themselves. As adults, they continued the beliefs and practices of childhood, had an ability to resist pressures to conform to beliefs different from the ones they held, had high self-esteem and low anxiety, and therefore had a closeness to and harmony with their families that remained central to their lives. College-age women who had experienced a moratorium in resolving identity issues felt much guilt and conflict. Twelve years later, three of these women had worked through their childhood selves, and six had returned to the life patterns that their families had exhibited during their childhoods. College-age women who had been diffusers were adrift, taking and changing self-definitions at will. As adults, three had attained adult identity, three were categorized as still diffuse but trying to understand their lives, and six others were still diffuse, without a personality structure, and relying on others for self-definition.

The work of Erikson, Marcia, and Josselson is fairly essentialist in its assumptions. They focus on individual traits presumed to be critical for the transition from childhood to adulthood and integral to all people. Josselson's work does include some acknowledgment that there may be different concepts of identity for women and for men, but it still puts all women together, assuming universal characteristics and ignoring race and class biases and the uniqueness of individuals. These studies limit the identity development of men and women to the adolescent and college years, with Josselson (1987, p. 168) concluding that "if we know a woman's identity status at the end of college, we can predict reasonably well the course of her early adulthood, which, we may suppose, will in turn predict her middle adulthood."

Identity Formation and Relationship

The relational view of women's identity is built on the notion that women develop in ways distinctly different from the ways in which men develop—that is, toward and with different values and processes. The relational view proposes that women develop and gain a sense of identity in a context of connections with others rather than through individuation and separation from others. In this model, women's sense of self is organized around building and maintaining relationships. The emphasis is positive, with women seen as proactively connecting with others rather than being dependent on them.

Carol Gilligan (1982), following the work of Nancy Chodorow (1974), places the centrality of connection in women's sense of self at the core of women's development. In Gilligan's study of women and moral decision making, women define themselves in relational terms that imply maturity, and they view growth as something to be found in intimate relationships. Both women's sense of self and women's sense of morality are integrally connected to issues of responsibility toward and care for other people. Gilligan proposes that the main goal of women's development is an effective balance of self-nurturance and care for others.

Jean Baker Miller (1986) continues research related to the development of women's sense of self. She suggests that the central interactions experienced by infants are those in which people tend to them, and so they begin to attend to the emotions of others, acting on others as those others are themselves in interplay with the infants' own emotions. In this model, the beginning notion of self is not one of stasis and isolation but rather one of dynamic interaction. Miller contends that an interactive sense of self is present for infants of both sexes, but that caretakers' culturally influenced beliefs about girls as future caretakers and boys as future providers play an important role. Girls are encouraged to attend to the emotional needs of others, whereas boys are diverted from this kind of attention. Consequently, for Miller, a person's sense of identity is linked very early with her or his own sense of being female or male. Women's sense of self becomes organized around building and maintaining relationships.

Judith Jordan and others (1991), having studied mother-daughter relationships, propose a "self-in-relation" model of women's identity development, also focusing on the self as developing within relationships. In this model, positive mother-daughter relationships, based on mutual empowerment and maturation, influence the development of a woman's healthy self. Identity development is based on a relationship-differentiation continuum rather than on a separation-individuation continuum. Being in relationships, picking up the feelings of others, and attending to the interactions between people is a "natural-seeming" way of being and acting for women; it includes self in relation to self and self in relation to others; "it is learned and assumed; not alien or threatening" (Jordan, Kaplan, Miller, Stiver, and Surrey, 1991, p. 51). The model also stresses the unity of the physical, the affective, and the cognitive, not as separate but as simultaneous and global (Emmanuel, 1992). There is a process of learning identity through personal learning and exploration based on affect.

The strength of the relational approaches is that they address and legitimize the connection with self and with others that so many women live and value. These theorists view development as the struggle to stay connected, to care responsibly for oneself, and to care responsibly for others. They believe that identity continuously and simultaneously evolves throughout childhood, adolescence, and adulthood (Stern, 1985). Relational theorists believe that women struggle a great deal as they seek relationships in a prevailing social context that promotes autonomy and separation.

Because they assume that all women are relational, the relational approaches become essentialist and fail to consider the differences among women. In fact, they can lead to behavioral expectations (such as the expectation that a woman should be a "natural" mother), and women who are different may be viewed as limited and deficient. A strong emphasis on similarity also fails to allow for women to unlearn or change their identities significantly. Although this approach acknowledges societal influences, so far it has neglected serious discussion of societal influences on identity, such as interrelationships among family structures or interactions between female identity and issues of race and class.

Identity Formation and Socially Constructed Identities

Views of women's identity development that are more nonessentialist focus on how social forces interwoven with individual interpretations contribute to shifting constructions of identity. Deborah Anderson and Christopher Hayes (1996, p. xiii), using the concept of "life-ties," recognize the influence of the contexts within which women's identity is formed: "Life-ties are a set of related experiences and the perceptions these experiences evoke within the lives of adults." In their research, life-ties (such as the positive and negative influences of parents, schools, and churches) were found to be strong influences on identity. Individual identity and self-esteem were "related to patterns of symbolic and idiosyncratic meaning that characterized a woman's or man's unique interpretation of their life-tie experiences" (p. 284). Self-esteem and identity changed throughout adulthood and had to do with growth as well as loss and setbacks. Adults rearranged, sometimes repeated, and often invented their life themes and self-views in the context of family, work, and education.

Anderson and Hayes found expressions of positionality among oppressed people, including women, as they survived by attending to the needs and feelings of others, keeping those who had power over them happy. They found differences by social class, noting that the blue-collar class and people living in poverty often seem to age physically and mentally much sooner than white-collar workers. They argue that skills for autonomy or relatedness may result more from one's location in the social structure than from one's own efforts. For example, "economic responsibility for one or more children may rule out the realization of autonomy for women, while societies that pressure men to be good providers seem to rule out affiliative roles for them" (p. 14).

Susan McCarn and Ruth Fassinger (1996) consider the interaction of personal and societal forces when they conceive of lesbian identity as consisting of two parallel processes. These are an identity-development process, whereby a woman becomes aware of and accepts same-sex erotic and lifestyle preferences, and a group-identity process, whereby a woman confronts societal oppression of women and accepts her status as a member of an oppressed group. According to Diane Resides (1997, p. 53), "The key point in this model is that one's individual sense of self can be separated from the extent that one identifies with or [publicly] participates in lesbian culture. . . . The model also assumes a reciprocal and catalytic relationship between the two processes of individual sexual identity and group identification."

Gendered Identity

The previous section focused on approaches to understanding the broad process of identity formation and the significance of gender in this process. It is also important to understand how the specific identities that women develop are gendered. Societal prescriptions of gender define women's identity. Furthermore, women's self-esteem is integrally interwoven with their responses to learned gender roles, gendered behavior, and ways of thinking. A great deal of the literature describes the nature of gendered identities and gender-differentiated activities for females and males. I will provide a few examples of key ideas in this literature.

Childhood and Adolescence

Gendered identities often begin to develop before birth. When parents know the sex of the fetus, they report different levels of prenatal activity. Movements of a male fetus are described as "vigorous"; movements of a female fetus are described as "very gentle" (Beal, 1994). This assignment of gendered attributes and expectations continues throughout childhood and adolescence.

Parents, friends, and relatives treat children differentially, giving three times more spatial toys (such as Legos and Erector sets) to boys and three times more dolls to girls (McHale, Bartko, Crouter, and Perry-Jenkins, 1990). They teach girls to be nurturers, caregivers, peacemakers, rescuers, model mothers and wives at any cost, and sexual seducers. Boys, by contrast, are taught to be strong, to master tasks, to be competitive, to be breadwinners, to keep feelings buried, and to be sexually assertive. Children's picture books, video games, and television shows also portray boys as instrumental and independent while characterizing girls as passive and dependent (Lindsey, 1997).

Parents, grandparents, teachers, and baby-sitters value different activities for girls and boys as they grow. They encourage boys to explore the limits of their play areas. They urge girls to remain close to their parents. By the time boys are three years old, their parents respond with more positive evaluation of their accomplishments than do girls' parents, and this pattern, too, continues throughout childhood and adolescence.

Research shows that gendered treatment and evaluation influence children's perceptions of themselves as capable. First, boys continue to perceive themselves as capable throughout their high school years. White girls perceive themselves as capable, confident, and assertive in elementary school, but by the end of high school they have a poor self-image (American Association of University Women, 1992; Orenstein, 1994). Among Hispanic girls, this decline in self-esteem is even more profound than in White girls (Valenzuela, 1993). By contrast, Black girls retain a high level of self-esteem throughout high school (American Association of University Women, 1992).

Second, by the age of six or seven, children know what boys and girls can do, and they know they differ from each other. By fourth grade, children state very clearly why it is better to be a boy. People listen to boys. Boys have more money. Boys can grow up to be president of the United States. Such attitudes continue throughout high school.

Studies show some gender-role socialization differs according to race, culture, and class. Black children experience much less socialization along mainstream gender-expectation lines than do White children. Black girls as well as Black boys are encouraged to be independent, to obtain employment, and to engage in childcare (Bardwell, Cochran, and Walker, 1986; Lewis, 1975). The pattern of assigning domestic chores to girls and maintenance chores to boys is much more intense in the lower economic classes than in the middle classes.

Adulthood

The gendered expectations communicated to women during childhood and adolescence continue to be reinforced and challenged in adult women's lives. Marriage and motherhood, as well as women's roles in paid employment, continue to be influenced by gendered expectations, although those expectations now take new forms. Through dealing with these gendered expectations, women continue to unlearn and relearn who they are and how they feel about themselves.

Marriage and Motherhood

A central expectation for girls and women is preparation for and achievement of marriage and motherhood. A study by Rachel Hare-Mustin (1987) found that women's roles in the family remain unfulfilling and a source of identity conflict for many women. Women are encouraged by social norms and institutions to meet their needs for achievement and support outside the family, in friendships with other women, and in the workplace rather than through radical transformation of family structures and roles. Seldom has the assignment of housework primarily to women been effectively challenged, even though the repetitive and unappreciated routines associated with housework have been found to be also associated with women's depression (Hare-Mustin, 1987). Thus women may have ambivalent feelings about their roles and identities in the home.

In Barbara Louis's study (1985), separated and divorced women reported wrestling with societal and family expectations, waiting to be rescued, and surviving without someone to protect them. The women talked about learning and unlearning identities. Their comments reflect the intensity of emotion associated with this learning process—for example, "I found it very confusing because you grow up and develop a certain pattern of everything. It's like a major explosion" (p. 85); "You take it all apart and you start over again; that I'll discard and this I'll put in that" (p. 43); "One of the things that I have to learn to cope with is not to feel ashamed of who I am" (p. 49); "Oh God, please, send someone to rescue me" (p. 43); "I'm scared to death. I don't know how to exude the fact that I'm number one; that it's OK to be interested in making a lot of money, and that I'm competent and have the ability to make a lot of money, and won't fall back into the helpless woman position" (p. 43).

Another study also illustrates how changes in marital status provide women with opportunities to learn and unlearn previous identities. This study explored the enormous issues surrounding decision making that were confronted by a group of widows, sixty and older, after the death of their husbands (Greaves, 1992). They had learned the gendered expectations for being a wife for their generation all too well. From childhood on, they were schooled to let men make decisions about buying and selling houses, taking care of repairs, and finances. As widows, they had to do tasks they believed were not women's work. The widows had to go against their own beliefs about what women do and had to learn the skills of decision making that they hadn't acquired previously.

Workplace Roles

Women may struggle in particular with perceptions of being incapable in male-designated roles in the workplace. Two examples give a picture of these struggles. A recent study of small-business owners across the country showed that women are less confident about their ability to succeed in business than men are (Beausoleil, 1997). Another study focused on women scientists, highly educated and well paid, who reported that their learning was constantly influenced by, and sometimes emerged as a response to, the tensions they experienced as outsiders in this predominantly masculine culture (Kerr, 1988). One scientist wanted to move in new research directions, but she was not confident about this move; the techniques in the new area were different and more difficult. This new emphasis was a field even more dominated by "macho and very aggressive men"; she said, "I was sure I was going to get creamed if I tried to do that without really knowing what I was doing" (Kerr, 1988, p. 65).

Women as Agents of Their Own Identity and Self-Esteem

The examples in the previous section might seem to portray women as primarily learning to conform to or being restricted by societal prescriptions for gender identities and roles. I would stress, however, as Elisabeth Hayes also notes in Chapter Two, that women are not just passive recipients of these societal prescriptions; rather, they are often very proactive, choosing change. Val Freysinger and I (1992), studying women and leisure, found that a group of women in their early thirties, influenced by the women's movement, by changing times, and by the experience of rearing daughters, began to search for their own identities. They wanted to find out who they were apart from their socially prescribed roles. Leisure provided time for doing this. One woman expressed it this way: "In leisure you can become a person again. You're not mum, you're not [number] 54 on your time-card, you're a person" (Freysinger and Flannery, 1992, p. 315).

Women are agents in fostering their own self-esteem as well as in developing their own identities. For example, studies have described how some working-class women have quit basic education and training programs out of resistance to being treated like children: the programs were regimented and rigid; to maintain their integrity as adults, the women needed to leave these kinds of learning contexts (Bingham, 1995; Gorback, 1992). Such resistance to demeaning approaches to education can be found among women at all levels of education.

Of course, women have varied responses to the gendered expectations of society and culture. Studying the process of how personal sense of control over identity intertwines with cultural identity for women, Lucy Earle Reybold (1997) found that women respond very differently to conflicts between personal and cultural identity. Some women construct their own personal models of self and ignore cultural expectations; others adapt their personal models of self, in a compromise with their culture. Some confront the culture directly; others choose not to confront the culture at all.

Gender, Race, and Class Identity

It is significant that much of what has been written on gendered identity is really about White middle-class women and has been extended to women of other races and classes. Yet, because women's identity and self-esteem are interrelated with the class, cultures, and ethnic groups to which women belong, women may be very different in how they develop and express gendered identities. For example, we can't assume that sexism affects White women and women of Color in the same way (Reid, 1995), nor can we isolate gender from class. Race, class, and gender are interlocking aspects of women's experience that entitle certain people and deny status and power to others. The examples that follow are illustrative of what is in the literature, not facts about all women belonging to the particular group.

One example of the interrelationship of race, gender, and identity is that Black women have not been expected to fit the dominant culture's stereotype of femininity: "The irony of slave women's history is that womanhood was redefined to allow for the exploitation of their labor, resulting in the development of independent, self-reliant characteristics" (Brown-Collins and Sussewell, 1986, p. 7). As another example of the effects of both race and class, bell hooks (1994) writes that for Black women and for working-class women of various races, mothering and childcare are seen as functions, as part of women's work, rather than as integral expressions of their identities, an attitude often attributed to White middle-class women. Further, many lower- and working-class women, forced by economic need to work outside the home, can't limit their work to the "home" sphere, as White middle-class women can. Therefore, their identities may be more likely to be defined by both work outside the home and work within the home. Yet, from another perspective, the growing numbers of middle-class women who are in the paid workforce may find their employment to be an even more influential source of identity than lower- or working-class women. Middle-class women may be able to obtain jobs that offer more opportunities for self-expression, development of skills, and personal growth.

In Wendy Luttrell's study (1984), White working-class women defined what it was to be working-class. The attributes they had learned and claimed were "being tough," "being rebellious," "being quiet and withdrawn," "being cute," "being the mother and marriage type," "not being smart," or "having common sense" (p. 162). They identified these shared traits as necessary for their survival as working-class women. These women saw themselves as entering adulthood earlier than middle-class women. By the age of twelve they were taking major responsibility for siblings, and not long after that they were expected to help support the family economically. When working-class women entered school or training programs, they experienced great difficulty with the institutional structures and lack of personal control, commenting that they had been adults for years and now were being treated as children. For these working-class women, the image of motherhood was conflicted: to become wives and mothers was to get autonomy from their families of origin, whereas at the same time to become wives and mothers involved a loss of self because they had to be subservient and submissive to their husbands. Aida Hurtado (1996) refers to these conflicted identities as "stigmatized identities": socially constructed identities that are associated with minimal amounts of social and economic power.

Little research exists on the effects of ethnicity and social class on gender-role development, but one study (Reid, 1995) suggests such effects. The researchers report that while Asian American families hold a conservative attitude toward women's place in the family, this gender-role attitude does not extend to the denial of women's participation in the workforce. In fact, Asian American women's rate of participation in the workforce is greater than that of any other group of women.

Women with multiple cultural identities must learn how to deal with sometimes conflicting expectations. Cherri Moraga (1983) writes, "I think: what is my responsibility to my roots—both white and brown, Spanish-speaking and English? I am a woman with a foot in both worlds; and I refuse the split" (p. 34). Gloria Anzaldúa (1987) uses the metaphor of "border crossings," meeting places between cultures, and perhaps identities, too, where one wrestles with leaving parts of one's culture and accepting aspects of a new culture, or where one lives on the margins of several cultures.

Adopting this notion of borders, Pablo Vila (1997) suggests that not all people choose to "cross" them; some choose to reinforce their cultural borders, or to create entirely new ones.

Women's Identity and Self-Esteem

One aspect of women's identities is how they view themselves as learners. Women often contrast their identities as learners in school and as learners in out-of-school contexts. Some women have a strong and positive sense of themselves as learners, regardless of their experience in formal education. In interviews by Carla Clason-Hook (1992, p. 258), one Latina woman said, "I didn't go to school, but life taught me many things. You know, it's true, life is a school. What we live during our lifetime is where we learn the most. Yes, life is a school. We learn by stumbling around." Other women contrast their views of themselves as learners in school and their identities as learners outside school. In Luttrell's study (1984), working-class women perceived that schooling did not validate their sense of themselves as knowledgeable and competent learners; the women saw themselves as lacking "schoolwise" intelligence but valued their own "common sense" that came from self-education and their daily experiences in the neighborhood. Irene Baird's study (1994) of single women on welfare who were heads of households again shows the distinctions women can make between school learning and common sense, and how this distinction is related to their identities as learners. For these women, common sense was what was learned through experience in the world. The two kinds of learning were so different in the mind of one woman that in the context of "school learning" she said she did not know how to read, and yet the researcher saw the woman using an automotive manual to fix a car. When the researcher asked the woman what she was doing with the manual, the woman said she didn't believe she was reading it because the manual wasn't a "real" book or, in her mind, a schoolbook; it was something she could actually use, unlike the texts she found useless in school!

Women's identities and self-esteem as learners are influenced by their experiences in many different social contexts. Early schooling experiences have a significant impact on women's identities as learners in adulthood. The classroom contexts of women's adult learning, the home, workplace, community organizations—all these and other contexts, as described in Chapter Two, are locations where women learn. Chapter Two provides a broad description of women's learning in these contexts; here, I will give more specific examples of how women's identities and self-esteem as learners develop in these settings.

Early Schooling

A number of studies document the negative impact of early schooling and its influence on other learning for women, particularly for women of Color and women with low socioeconomic status. Examples include the stories of economically disadvantaged women on welfare in a workfare program in California (Gorback, 1992), Native American women enrolled in a skills-upgrading program (Nesdoly, 1993), Appalachian women learning in community organizations (Bingham, 1995), and displaced homemakers, rural women, disabled women, and women of Color in four special readiness programs (Safman, 1988). For all these women, school had been a place where they didn't fit in. As children they had been poor, minority, unable to dress or speak the way other children did, shy, and so forth. Their low school-related self-esteem as adult women often stemmed from unhappy memories of these past experiences and failures.

The negative effects of previous schooling, and hence feelings of low self-esteem, can be diluted under some conditions. For some women, just attending an adult education program enhances self-esteem because it gives them the socially acceptable status of "student," one that legitimizes them in the eyes of their children and the broader society and reduces their feelings of inadequacy (Gorback, 1992). Phyllis Safman (1988) identifies a link between feelings of control and women's self-esteem as learners, particularly for women of Color and economically disadvantaged women. In her work, if women saw connections between basic educational programs and future or present employment, they felt better about themselves as learners, perceiving that with education they could better control their own destinies. Karen Gorback's work (1992) illustrates another kind of control related to women's identities as learners: control as reflected in school attendance itself. One of the women in Gorback's research expressed her story eloquently: "I grew up with a family of six siblings. My parents took me out of the eleventh grade to take care of my mother when she got sick, so I didn't get to finish. Twenty-five years later here I am, finishing high school. I mean, I was stuck down in a corner so many years and they kept tellin' me how stupid I was and dumb. From my parents to my 'ex' I felt useless, worthless. . . . I'm in control now. I have more confidence in myself. By being in the program I'm sure of myself" (p. 103).

Classroom Cultures

The culture of the classrooms that women experience as adult learners can also strongly influence their self-doubt or lack of confidence in their learning abilities. Women's alienation in traditional classroom cultures is widely documented (see, for example, Association of American Colleges, 1989; Crawford and MacLeod, 1990; Chapters Two and Four of this volume). Lani Guinier, Michelle Fine, and Jane Balin (1994) suggest that for women students to participate successfully in the classroom, they must perform as their male peers do—engaging in combative argumentation, asserting their opinions, and challenging faculty and peers. Such behavior may be at odds with their views of themselves as learners. Jill Tarule (1988) writes that in higher education, traditional emphases on competition and the often impersonal climate of classes have played a role in fostering self-doubt and silence among women, characteristics that may not typify their self-esteem and behavior in other settings. Individual research studies on women in the classroom often reveal this same alienation. Ana Martínez Alemán (1988) has found that the college classroom is at odds with women's socialization as girls and women. The women in her study said people in the classes were strangers, that they didn't have trusted friends in the classroom, and that they felt people would judge their answers: "You don't know what they are going to say. You don't know if they're going to totally criticize you, if they're going to think that you're an idiot" (p. 6). A unique finding of this study is that women's self esteem as learners was positive when talks with friends were places of learning. Outside the classroom, meeting anywhere they could, the women in this study viewed their friendships as places to take risks with their thinking, risks based on trust and intimacy. The women were confident in trying out ideas, in helping each other learn, and in developing interdependence through searching to understand what the class material was about.

Joan Gallos (1993), Sandra Harding (1991), Mary Belenky, Blythe Clinchy, Nancy Goldberger, and Jill Tarule (1986), Nell Noddings (1984), and other feminist thinkers see the problem in academic environments as one of the absence of women's ways of knowing, women's knowledge, and women's experiences. Without these, women in the Belenky, Clinchy, Goldberger, and Tarule study (1986) reported classrooms as doubt-inducing or debilitating. (See Chapter Six for the use of narrative as a way of transforming women's identities and self-esteem as learners, and Chapter Seven for examples of feminist pedagogy in the classroom.)

Home

Experiences in the home are another source of self-doubt for women that can influence their learning. These experiences include women's childhood homes or families of origin and their adult households. Self-doubt can occur when women return to school as adults and feel guilty or inadequate and blame themselves for the difficulties they experience in handling multiple roles (Rice and Meyers, 1989). In fact, such feelings of inadequacy and guilt are often portrayed as major barriers to women's persistence in formal education.

Kathleen Rockhill (1987), in a study of Hispanic women's efforts to become literate in English (also described in Chapter Two), demonstrates two other aspects of home situations that influenced Hispanic women's self-esteem as learners: power issues between men and women, and the "double day" for women.

The power issues were reflected in the women's tendency to defer to their husbands as the more proficient speakers of English. They saw themselves as not good at communicating in English and saw their husbands as much better at it. The husbands also saw themselves as better at communicating in English than the women were, and yet when the actual skills of the women and their husbands were compared, the women often had better skills than their husbands did. The women described in interviews how "their husbands 'call them down,' tell them they are stupid, illiterate, even whores" (Rockhill, 1987, p. 321). Husbands opposed their wives' participation in literacy education, but the women saw no connection between these abusive experiences in their homes and their own beliefs that their English was not as good as that of their husbands.

Rockhill identifies the "double day" as another influence on the women's views of themselves as learners. The women tended to blame themselves for not learning English, explaining that they were too preoccupied by family concerns to study. Most of the women worked outside the home and were responsible for the bulk of the work in the home as well as for the emotional support necessary to sustain the family. As Rockhill notes (1987, p. 320), "the acquiring of English for these women is regulated by material, cultural and sexist practices that limit women's access to the public [sphere], confining them to the private sphere of the home."

Other Contexts

Their experiences in many other contexts can have direct and indirect impacts on women's identities as learners. Here, I will offer just two examples.

First, in the 1940s, with the enlistment of men in the armed forces to serve in World War II, working-class women were recruited to play professional baseball. Members of the first All American Girls Professional Baseball League associated their experiences in the league with fostering self-confidence, decision-making skills, risk taking, and a sense of relatedness and relationships with others (Hensley, 1996). These outcomes may have been partly due to their engagement in a typically male-dominated profession and to their overcoming the initial skepticism and outright derision that greeted their first public appearances. The women also reported that because of these experiences they participated in continuing education for the rest of their lives. The specific connections remain unclear, but we can speculate that the women gained confidence in their ability to learn difficult new skills, as well as the motivation to meet new challenges.

Second, in a study of women's learning experiences in a community center, one woman reported that she developed a new perspective on her own intelligence as a result of serving as a volunteer tutor: "It took me the longest time to figure out that I was smart. . . . I was volunteering and I was helping a lady. I was tutoring her in second year college algebra. And I thought to myself, 'Hey! I'm smart! if I can do this, then I'm an intelligent lady—'cause when I worked it and nobody else could I thought, I'm not stupid.' And it's helped me ever since then. It made me realize that I wasn't stupid, that I could be taught. I could learn. And from then on I've just been learning as much as I have been able to learn" (Bingham, 1995, p. 156). Thus experiences in different contexts may give women opportunities not only to learn new skills but also to recognize the abilities they already possess as learners.

Summary

Women's views of themselves as learners are varied. Individual women may name themselves as learners at some times but question themselves as learners at others. Their identities and self-esteem as learners are clearly influenced by their experiences in many different social settings. Nevertheless, such settings influence but do not determine women's identities as learners. Women are actively engaged in reinventing these identities, just as they continually reconstruct other aspects of their identities.

The value placed on being a "successful" learner, particularly in formal education, is growing. Women's identities as learners can have significant influences on their general sense of self-esteem and on their other identities. There is considerable stigma attached to lack of success in formal education and schooling. Women who have not been high achievers in such settings may be particularly prone to self-doubt with respect to their learning abilities. It may be important for educators to help all women become more aware of the learning they accomplish outside formal educational settings, to validate this learning and connect it to classroom learning experiences.

Conclusion

There are many influences on women's identity and self-esteem, and thus on their learning. Gender is a particularly powerful influence, and yet we may be unaware of how gender affects our identity and self-esteem. After her friend's comment that she had left herself out of her work on self-esteem, Gloria Steinem realized how true this was; she gave up "those elaborate and intellectualized pages," she says, adding:

> But it took much longer for me to give up my image of myself as someone who helped other people through crises and never had any of my own . . . my patterns of childhood taking care of mother. I finally had to admit that I, too, was more aware of other people's feelings than my own; that I had been repeating the patterns of my childhood without recognizing them. . . . most of all I was "codependent with the world" [Steinem, 1993, pp. 7–8].

Its influences may seem invisible, but gender does not disappear whether we are addressing identity, self-esteem, or some other aspect of our lives as women. Rather, women's identity and self-esteem are intertwined with learning, unlearning, and relearning who we are and how to value ourselves. Steinem (1993) does a good job of stressing the "revolution from within" in which women must engage in order to find themselves in the midst of their relationships, work, and all other aspects of their lives. I would also suggest, however, that the revolution must take place from without, in society, if women's selves, identities, and attributes are to be valued and appreciated in all settings. I wish all women to have the experience of Judy Chicago, who came to see herself as a person and as an artist, who liked what she liked and valued what she valued and no longer needed either to prove herself in a man's world or to abandon her paintings in order to be accepted by men. "Moving through the flower," she writes (1974, p. 206), "is a process that is available to all of us, a process that can lead us to a place where we can express our humanity and values as women through our work and in our lives, and in so doing, perhaps we can also reach across the great gulf between masculine and feminine and gently, tenderly, but firmly heal it."

4

Voice

Elisabeth Hayes

M arie left the first session of the training seminar with feelings of frustration. "I didn't feel like I had a voice at all in that group," she confided later to a co-worker. "Every time I tried to make a point, I was interrupted by one of the men. I don't think I'll even try to say anything in the next session."

Julia was talking with several other women who were participating in a support group for recently divorced women. "I am really learning a lot about myself in this group," she commented. "What's really important is that I am finally developing my own voice as an individual, rather than being dependent on a man for my identity. The group is helping me get in touch with who I really am inside."

At the initial meeting of a community leadership development program for women, the facilitators told the group, "One of our primary goals is to help women gain a greater voice in community decision making. We hope that you will learn how to challenge the sexist practices that often prevent women from achieving leadership roles."

Voice is a pervasive and powerful image in women's stories about learning and in the academic literature on women's learning. Why is voice so compelling and readily linked with learning for women? One reason, as suggested by the authors of *Women's Ways of Knowing* (Belenky, Clinchy, Goldberger and Tarule, 1986), is that voice implies communication and connections with other people, an orientation to relatedness that has frequently been associated with women in dominant United States culture (see Chapter Five for further discussion of women and connection). Voice also is active, implying the ability to express thoughts and feelings so that they can be heard and understood by others.

Voice as an image, and its associations with learning, are complex, with many layers and facets of meaning. In an effort to give some clarity to the concept, I will distinguish among three different meanings or uses of voice in connection with women's learning. First, the word *voice* can be used in a literal sense, to signify women's actual speech or speaking style; this use of the word, to mean *talk*, focuses on how women use spoken language in learning situations and on how their learning preferences may be reflected in their use of talk. Second, the word can be used in a metaphorical sense, to represent the expression of women's identity; this use of the word, to indicate *identity*, focuses on how women's identity is reflected in what they say, in the ideas they express, and in the confidence they express in their own thoughts and opinions. Third, the word can be used in a political sense, to reflect the power and influence that women have in a particular situation; this use of the word, to mean *power*, emphasizes women's development of a consciousness of their collective identity and oppression as women, and of the means to challenge this oppression.

Voice as Talk

Whenever people learn together in groups, talk, in its literal sense, is usually an aspect of the learning process. Talking can be important for clarifying ideas, asking questions, and so on—in other words, for enhancing the quality of learning. In addition, talk can be important in demonstrating and getting affirmation of one's ideas and abilities and of oneself as a learner. And, as many feminist educators have pointed out, talk is one means of participating in collective knowledge creation, a process that historically has excluded most women. Educators have used sociolinguistic perspectives on women's communication styles to understand how women may prefer to use talk in learning.

Women's Talk: Making Connections

Deborah Tannen (1994) has used the term *rapport talk* to describe a communication style that is believed to be favored by many women. The emphasis in rapport talk is on maintaining relationships through talk. In this hypothetical example, Carolyn is telling Sue and Joan the story of how she is learning to use her new computer:

CAROLYN: It just took me forever to figure out how to connect everything together, and the manual was impossible to understand, you know?

SUE: [*groaning*] Uh-huh.

JOAN: Oh yeah, terrible. What did you do?

CAROLYN: Well, then I got the thing running, but I couldn't get into the word-processing program. And I got really confused by all those, those little, umm, icons, you know what I mean?

SUE: Mmm . . . those pictures are too tiny!

JOAN: So how are you feeling about it?

CAROLYN: So, anyway, I got really frustrated and felt so stupid—

SUE: I had exactly the same feelings with mine. You just think, Why can't I do this?

JOAN: Me, too.

SUE: But you learn to do it. I know you will. Then you feel smarter, like—

JOAN: Like then you know you can figure it out, and it's something you thought you couldn't do before.

CAROLYN: Part of it, I think, is being a woman, and not believing that women are good with technology, maybe?

SUE: Exactly—

JOAN: So we are talking about stereotypes, right?

Carolyn, Sue, and Joan's conversation provides examples of many features associated with rapport talk. While Carolyn shared her story of learning to use the computer, Sue and Joan indicated their interest and support by brief remarks, "uh-huh"s, and so on. Carolyn checked with her listeners to make sure that they were understanding her. Sue and Joan responded by offering reassurances and sharing their own experiences with learning to use a computer. Joan used questioning to encourage Carolyn to share more about her experiences. The topic of the conversation developed gradually, never losing the connection with Carolyn's experience but broadening to the idea of stereotypes and their effect on women's use of computers.

Apart from the use of these conversational strategies, the content of women's talk also has been characterized as more relationship-oriented. According to many sociolinguists, women's talk reflects a concern for the personal, is descriptive of feelings as well as of thought, and is oriented to the details of a narrative or experience.

Tannen contrasts women's rapport talk with "report talk," a communication style that seems to be used more commonly by men. Report talk is focused more on using talk to establish individual power and control than on relationships. It is characterized by lengthy monologues, competition among speakers for control of the conversation, and abrupt shifts in topic.

How do women and men learn such talk strategies? According to some theorists, girls and boys learn at a very young age that females and males are supposed to communicate differently. Pamela Treichler and Chris Kramarae (1983) summarize research indicating that parents and teachers interact differently with girls and boys, giving them encouragement for different kinds of talk. Children's interactions with their peers in play groups quickly begin to reproduce these sex-linked communication styles. For example, in groups of boys, talk tends to be used to assert dominance and authority. Groups of girls use talk more to foster relationships, tending to exert control indirectly and to avoid direct confrontation. Thus, through these informal experiences, women and men develop and practice different conversational strategies that can become relatively consistent patterns of communication.

The idea that many women use rapport talk has considerable appeal. It seems to reflect the way in which many women perceive their own experience. Nevertheless, some scholars have been critical of efforts to characterize women's speech in such global terms. Mary Crawford (1995), for example, argues that describing women's talk as relationship-oriented simply reflects and reinforces society's stereotypes about women, ignores differences among women, and obscures the effect of context on women's talk. Susan Gal (1991) has pointed to research indicating that women in different cultures use different communication styles; in the United States alone, such factors as race, ethnicity, and class can have a significant effect on women's typical communication styles.

Tannen (1994, p. 14) makes a helpful distinction between gender patterns and gender identity. She argues that there is nothing intrinsically female or male about particular ways of talking, but that women and men learn to use talk in particular ways because those ways are associated with gender. Not every individual may fit the pattern, and patterns will vary across cultures. The problem arises when gender patterns become associated with gender identity, that is, with absolute differences between women and men that are intrinsic rather than socially determined.

I believe that it is possible both to be aware of general patterns within our own culture as well as to be sensitive to variations among individuals and across cultures. I also agree with Crawford (1995) about the importance of understanding how context shapes women's talk. Rather than focusing exclusively on how and what women say, we need to examine the situations in which this talk takes place. Let's take a look at one context of particular relevance in learning: the higher education classroom.

Talk in the Higher Education Classroom

It was an all too familiar pattern in my graduate seminars: during the second class session, we quickly became engaged in a discussion of an issue that I now can't recall, but what I do recall is suddenly becoming aware of who was talking, and how. My male co-instructor and I had sixteen students in the class, only four of them men. These four men were rather loudly asserting their opinions to each other across the room. The women in the class remained silent throughout this long exchange until I broke in to shift the topic and invite more participation.

After class, I said urgently to my colleague, "We can't let that happen again!"

"What?"

"The way the men were dominating the class in that discussion!"

"I didn't notice it," he replied with some surprise, "though now that you point it out, I guess they were."

What happens to women's talk in the context of higher education? In more traditional college classrooms, the norms for student talk may conflict with women's typical communication styles. When student talk is encouraged at all (frequently it is not), the traditional academic model is more similar to the mode of report talk than to rapport talk. Tannen (1994, p. 57) characterizes this approach to the discussion of ideas as "ritual opposition": individuals are expected to present their ideas in a convincing and absolute manner, and others are expected to identify and challenge whatever weaknesses may exist in those ideas; presumably, such back-and-forth argumentation will contribute to the rigorous scrutiny of ideas and lead to new insights. As Tannen points out, however, people who are not used to ritual opposition, or who do not feel comfortable with it, will not find it conducive to learning. What is perceived as an attack on their thinking can make these people doubt their own ability and stifle their thinking rather than enhance it. Many women, particularly those who enter higher education after years away from schooling, and whose experience has been in settings where ritual opposition is not a predominant style of talk, may be among those who do not thrive in such a climate.

What, to be more specific, is the effect on women and their talk? Of course, women will respond differently to this climate. Some women may find this model of talk so uncomfortable that they simply choose not to participate. Other women gradually learn to adopt the academic model of debate and can become quite successful at it. In general, however, research suggests that women talk less in higher education classrooms than men do, and that they talk for shorter periods. As Treichler and Kramarae (1983) point out, this may be more the result of male dominance than of a simple difference in conversational style. If women attempt to join discussions, they can find themselves quickly cut off or ignored by male students—and even faculty. Jean Kelly (1991) found examples of these patterns in her study of adult students in a training course for supervisors. In her analysis of the discussions, Kelly found that men used the types of talk strategies associated with report talk to control the interactions, and that they tended to prevent women from participating. The women's use of strategies to support other speakers, such as asking questions to elicit more information, gave the men still further opportunities to maintain control of the discussions. This description makes it appear that the men were deliberately trying to sabotage the women's conversational styles, but that was probably not the case. Nevertheless, because the men's talk strategies were aimed at self-assertion rather than connection, the net effect was that the women tended to be pushed out of the discussion.

Of course, it is difficult to generalize about women and men's talk even in one type of learning setting, such as higher education, because of the many factors that can shape communication patterns. Higher education researchers have found some interesting potential relationships between certain aspects of the classroom and patterns of talk for women and men. For example, a number of studies suggest that both female and male students talk more in classrooms led by female instructors, and male-female participation tends to be more equal. One possible explanation for the greater female talk is that a female teacher provides a positive role model for women, increasing the likelihood that they will believe it is okay for women to con-tribute to the discussion. Men may also talk more because the sta-tus differential between teacher and student is reduced somewhat if the instructor is female. Another explanation is that the sex of the teacher is not in itself the critical factor affecting student talk, but rather that female teachers are more likely to use teaching strategies that encourage student participation, such as group discussion. In a recent study, Polly Fassinger (1995) found that norms of classroom interaction, among all classroom factors after class size, had the strongest influence on men's as well as women's self-perceived class participation, and that the sex of the teacher did not in itself have a significant influence. These norms included beliefs such as "My peers listen attentively" and "Students respect each other's views" (p. 87). Interestingly enough, these norms seem more closely aligned with the characteristics of female-associated rapport talk than with male-associated report talk.

From a somewhat different perspective, the critical factor may be the relative self-confidence that women feel in a learning situation, not simply their preferred styles of communication. In Fassinger's research (1995), male as well as female students' self-confidence had the most influence on their self-perceived participation; its influ-ence was greater than that of any other classroom factor, including classroom norms. Even more notable was that self-confidence was more influential for women than for men in determining class par-ticipation. Nevertheless, women were less confident and partici-pated in class less than men did.

Most research has focused on how women's talk is limited in higher education, but there are some studies in which women are described as talking more than other students in the class. For exam-ple, in one of my one studies (Hayes, 1992) that included both adult and traditional-age college students, women were perceived as participating more actively than men in classroom discussions. Adult women in Tanya Furst's (1991) and Diane Horwitz's (1994) dissertation research stated that they talked more than other students, and even that professors relied on them to keep class discussions going. What would make women in these studies so much more talkative than what seemed to be the norm in other studies? One explanation is that there may have been a discrepancy between perceptions of women's behavior and their actual amount of talk. Dale Spender (1980) suggests that stereotypes about women as "talkative," combined with the implicit norm of silence for women (in public settings), affects women's perceptions of their own talk, as well as others' perceptions of their talk. Women can easily be perceived as taking up more talk time than they actually are, particularly in relation to men.

In the studies of Horwitz (1994) and Furst (1991), the women were comparing themselves with younger, traditional-age students, and in fact it was unclear from their descriptions whether any adult men were in the classes. We can only speculate about the impact of having adult men in the class, but the more obvious point is that the women's age was related to their classroom talk and distinguished them from younger students of both sexes. It's likely that in this case sex was not the critical factor, but rather that the women's range of life experiences and motivation to learn was what made the difference in their amount of talk.

Cultural norms for communication can also affect women's and men's participation in classroom talk. Unfortunately, much research (such as the studies cited earlier) seems to have ignored such factors. Nancy Goldberger (1996), for example, points out that in some cultures silence and respectful listening are valued as much as speaking out. In contrast, Aida Hurtado (1996) points out that for some women of Color, being too "outspoken" in the classroom may be more of a problem than being too quiet. Patricia Hill Collins (1990) and Thomas Hochman (1981) suggest that Black students may expect and demonstrate stronger emotions and greater personal investment in debates, which can conflict with the emphasis on detachment and objectivity typically expected in the classroom.

Impact of Talk on Women's Learning

The nature of talk in many formal learning situations can put many women at a disadvantage in learning. If their ideas are ignored by teachers or other students, women can learn to doubt their ability, even though their comments may not be ignored because of their content; a woman's comments may be overlooked or discounted because of how they are presented—in what seems to be a tentative or uncertain manner—or simply because the speaker is a woman. We know less about how talk patterns affect women's learning of subject matter. In fact, since women tend to outperform men in terms of grades, there may not seem to be a negative impact. Comments from women suggest, however, that one effect may be a dampening of their motivation to pursue particular areas of study in formal learning.

Women's talk can influence how their learning and abilities are perceived by others. When those others are teachers who assign grades, or supervisors who evaluate job performance, women can be treated unfairly. Tannen (1994) tells the story of a physician who received a low grade during her internship from her supervising physician. She was surprised because she knew from her contact with other interns that she was the best in the group. When she questioned this grade, the supervisor replied that she had less knowledge than the other interns. When she asked him for evidence to support this assertion, he replied that she asked more questions than anyone else in the group. Tannen also describes Kate Remlinger's classroom research on asking questions: when Remlinger interviewed three women and three men about their question-asking behavior in class, all three men indicated that if they didn't know something, they would look for information on their own, ask a friend, or otherwise avoid asking questions in class. Tannen observes that women seem to be less aware that asking questions may create an unfavorable impression of their abilities.

Other talk strategies commonly associated with women may affect the extent to which others find them credible. The use of tag questions ("That author's argument was not very persuasive, was it?") and other strategies of rapport talk do not communicate a sense of certainty or confidence. In my own research (Hayes, 1992), even though they were perceived as participating less actively in class, men were perceived as being more self-assured than women.

Changing Patterns of Talk and Silence

Many educators have argued that to support women's learning we must change patterns of talk in learning situations. Some argue that women need to become more assertive—in other words, to learn to talk "like men." Others argue that we should change patterns of talk to be consistent with the modes preferred by women.

There are some difficulties with both alternatives. Teaching women to talk the way men talk assumes that male talk is the most preferable mode for learning. We have little evidence that this is so. In fact, report talk reflects an orientation to individualism and "one right answer" that is incompatible with the move toward more collaboration and tolerance for ambiguity in the workplace, in the academic world, and in daily life. Unfortunately, the focus in discussions of women's talk has more often been on how women's talk places them at a disadvantage in learning, rather than on the strengths of women's talk in learning. One of my graduate students, in a discussion of how women tend to be more tentative than men in expressing their ideas, exclaimed, "That's because women are smarter! They can see many sides of an issue and know how difficult it is to be certain!" Horwitz (1994) points out that women's willingness to express their uncertainty could be a strength in learning, allowing them to clarify ideas and be receptive to new perspectives. Moreover, even if women do change their way of talking, they still may experience problems in how they are perceived by others. As Robin Lakoff (1975) has stated, women are at a disadvantage, regardless of their talk patterns: if they do talk "like men," they can be perceived by others as too aggressive or too confident;

in other words, they don't fit our image of how a woman should behave, and so they are negatively evaluated. Women can also be put in the position of adopting a persona that does not feel comfortable to them.

Nevertheless, changing talk patterns to be more supportive of women's talk is not an easy task. It is not just a matter of using group discussion or inviting personal experience or feelings. Simply equalizing female and male contributions to a discussion is not sufficient for creating a supportive learning climate for both women and men. The research of Virginia Hardy, Vivien Hodgson, and David McConnell (1994) provides a good example. These researchers looked at how computer-mediated conferencing (CMC) affected the talk patterns of adult students in several small learning groups. In CMC, participants cannot interrupt one another, and they do not need to take turns participating. The researchers found that the participation of women and men was relatively equal, but that the women students described the men's talk as too cerebral. The men tended not to share their own feelings, and they asked the women to explain reasons for their feelings, thus shifting the discussion more toward intellectual analysis. The issue was not that the women felt incapable of intellectual conversation but that they expected and valued a different sort of discussion, with interactions that were, in the words of one woman, "more holistic" (Hardy, Hodgson, and McConnell, 1994, p. 410).

One solution to the difficulty of making mixed-sex groups more equitable has been to create all-women learning situations. There are many potential benefits of single-sex learning groups, but inequitable patterns of talk and domination can exist in all-female groups as well. Saundra Gardner, Cynthia Dean, and Deo McKaig (1989) describe a class in women's studies that was intended to create a "feminist" classroom environment. Unexpectedly, women students with greater prior knowledge of feminism began to dominate the discussion and "lecture" other students. Ultimately, the instructor had to take a more active role in equalizing participation and preventing domination. As Crawford (1995) has pointed out, the cooperative mode of discussion used in feminist consciousness-raising groups was the result of considerable practice and hard work, and many women had great difficulty with it; it was not the natural outcome of establishing all-women groups.

There are many fascinating questions to be answered about the role of talk in women's learning. Given our current understanding of the positive and negative consequences of female and male communication strategies, it may be helpful for adult educators and learners to make talk patterns an explicit focus of learning. Talking about male-female participation patterns, and about women's and men's different perspectives on appropriate communication strategies, could be a first step. Women may find it helpful to learn report-talk strategies if they are in situations where such communication styles are valued and rewarded. Nevertheless, we can also strive to create, in the classroom and in other learning situations, norms that encourage and support varied forms of talk and interaction.

Voice as Identity

"The support group at the women's center is really incredible," Maria told her counselor. "I am learning so much about myself. This is the first time I have been able to talk about how my husband has abused me. I feel like I am giving voice to a part of my experience, a part of myself that I was afraid to express."

As Daniele Flannery discussed in Chapter Three, women's stories of their learning are pervaded by issues related to changes in and development of identity. Often, women describe these issues in terms of voice: "I learned that I had something to say"; "I gained a new voice"; "My voice got stronger"; "I learned to speak in my own voice, not the voice of others." George Lakoff and Mark Johnson (1980) have suggested that a metaphor can be used to express a complex set of ideas that are not yet fully elaborated or theorized; I believe that voice is such a metaphor.

The example of Maria illustrates one way in which voice can be associated with women's identity-related learning. Maria describes herself as "giving voice" to an aspect of herself and her experience that she previously felt unable to put into words. Women also talk about "developing a voice" as they craft new identities. "Reclaiming a voice" is another common metaphor in women's learning, referring to women's feelings of reasserting ownership of an expressive mode that they lost in childhood or adolescence as they conformed to social expectations for female-appropriate behavior. The distinctions among these three metaphors may seem subtle, but each metaphor offers a different perspective on voice and women's learning. In the next sections, using examples from some representative scholarship, I discuss the nature of each of these metaphors and each one's association with a particular aspect of women's learning.

Giving Voice

The term *giving voice*, as I use it here, refers to a process of naming experiences that were previously unarticulated. This can be an extremely powerful process. One power of words is that they seem to be able to make such unnamed experiences real, give shape and meaning to them, and allow them to be communicated to and reflected on by others. The act of naming our experiences is an integral part of establishing who we are; in many ways, we *are* our experiences. In the case of experience that has been unspoken because it is considered socially unacceptable or taboo, the act of giving voice can be transformative. (In Chapter Six, Ann Brooks describes examples of such transformations for women who were able to give voice to experiences of sexual and cultural discrimination.)

Although giving voice to or naming experiences is typically assumed to be affirming and liberating, it can also be constraining. For women, and in particular for women of Color, it may be oppressive to adopt existing labels for themselves and their experience. For example, consider the term *codependent*, which has become a popular way to characterize relationships assumed to be unhealthy.

Using this term to describe her relationship with her alcoholic husband may lead a woman to identify herself both as the perpetuator of her husband's drinking and as someone who is too dependent on another person; naming her experience in this way may diminish her self-esteem instead of contributing to a positive self-image. Even naming oneself as a woman can be detrimental in a society where the characteristics associated with women (passivity, emotionality, dependence) are considered inferior to those associated with men (assertiveness, rationality, independence). The act of giving voice to her experience may require a woman to challenge the existing names for that experience. For example, women have begun to use the term *breast cancer survivor* (instead of *victim*) as a way of portraying the active role they have taken in overcoming the illness.

Developing a Voice

The term *developing a voice* evokes images that differ in significance and meaning from the metaphor of giving voice. The term *development* suggests a process of evolution, of gradual unfolding, with voice taking on different forms as it develops. Used as a metaphor, the idea of developing a voice is an attempt to illuminate how women learn to express their identities as they change and develop. A woman may need to learn more about herself in order to express herself more fully and truthfully. In turn, as she develops a voice and listens to her own words, a woman may learn more about herself, and this new knowledge may further contribute to changes in her identity. The expression of identity may not always be consistent with women's internal experience of self, and one challenge may be for women to develop a voice, a means of self-expression, that corresponds to who they know themselves to be.

One aspect of developing a voice may be finding a voice, an act of discovery: it is not uncommon for women to link finding a voice with a creative act by saying, for example, "I found a voice through writing poetry" or "Becoming a mother helped me discover my own voice" or "My drama class led me to find a voice for the first time."

But developing a voice can also be a deliberate process of fashioning an identity as a woman strives to achieve goals or resolve conflicts.

The need to be known by others, and to know others more fully, can prompt women to learn more about themselves and develop new voices to better express themselves. It can also involve learning more about others and learning to speak in ways to which others will be receptive. For example, Patti, a woman described in *Women's Ways of Knowing* (Belenky, Clinchy, Goldberger, and Tarule, 1986), was experiencing continuous conflict with her parents. She learned not only that she needed to really understand her own feelings in order to express them but also that she needed to "translate her inner voice into words her parents could understand" (p. 90). Patti's story suggests that developing a voice may involve learning not just to speak out but also to modulate one's speech.

Is development of voice a linear process? Development is frequently interpreted as a process of moving from a lesser to a greater degree of realization or potentiation in some area, but scholars and women themselves increasingly point to the development of voice as a nonlinear process that is highly affected by context. For example, a woman may have a strong personal voice in the context of her family but may feel herself to be inarticulate when she enters a college classroom. Development of voice in one context may affect voice in another context. Women's stories of developing voice in the classroom are often accompanied by stories of developing a new voice in the family context: "I began to speak my mind to my husband"; "I was able to talk to my children in a new way."

The construct of development and the issue of linearity also raise questions about what sort of voice may be better than another. Might this judgment vary according to the context in which a woman finds herself? Should our understanding of developing a voice include more attention to how women develop different voices and use different voices in different situations? (See "Multiple Voices, Multiple Identities," p. 97.)

Reclaiming a Voice

Annie Rogers (1993, p. 285) tells an evocative story of her own experience of reclaiming a voice in an acting workshop; she was performing one of her poems, one that reflected how she had lost voice in childhood, and her instructor was prompting her, often forcefully, to reconnect with what her physical being and her feelings had been at the time described in the poem: "The white ceiling became a dark sky, filled with cold stars, then black—and the voices, once cut off from me, came back to me. My own voice came from within my body, resonated through the tiny bones of my face. My lips and arms tingled from the vibrations." This anecdote illustrates several dimensions of reclaiming voice.

A key assumption in connection with this metaphor is that women lose or deny their "true" voices in response to the oppressive nature of social and cultural expectations for women. The studies done by Rogers and other psychologists associated with the Harvard Project on Women's Psychology and Girls' Development indicate that in adolescence girls lose "trust in the authority of their own experience" (Rogers, 1993, p. 273). This loss of trust, and of voice, happens differently for girls of different racial, class, and cultural backgrounds. White middle- and upper-class girls' loss of voice seems to result from their efforts to conform to social expectations for female-appropriate behavior and self-expression. They learn that it is unacceptable to talk about certain topics or to express certain emotions, such as anger or hatred. To conform to the conventions of "female goodness," these girls stop saying what they really think and feel. Mothers and female teachers may be powerful role models for such behavior, as girls observe what these women say—and don't say—about their experiences and relationships. Silence is first used as a means of self-protection, to avoid the threats to relationships that could result from the voicing of unacceptable thoughts and emotions. Ultimately, this public silence affects girls' internal voices as well, becoming what Rogers describes as "psychological resistance—the disconnection of one's own experience from consciousness" (p. 289).

Poor and working-class girls and women of varied racial and cultural backgrounds also seem to experience this disconnection from their selves, their emotions, and their voices, but research by Jill McLean Taylor, Carol Gilligan, and Amy Sullivan (1995) indicates different causes and outcomes of this loss of voice. Many of the girls in this study seemed to feel less pressure to conform to the mainstream culture's norms for and ideals of feminine behavior (being "nice," not expressing anger), but some learned to suppress their emotions out of a desire to appear strong and self-sufficient. Silence and self-isolation became strategies that many girls used to protect themselves from becoming objects of hurtful gossip among their peers.

Reconnecting with emotion-laden experience may be central to women's recovery of voice. Reclaiming a voice involves the recognition that voice is emotional and physical, not simply intellectual. A significant learning experience for women may be recognizing and accepting emotions that they have learned to regard as unacceptable, particularly those emotions that are considered unacceptable in relation to cultural ideals of femininity or other societal or religious prescriptions. Rogers (1993, p. 271), arguing that courage is integral to the expression of self, and tracing what it has meant through history to be courageous, finds a definition that illustrates the connection of voice, mind, and emotion in a compelling manner: "to speak one's mind by telling all one's heart."

For women of Color, a central issue in reclaiming a voice may be regaining the ability to articulate identities that have been repressed because of experiences in a racist and sexist culture. For example, Olivia Castellano (1992) describes her experience growing up as a Mexican American, as well as the self-hatred she developed for her Chicana identity. As a high school student, she was assumed to be stupid by her teachers because she was Mexican American, whereas her friends and family criticized her for studying rather than finding a husband. As a college student, she became very shy and unassertive, choosing to be silent in class out of fear that she would appear to be either an unfeminine woman or an angry Mexican. Only when she enrolled in a graduate program specifically designed to support Mexican American students did she learn to reclaim her voice and identity as a Chicana. Particularly important in her story is how she was able to acknowledge the deep anger that she felt in response to her experiences of racism. Rather than fearing this anger and suppressing it, she became able to express it and use it in ways that enabled her to challenge further oppression.

The stories (like Castellano's) of women of Color are particularly useful in illustrating the conflicts that women can experience in expressing their identities. They also illustrate how women's voices can reflect multiple rather than singular identities. Castellano's struggles with her identity as a Mexican American were complicated by her identity as a woman: if academic achievement was considered beyond the ability of a Mexican American, it was even more out of character for a Mexican American woman. Such stories point to a somewhat different perspective on identity and voice, one that allows us to see how each of us experiences multiple identities and voices.

Multiple Voices, Multiple Identities

"Some days," Paula told her friend Shannon, "I just become aware of all these voices inside my head, clamoring to be heard. I don't know who I am sometimes—are all these voices mine? And a problem is that they don't all agree. So it's really difficult to express the 'real me'—I feel like I'm making myself up, using a new voice, in every situation."

If you were Paula's friend Shannon, how would you react to Paula's comments? Your first response might be to assume that she is demonstrating signs of a personality disorder. On reflection, however, you might recognize some of your own feelings and thoughts in her words and assure her that this is a common and normal experience for all of us. Typically in our culture we have placed value on, and treated as the norm, the development of a unitary, coherent sense of identity, reflected in a consistent and confident individual voice. Nevertheless, such an ideal identity and voice may not reflect the actual experiences of most people, particularly women and people of Color. Further, this image of identity and voice may not really be ideal in terms of promoting positive human growth and change. Trying to conform to this image may in fact create feelings of inadequacy and self-doubt for women and may stifle rather than strengthen their voices.

Recently, authors writing from a feminist poststructuralist perspective have offered new ways of understanding identity and voice. I find three ideas from this perspective to be particularly helpful: multiple voices as reflective of multiple aspects of identity, voices as constituted by social factors as well as personal experience, and voices as constantly in process.

First, the idea of multiple voices reflects the assumption that as individuals, or "subjects," we have diverse identities that are expressed differently in different situations. We can probably all think of examples of how we change our voices, consciously or unconsciously, according to the context in which we find ourselves. For me, a striking example of this change in voice involved an older woman who was one of my adult literacy students. In the literacy classroom, she spoke softly and tentatively, in a voice I would have characterized as uncertain and lacking in confidence. But I attended several church services where, as the wife of the minister, she led the congregation from the pulpit in prayer and song. In the church, her voice was one of strength, self-assurance, and authority. I also had dinner with her and her family on several occasions after church. In the home, she became a dutiful wife, speaking to her husband with a voice of deference and responsiveness. Clearly, these examples suggest that a key factor in voice can be the nature of the power and authority that we experience in our relationships in different situations.

Second, our multiple voices do not just reflect feelings of power and authority in particular contexts. These voices are also products of broader social and culturally determined identities (such as those influenced by class, race, and gender) that shape who we are, as well as of our personal histories and personalities. Inconsistencies and contradictions among these identities can contribute to our experience of multiple voices. A woman may find that her working-class voice clashes with her voice as an academic; another may find contradictions in speaking as a woman and as a Roman Catholic. We may suppress some voices, to reduce this sense of conflict or because certain contexts make it difficult or unsafe to express certain voices. An important learning process for women may involve becoming more aware of the voices, the aspects of our identity, that we express as well as of those we suppress. This awareness may also help women become more critical of their "voices": Do they reflect the incorporation of social or cultural images that are oppressive? Castellano (1992), for example, describes how, even though as a young woman she was challenging traditional female roles by going to college, her ability to express herself was still deeply affected by traditional images of appropriate feminine behavior, images that dictated silence and submissiveness.

Third, our identities, and our voices, are continually in process. We are constantly creating and recreating ourselves through voice; giving voice to ourselves is a process of identity development itself, not simply a reflection of what already exists. This idea is reminiscent of the metaphor of developing a voice but it adds the perspective that the goal of this process is not to attain a single, "authentic" voice. Instead, the goal might be better understood, not as the development of a voice or of voices, but as the voicing of self that may develop as we become increasingly responsive to change, to new understandings of ourselves, to overcoming the limitations of our previous identities, and to creating new means of self-expression. Viewing our identities and voices as continual works in progress may offer important opportunities for the transformation of limiting assumptions about and labels for who we are and how we can express ourselves.

The Role of Dialogue

Typically, dialogue plays a prominent role in this process of "voicing self" for women. Dialogue helps us experience ourselves and our voices as they are created. The experience of dialogue is a powerful source of learning because it engages us on physical and emotional as well as intellectual levels. We can hear our voices as we speak them and they are reflected back to us in the voices of others. We can feel our own emotions as well as hear them in our voices and feel the emotional reactions of those with whom we speak. Women's descriptions of their experiences of voice reflect this impact. Some of these examples may sound familiar: "I was shocked by the anger in my voice—I didn't realize I was capable of sounding so forceful"; "Their lack of interest made me realize that I needed to make my voice more convincing"; "I was shaking as I tried to give voice to my experiences of abuse."

At a most basic level, dialogue can refer to any kind of conversational exchange between two or more people, but certain forms of dialogue have been proposed as more conducive to the development of women's voices. Not surprisingly, these forms of dialogue have many of the elements associated with rapport talk. The emphasis is on understanding and appreciating others' perspectives through careful listening and responsive questioning. Of course, dialogue as an ideal may not be fully realized in many situations, but conversations that come close to this ideal seem to be those that women link to their experiences of giving voice, developing voice, and reclaiming voice.

At a fundamental level, the context of a trusting and respectful relationship provides women with a safe environment in which to speak. Some women may have few opportunities to speak their minds in a relationship without feeling the need to censor their ideas and feelings. Attentive and supportive listeners, through their responses, can help women find their voices—by affirming those voices, asking questions to draw out voice, and prompting reflections on what has been voiced. Through dialogue, women may provide each other with models for voicing self that challenge limitations fostered by social and cultural prohibitions.

Most of the emphasis in feminist writings about voice and dialogue has been placed on this mutually supportive type of conversation, but I don't think we should overlook how women may develop voice through other types of dialogue. A woman may gain a sense of confidence and a more powerful voice from successfully participating in a confrontational debate. For example, I developed a professional voice based on logical argumentation in my graduate courses and professional presentations, one that served me quite well in certain contexts of my life. I also have a good friend who often sees the world quite differently from the way I do. She has the annoying habit of bluntly pointing out how she thinks I am misinterpreting things or misunderstanding myself. At times I don't feel very supported in such exchanges, and they can be frustrating; our conversations sometimes seem like hard work. But I am forced by her comments to take different perspectives, which can help me name my experiences in new and more helpful ways. Our form of talk may not fit the model of rapport talk, but we do have a caring relationship that provides a safe context for us to challenge and draw out each other's voices.

Voice as Power

The metaphor of voice as power draws our attention to how relationships of power and authority shape and are shaped by women's voices. Although this chapter has raised issues of power in connection with voice as talk and voice as identity, in this case voice can be understood more directly as an expression of power. Shulamit Reinharz (1994) has pointed out that, historically, women have been denied the right to speak, and women's efforts to claim a voice can be acts of resistance and rebellion against domination. Voice is a particularly powerful image because it places the powerless in a proactive role. In terms of learning, voice as power suggests that women learn to use voice in response to their experiences of power relationships. Their use of voice may conform to inequities of power; they may also learn to use voice in ways that subvert power. An important goal for women can be learning to use voice to gain greater power and authority.

The metaphor of voice as power can be expanded to encompass women's individual and collective voices. Women can claim voice and power as individuals and as a group, and these individual and collective efforts are frequently intertwined. In this discussion, I feel it is important to acknowledge that women have very different experiences of power and oppression. Sexism in our society creates a common experience of oppression for women, but this experience is modified by a woman's race, culture, class, and other factors. All these factors affect women's use of voice in relation to power. A key issue in women's development of collective voices has been learning about differences among women and striving for ways to articulate a common voice that acknowledges rather than ignores this diversity.

Individual Voice and Power

How does power affect women's voices? It affects both what they say and how they speak. Women's use of rapport talk (asking questions, speaking tentatively, not interrupting) can be interpreted in light of power relationships. Women in a patriarchal society need to be responsive to the powerful so that they adopt certain kinds of talk strategies that enable them to learn more about the needs, desires, and feelings of the powerful. Power also affects the extent to which women are heard in any given situation. In a group of women and men, women's comments may be ignored by men, and even by other women, because women are not perceived to have significant status or authority. I've observed this in professional meetings time after time. When women have managed to squeeze comments into the discussion, their comments typically have received no response from the rest of the group.

This perspective on voice may suggest that women simply learn to conform to existing power relationships, but this is not the case. Women can also use their voices in ways that subvert power relationships. Women's use of silence provides some good examples. Nancy Goldberger (1996) distinguishes between those who are silent because they truly feel powerless and without words—the "silenced"—and those who have a sense of choice about whether to speak and choose not to. Silence, particularly in educational settings, has frequently been considered a reflection of women's powerlessness and "internalized oppression"—lack of confidence, feelings of inarticulateness, or lack of knowledge. In some cases, women themselves do attribute their own silence to beliefs that they have nothing worthwhile to say, or to feeling stupid. But many women's accounts suggest somewhat different reasons for silence. As Carmen Luke (1994) argues, women's silence may represent a deliberate strategy to maintain safety. This safety may include protecting their sense of integrity and self-worth; it may also mean protecting their ability to achieve certain goals. Juanita Johnson-Bailey (1994) describes how Black women refused to answer questions in class or participate in class discussions as a means of self-protection. Describing a class on civil rights issues, one woman stated, "There were lots of times that questions were asked that even I did not respond to at all because I did not want to respond honestly or from my true feelings. A lot of times, I just suppressed my own answers or my reactions" (Johnson-Bailey, 1994, pp. 191–192). This woman felt vulnerable in class because she was the only Black student, and the professor seemed uncomfortable with her presence. In such a classroom situation, a woman may silence her voice to avoid the risk of harming her grade by being perceived as argumentative or simply too noticeable. Women can deliberately adopt a powerless voice to achieve their own goals. One woman in Johnson-Bailey's study (1994, p. 206) described how she learned to talk with professors to get the assistance she needed: "'Would you help me please?' If that pleading tone of voice is part of the inquiry then they are usually receptive."

As discussed in Chapter Two, silence can be used to resist what women perceive to be acts of domination and control, and it gives women a certain kind of power from not conforming. Women's silence may be resistance, but it does not necessarily lead to changes in power and authority, nor may speaking out. Hurtado (1996, p. 379) argues that "outspokenness," in order to be effective, must be employed strategically by women; as a child, she "learned that my mouth was my most powerful weapon" for survival in a racist and sexist society, whereas in college she became skilled at systematic argumentation, able to dismantle racist and sexist positions held by professors—those in power—with "humor, logic, belligerence, outspokenness and direct confrontation." Hurtado's voice was powerful because she was able to use the "tools of the master," which included persuasive logic as well as a forceful speaking style, to challenge the authority of the professors' positions.

Acquiring a strategic or tactical use of voice may be important in how women use voice in ways that give them more power. Hurtado (1996, p. 387) describes "tactical subjectivity" as an attribute of women of Color, referring to their ability to shift their identities and points of reference in response to the type of oppression they are confronting in a particular situation. Likewise, women may need to acquire a tactical voice, one that changes strategically on the basis of an understanding of power in the immediate context. For women, gaining an understanding of power may include developing new perspectives on the nature of power and its potential expression. A key question can be how we can develop powerful voices that do not dominate or oppress others.

Finally, we should recognize that the connections among voice, silence, and power are culturally determined. As already noted, in some cultures, silence does not indicate lack of power; for example, Patrocinio Schweickart (1996) observes that silence is highly valued in her native Filipino culture, and that among Filipino people, who love to talk, someone who talks too much may be seen as over-estimating the power of his voice. Further, silence can be seen as a sign of deep thinking rather than as a sign of stupidity or lack of voice. Goldberger (1996) also describes cultures, such as those of Native American peoples, in which silence is considered an act of respect for another person yet is freely chosen, not adopted in response to powerlessness. Therefore, the nature of a powerful voice for women may vary across cultures; in fact, we may learn a great deal from further exploration of voice in different cultures.

Collective Voice and Power

Collective voice and power can be viewed from two perspectives. From the first perspective, we can think of collective voice as reflecting how individual women identify with the collective experiences of women (or another group) and learn to speak in a collective voice—as "we" rather than "I." From the second perspective, women's development of a collective voice moves us from viewing learning as an individual process to viewing learning as a group process. A collective voice involves groups—in this case, groups of women—learning to speak a common language for the explicit purpose of achieving greater power and influence.

What does it mean for individual women to speak in a collective voice? Karyn Hollis (1995) gives several examples of collective voice in her fascinating analysis of autobiographical writings by women in the Bryn Mawr Summer School for Women Workers. In their writings, some women used a collective voice to reflect their collective identity as workers ("We workers do not want our employers to give us community houses and cheap rent, with lights and water free. We want wages that will enable us to live in better houses on better streets") and specifically as women workers ("It is a very difficult life for us girls in these days; we have to fight our boss on one side, our union that should otherwise protect us on the other") (Hollis, 1995, pp. 80, 88). What is particularly notable, as Hollis points out, is the sense of power associated with many instances of the collective "we" of the worker, which tended to be active, confident, and resistant to oppression. Hollis attributes this powerful voice to the Bryn Mawr program and to the social context in which other worker collectives were successfully organizing. At Bryn Mawr, the women were exposed to a "discourse of collective experience, protest, and power" (Hollis, 1995, p. 97) and given opportunities (such as the autobiographical writing) to adopt a collective voice as their own.

There are difficulties in learning to use a collective voice, particularly for White women. One factor is the individualistic orientation of mainstream Western culture, which works against identification with any group. I became particularly aware of this in a class discussion involving some women guests of diverse nationalities and cultural backgrounds. These women of Color seemed to speak in voices that readily connected with those of their mothers and other women of their cultures. When we asked them about how their experiences of learning were affected by gender in their cultures, they intermingled their own stories with stories of their mothers, aunts, and female neighbors, using phrases like "This is what it was like for us." This tendency was a striking contrast to that of many White women in the class, including myself, who tended to distance ourselves from the experiences of our mothers in particular and to emphasize our own individual stories. In an effort to reject the traditional roles that our mothers had taken on, we deemphasized or denied the ways that our lives were integrally connected with those of our mothers and other women in our childhood communities.

The frequently covert nature of oppression for White middle-class women can also work against the development of collective identities. Women of Color in this country typically are more aware of their group identities, given their experiences of multiple oppression. A difficulty particularly for women of Color may be, as Hurtado (1996) suggests, how to create congruence among their multiple collective voices without compromising their complexity or rejecting their communities.

When women as a group seek to develop a collective voice, learn-ing becomes a group rather than an individual process. Mary Belenky, Lynne Bond, and Jacqueline Weinstock (1997, p. 8) describe such a collective voice as "a metaphor for a community that is constructing and articulating their thoughts as well as exercising their right to seek justice." Their description suggests that creating a common knowledge and the means for expressing it is central to a group's collective voice. Together, women may be able to name or rename their experiences, an act of power in itself. Further, the powerless can create conversations among themselves, which can lead to power even when the powerful refuse to listen. Through such con-versations, women can begin to realize the collective power of their minds, to "feel, see and hear the power of minds gathering" (Belenky, Bond, and Weinstock, 1997, p. 8).

The Mothers' Center movements in the United States and Ger-many, which I briefly described in Chapter Two, provide informa-tive examples of women learning to develop a collective voice. As described by Belenky, Bond, and Weinstock (1997), the decision to name themselves groups for mothers, rather than for families or par-ents, was itself a collective claim for power in light of negative reac-tions from some feminists and potential supporters who questioned the values and attributes associated with mothering. The naming process was an important aspect of challenging the devaluation and stigmatization of mothering in society.

Women must learn to confront some difficult issues in develop-ing collective voices. One issue is how to establish a sense of unity while acknowledging differences among members of a group. A related issue, and one often suppressed, is acknowledging and deal-ing with the power differentials that exist within the group. How are different individual and group voices given different power in devel-opment of the collective voice? Does the term *collective voice* express a false sense of unity and equality? Feminists of Color, for exam-ple, have been quite critical of early feminist work that assumes all women share similar experiences of oppression, and that ignores how women can contribute to the oppression of other women.

The expression of diverse voices may be preferable in a classroom situation, but in other contexts, where action is a goal, the issue may become more complicated. Is a "unified" voice more advantageous from a political perspective, in terms of gaining power for a group? For example, would the work of the Mothers' Center movement have been compromised if the mothers had emphasized their differences rather than their commonalities?

Summary and Conclusion: The Many Meanings of Voice

Voice has many meanings related to women's learning. In this chapter, I distinguished among three meanings of the term *voice*: voice as talk, voice as identity, and voice as power. Each of these meanings draws our attention to a different aspect of women's learning. Voice as talk suggests the importance of gender-related patterns of speech and communication in learning. Voice as identity emphasizes that how women develop and express identities is a key dimension of learning. Voice as power reflects the perspective that women's learning is affected by unequal power relationships, and that for women a goal of learning can be to acquire individual and collective power through the expression and validation of their interests, needs, and experiences.

This diversity of meanings can make *voice* seem to be a catchall term, used too indiscriminately and excessively to have any real value. I think that is a danger, but I also think that voice remains a compelling and evocative metaphor. As educators and learners, we may find all its connotations useful, or we may pay more attention to selected aspects of voice in our teaching and learning. For example, we may wish to become more aware of patterns of talk in group learning situations. Are some individuals excluded from discussions?

What style of talk best suits our learning goals and philosophies—
report talk, rapport talk, or some combination? Do we wish to promote the expression of voice as identity in our teaching? How do
learning activities encourage or discourage the naming of unexam-
ined aspects of self, the exploration of multiple identities, the reconnection of self and emotion? What is the role of voice as power in
our learning and teaching? How might we support women in developing voices that enhance their individual and collective power? As
these examples suggest, the concept of voice gives us a starting point
for asking deeper questions about the nature of women's learning.

5

Connection

Daniele D. Flannery

The purpose of this chapter is to explore the concept of connection and learning. There has been a significant amount of literature in the past years suggesting that connection, in some form, is integral to women's learning. In this chapter I lay out some of the different meanings of the term *connectedness* as used in the literature and in women's stories of learning. The goal is to begin to differentiate among the ways in which the notion of connection is used, and thus to add greater richness to our understanding of women's learning. At the chapter's conclusion, I consider several issues raised by linking connection with women's learning.

Before beginning, I want to point out that in the literature, the concepts of knowing and learning are often used interchangeably in reference to the concept of connection. Nevertheless, I do believe that a distinction should be made between the two concepts. Let me illustrate the difference with the following example.

While teaching a research course, I stressed several points that were to be part of all research. Using the analogy of being a lawyer, I frequently said, "Think of yourselves as lawyers trying your case before a court. You want your case to be clear, the pieces to fit together well, and the argument for your point to be so tight that the listeners cannot but think what you want them to think." Janet, a student in the class, said that she just didn't get it. We had been over and over the points. They weren't clicking with her, but she said she would work on understanding them. Much later, she came to class with a small picture of a famous art work in black and white. "I've got it," she said. "Finally things make sense to me. The lawyer idea was in the way. I couldn't relate to it. It has no meaning for me. So I sat down and said, 'Who am I?' What kinds of things are important to me?' And—I'm an artist! Pictures with lines and shapes, dark and light, innuendos of contrasts—this is how research now makes sense to me. Now I get it!"

Ways of knowing can be thought of as "coherent interpretive frameworks" (Belenky, Clinchy, Goldberger, and Tarule, 1986, p. 9) that people use to give meaning to their learning. Our knowing is deeply intertwined with our worldviews, with our histories, our families, our social groups, our experiences, and so forth. We construct or create our own knowledge, whether we would use these terms to describe it or not. Unfortunately, because many institutions, such as schools and churches, have told us, didactically, what we should know, we may think of knowing and knowledge as valuable only when they come from outside ourselves. The act of coming to know became possible for Janet when she used art to understand the research principles. She had a strong worldview as an artist, but no sense of what it might be like to think the way a lawyer thinks. Art had been part of her entire life. Regardless of the different positions she had held, the artist part of her always came through. The world of art had shaped her way of knowing, but she was trying hard to know in a way that was unfamiliar—to understand how the research process was like trying a case in court. She couldn't do it. It wasn't her way of knowing.

The more specific processes of acquiring, maintaining, and changing knowledge within an interpretive framework relate to what I define as learning. The term learning refers to the processes, often cognitive, by which we come to know. How did we go about learning the facts, ideas, and skills we acquired? What were the processes we used to understand our feelings, to weave ideas into meaningful patterns, and to really understand something? Once

Janet was able to attach the research concepts to ways of knowing that were meaningful to her, her learning processes took over. She learned the material in the same way she would usually go about learning. She looked at the whole picture, seeing the artwork—or, in this case, the research process—as a whole. She asked herself if it felt right—that is, was everything contributing to the whole? If not, then her learning process was to look at what was contributing to a sense of the whole and what was not—a shape didn't fit with the rest, the shading was not subtle enough, and so forth. When she made changes, she used her own previous experience with artworks to determine what now felt right.

In the rest of this chapter, I use the terms *knowing* and *learning* as they are used by the authors whose work I include as source material. This usage will not necessarily reflect the distinctions that I have made here between the two concepts. Nevertheless, I urge readers to keep in mind the two different meanings of knowing and learning that I have just described: the theme of connection appears both in relation to the broad ways of knowing and in relation to the specific processes of learning.

Connection: Self and Others

For many, Carol Gilligan (1982) began a public conversation about a mode of being popularly called *connected*. In her work on women's moral decision making, Gilligan found that women saw a world that was composed of relationships. In her theory, a woman's self is delineated through connection with others. In reality, this was not a new idea. Other psychologists looking at women's development as relational (as discussed in Chapter Three) were also exploring the same kinds of phenomena. Jean Baker Miller (1986) portrays women's sense of self as organized around making and maintaining affiliations and relationships with others. Gilligan noted that women use this affiliative mode when making moral decisions. For example, in Gilligan's interviews (1982) a woman named Ruth says, "I have a real thing about hurting people and always have, and that gets a little complicated at times, because, for example, you don't want to hurt your child. I don't want to hurt my child, but if I don't hurt her sometimes, then that's hurting her more, you see, so that was a terrible dilemma for me" (p. 103). Women's experiences of themselves, as seen in Ruth's struggle, were tied to activities of connection and care.

Several years later the work of Mary Belenky, Blythe Clinchy, Nancy Goldberger, and Jill Tarule (1986) popularized the notion of ways of "knowing in connection" for women. Two of the five ways of knowing that their work identifies emphasize different types of connectedness in knowing. These two were "subjective knowing" (knowing in relation to oneself) and "connected knowing" (knowing in relation to others, a subset of the broader category of procedural knowing that also includes "separate knowing"). Collectively, these writings influenced many, who began further exploration of the notions of connection and women's learning. As a starting point for organizing the different ways in which *connection* is used, I distinguish between two aspects of connection: connection with/in the self, and connection with others. These aspects are meant to be a way of looking at the different perspectives on connection and women's learning. They are not meant to be the only ways to understand the nature of connection in women's learning, nor are they to be seen as independent of each other. In fact, they are very interconnected.

Connection with/in the Self

Connection to oneself is about knowing and learning in relation to oneself, one's own inner world. Connection with oneself can be expressed with many terms. In the sections that follow, I include *global processing, subjective knowing,* and *intuition* as aspects of connection with/in the self. Subjective knowing and intuition are more commonly associated with ideas in the literature about connection and women's learning. I have added global processing as a key topic, although its associations with connection are less frequent; nevertheless, the theme of connection is implied in many of its characteristics.

Global Processing

Laine Melamed (1985, p. 127), in her work on play and women's learning, writes, "Human activity is a playful blending of adventure, surprise, energy, circularity, trial and error, and interconnectedness. In order to know and understand, the many parts of the self must interact and bounce off each other, in a somewhat random manner. Rather than ordered, sequential knowledge-building, most of us 'follow our nose,' filling and refilling the moving empty spaces within a lifetime." Melamed is writing about global processing, a kind of cognition. In the literature, the term *cognition* refers to the way an individual experiences, processes, organizes, stores, and retrieves information. Cognitive styles are "information processing habits representing the learner's typical mode of perceiving, thinking, problem solving, and remembering" (Messick and Associates, 1976, p. 13). Global or connected ways of processing information are present in the literatures of three separate but related fields: cognitive psychology (Cohen, 1969; Bruner, 1985), brain research (Herrmann, 1990; Levy, 1974; Luria, 1973) and field-articulation research (Witkin, Moore, Goodenough, and Cox, 1977). Cognitive psychology uses the term *global cognition* or, more recently, *narrative cognition*; brain research, or hemisphericity research, uses the *right brain* in this connection, whereas the field-articulation literature uses the term *field-dependent* (or *field-sensitive*). The characteristics of the learners described in these three literatures are similar (Flannery, 1993). Learners who are global, right-brained, and field-dependent put things together to form wholes. They process pieces of information simultaneously and perceive the overall patterns and structures of what they are learning. Global learners perceive information concretely, relating to things as they are at the present moment. They see likenesses between things and understand metaphorical relationships. Global learners lose themselves in the moment; time is inconsequential. They make leaps of insight that are based on what may seem to be incomplete patterns, hunches, feelings, or visual patterns (Edwards, 1989). Global learners perceive information in a subjective manner, connecting it with their own personal experience. If the information does not connect to what is personal to them, they discard it as unimportant. They use deductive or intuitive reasoning.

The literature portrays women as more global (Haring-Hidore, Freeman, Phelps, Spann, and Wooten, 1990), more field-dependent (Witkin, Moore, Goodenough, and Cox, 1977), and more right-brained (Sagan, 1998) than men—that is, women tend to connect and interconnect ideas, events, and people in whole pictures rather than focusing only on one part of a picture. Women tend to demonstrate connected patterns of knowing and learning. They connect what is to be known to their own experience and to what is familiar to them. They connect cognition and affect. They use intuition, a connection among body, mind, and spirit. Wingfield and Haste (1987) name the learning styles of such connected learners "holistic," a description that implies a preference for both thought and feeling. As noted in Chapter One, generalizations about women's learning should be viewed with caution, and these generalizations are no exception. They reflect a dominant perspective in the literature, but in the last section of this chapter I will raise some issues about the support for such beliefs.

Subjective Knowing

Mary Belenky and her colleagues (1986) introduce the concept of subjective knowing, a kind of knowing connected to the self. It is a personal knowing from within, or from one's inner voice. Subjective knowing is based on one's firsthand experience. Subjective knowing is an awareness of the existence of inner resources for knowing and learning. Sometimes it is expressed as "just knowing," sometimes as one's "gut feeling."

For subjective knowers, truth is personal. It involves the connection of the affective with learning. For subjective knowers in *Women's Ways of Knowing* (Belenky, Clinchy, Goldberger, and Tarule, 1986), learning occurred when the women observed themselves and others who were like them. The women trusted an inner feeling instead of depending on outside authorities to determine right and wrong. Many women in this study expressed this position of subjective knowing, and it cut across age, race, class, ethnic, and educational boundaries.

In subsequent work by these and other researchers, the concept of subjective knowing was broadened and clarified (Debold, Tolman, and Brown, 1996; Clinchy, 1996). Studies of adolescent girls suggest that for the subjective knower there is a mind-body integrity: use of one's own multiple experiences and of multiple aspects of oneself in order to learn. According to Nancy Goldberger (1996, p. 96), "Subjectivity is not unitary, but [is] created by dialogue with[in] varying power relations[hips]." In fact, in clarifying this concept, Blythe Clinchy (1996, p. 211) writes that subjective knowers do not "wallow in subjectivity"; rather, they "respect views that differ from their own; they seem to listen and refuse to criticize. They value the sort of knowledge that emerges from first hand experience, and draw on feelings and intuition as sources of information."

Issues of agency and power are included in the concept of subjective knowing. As subjective knowers, our knowledge can be totally based on ourselves as authorities (Belenky, Clinchy, Goldberger, and Tarule, 1986). We may be our own total referent for knowing and learning, for right and wrong. Even at times when we just don't know, we stubbornly may take refuge in ourselves for safety, for quiet, and for centering.

From the perspective of subjective knowing, we can fight to be connected to ourselves as we struggle with what doesn't fit with our knowledge, what oppresses us. The work of Elizabeth Debold and Lyn Mikel Brown (1991) gives us a prime example: the struggle of adolescent girls against culturally sanctioned forms of knowledge and behavior that challenge their bodily and psychological sense of themselves. It is important to note that in these studies, the girls' ways of knowing, although centered on the struggle to maintain and clarify self-connection, were multiple. The girls talked about what was happening, what wasn't fair; they were talking about knowledge as constructed, changing, and contextual. Not totally self-absorbed, the adolescents were actually engaged in working things out within differing power relationships.

Women's experiences with conflict between inner voice and external authority are myriad. Elisabeth Hayes does an excellent job of dealing with this in Chapter Four, and so perhaps two somewhat different examples of such conflicts will suffice here. The first example is of women who were initially unaware of their disconnection with the self as knower but became more aware of this disconnection and struggled to overcome it. The second example is of a woman who struggled to retain her personal authority despite lack of support from her peers.

Example 1

A group of women school leaders had formed a support group to learn how to survive in institutions where male-based formulations of leadership were dominant, and to learn how to figure out the prevailing rules of behavior for leaders in these settings (Regan and Brooks, 1995). Over time, they realized that they had learned the rules and behaviors but weren't comfortable with them. As they told their stories of discomfort, they realized that the rules by which they were living weren't their own. They used the term "points of rupture" to describe the places where the rules conflicted with their own ways of knowing and valuing.

Only when the women had managed to get in touch with themselves and their ways of knowing and valuing were they able to begin connecting themselves to the kinds of leadership with which they were at ease and that they wanted to practice in their schools. They finally worked to become their own authorities. They defined the characteristics they wanted to embody in their work settings, and they supported one another in trying to live up to them.

Example 2

As a woman, a Black intellectual, and an academic, Alice Walker (1983, p. 244) talks about her experience as an "outsider-within," as one without position in the academy or among intellectuals: "I believe . . . that it was from this period—from my solitary, lonely position, the position of an outcast—that I began really to see people and things, really to notice relationships." Walker had a strong belief in her own authority as a creator of knowledge, despite lack of recognition from others. Notably, this lack of recognition enabled her to enhance still further her knowledge and the value she placed on her own knowledge. Walker adds (p. 264) that "the gift of loneliness is sometimes a radical vision of society or one's people that has not previously been taken into account."

Intuition

There is a large literature on intuition in general, and within this literature, discussions of intuition as a particular aspect of women's learning are especially prevalent. I will provide some examples to illustrate key themes in this literature.

As already mentioned, for Belenky, Clinchy, Goldberger, and Tarule (1986, p. 34), intuition is a part of subjective knowing, which is "a way of knowing based on intuition and/or feeling states rather than on thought and articulated ideas that are defended with evidence." As these words suggest, intuition is often linked with feelings and contrasted with rational thought.

I can use my own experience as an example. My own most natural learning might be characterized as intuitive. For me, "it feels right" is a visceral, bodily experience. I use this phrase about ideas I think and write, things I read and hear, decisions I make for today and tomorrow. When something doesn't fit, I have an overall feeling (not located any particular place) of discontent, of dis-ease. If something is right, I feel right and certain and settled. Sometimes I have more specific bodily responses to things. I will feel very peaceful within, calm, quiet, or I will have whirling in my stomach, pressure in my chest, quick lower-back pain. These responses are usually about situations that occur, decisions that must be made, and similar things. I see them as different kinds of responses. With these latter situations, if I as the knower am in touch with these feelings, I know immediately what is true for me.

This kind of intuitive knowing is not more effortless than logical, rational thinking. Those of us who know this way hone our affective abilities just as others hone their cognitive abilities. Our claims to validity lie in the synchronicity of our knowing.

Discussions of a slightly different form of intuition can also be found in the literature on women's learning. This expression of intuition emphasizes "the process of reaching accurate conclusions based on inadequate information" (Schultz, 1988, p. 19). The emphasis is less on the use of feelings as a source of knowing than on "coming to know" as the process of generating insights that are perceived, without the typical, logical sources of support, to be valid. This form of intuition involves "confidence in the process of intuition, certainty of the truth of intuitive insights; suddenness and immediacy of knowledge; emotional affect; [the quality of being] non-analytical, nonrational, nonlogical; [recognition of the] Gestalt nature of knowing, difficulty putting images into words and a relationship to creativity" (Schultz, 1988, p. 29).

A Black woman whom I will call Bea (her name is not reported in the original source), and who was interviewed in Janet Delany's (1999) study of Black women leaders in occupational therapy (OT), provides a good example of the nature of intuition and some of the issues associated with it. Bea never named her approach to learning as intuitive, but she told several stories that implied a kind of knowing associated with intuition. She explained, for example, "When I graduated from OT school, I already knew that I wanted to work in psychiatry because I had had a very good experience in my acute psychiatric fieldwork. I had, for some reason. I knew that I could look at this person and I could sort of tell what they needed" (Delany, 1999, p. 6).) Asked to talk about how she knew, Bea said (p. 25), "I know what to do sometimes. I don't think it's thinking, the rational, logical. So I think it's the way I put things together or the way I see patterns. I feel it as a sensation in my body. It's like a sensation, yea. I don't know, a sort of tingling, I don't know how to describe it. It's like tingling, then I kind of get a flash of what's needed here is something." A reliance on intuition is not without its problems and difficulties, however, which may be associated with resistance to or self-doubt about this type of knowing:

> There are times that I know when I don't want to let myself know or I don't think I have the right to know or there are lots of ways in which I put the knowing down. Or, I give way to someone else when I have these. . . . part of the question that you're raising is how do you honor the knowing. Because I'm sure everybody has this in some way, but how do you, what is the setting in which you can let yourself fully experience it, and not only that, but act on it. I think in the work that I currently do, I don't allow that knowing to come up as fully. It's beginning, but it's taken a very long time for me to allow it, to allow myself to use that knowledge [Delany, 1999, p. 26].

Such resistance and doubts may well be linked to society's general devaluation of this mode of knowing. Bea describes how public expression of intuitive knowing can risk negative judgments from others. Interestingly, she links this kind of knowing to her understanding of racism, often a particularly controversial topic of discussion:

I think sometimes it's not safe to know. I think this comes up around issues of race. Who can know and who can't know. I can see it, it plays itself out sometimes with my colleagues. Sometimes you're not supposed to know all of that or say it all, or be too off centered. . . . So, I think you have to maintain the integrity of your knowing. It's not always easy. Especially if what you know is different from how other people would put it or know it or what their experience is [Delany, 1999, p. 27].

Bea also provides some examples of how she hones her intuitive skills. She describes intuition as a form of "meditative practice. I think that one becomes grounded in one's knowing" (p. 28). She goes on to describe in more detail the process that she uses:

First, take in a breath and feel it in your gut. And that's real important, because I'm discovering that when I feel that, one can carry tensions like all over your body. And when I'm able to push that into my gut, that's the place from which I can act and its not flailing action. . . . It's like pulling all of the water from a tributary back into a pool, something like that. . . . then ask yourself this question. Is the front of my field equal to the back of my field? Now the front of your field, where people enter your field and come out of it; be aware of the back of your field, . . . the things that will come back to haunt me, you know, if I don't pay attention to them as I go pushing forward. . . . The third thing is to feel your self grounded to the center of the earth. And the fourth thing is to have selected a quality that you want to work on for a time. And the quality just pops into your mind. . . . So I'm describing a way of producing a kind of openness to knowing [Delany, 1999, p. 28].

Of course, Bea's explanation provides only one perspective on how intuitive knowing might be developed. As another example, Joyce Victoria Moon (1993) found that engaging women in the act of singing promoted intuitive learning. In Moon's study, singing was a tool that enabled the reconnection of body to mind, spirit, emotion, intuition, and memory. The women said singing enabled them to bypass thinking in order to bring new information into consciousness, and it predisposed them to be in touch with natural rhythms in the self and in the world. Moon's explanation was that "singing appears to access and strengthen the right brain. The right brain controls harmonics, intuition, metaphor, simultaneous, lateral thinking and whole, connective awareness" (Moon, 1993, p.111).

Common Elements of Connection with/in the Self

Global processing, subjective knowing, and intuition have much in common. They deal with connection to one's body, one's experiences, one's feelings. They emphasize the importance of and the validation of personal experiences. The concepts differ in their emphases on different aspects of knowing and learning. Global processing tends to focus more on the cognitive dimensions of learning. Subjective knowing emphasizes the way women go about connecting with themselves, rely on their own knowledge, and struggle with broader issues of power and control related to acknowledging themselves as authorities. Subjective knowing overlaps with descriptions of intuition in its emphasis on what women sense and "just know," and yet discussions of subjective knowing have not considered these aspects in depth. This is the realm of the literature on intuition, which considers both the inner "Geiger counter" of knowing that women often report and a knowing that requires the suspension of rational thought processes.

Laine Melamed (1985, p. 167), concluding her study on play and women's learning, writes that "the feminine mind knows relatedness, has an intuitive perception of feelings, and has a tendency to unity, rather than separateness." This conclusion aptly summarizes the important aspects of women's learning discussed in this section on women's connection with/in the self.

Connection of Oneself with Others

The connection of oneself with others is about learning and knowing where affiliative connection with others occurs. In this section, I just give a taste of the vast literature that emphasizes how women learn through interactions and relationships with other people. I then focus on connected knowing, as Belenky, Clinchy, Goldberger, and Tarule (1986) have developed it in *Women's Ways of Knowing,* and on literature that gives further insight into and support for aspects of connected knowing.

Learning Through Interactions and Relationships

Much literature, reflecting dominant assumptions about women's orientation to relatedness (see Chapter Three), has focused on how women rely on interactions and relationships with others in their learning. The dominant theme across studies is that women both prefer to learn with others and prefer a certain kind of learning relationship with others, one that emphasizes mutual support and caring. A number of studies in different contexts describe how women learn through interacting with other people, especially in ongoing relationships (Hoy, 1989; Van Velsor and Hughes, 1990). These include studies of women's learning in work settings, such as Laura Bierema's research (1995) on how executive women learn organizational culture, research that notes the importance of mentoring and of peer and networking relationships. Studies have also investigated women's connection with others in learning in the home and family. For example, Carolyn Brown (1994) explores how friends and various social networks supported first-time mothers in learning about pregnancy and childbirth. Ana Martínez Alemán (1998) uses the term "interdependent cognition" to describe the talk of female friends as a primary vehicle for cognitive growth.

A common assertion is that women tend to learn best in environments that promote mutual openness and an ethic of care, cooperation, and collaboration (Gilligan, 1982; Noddings, 1984;
Melamed, 1985; Kazemek, 1988; Ravindran, 1989; Clason-Hook,
1992). Women's preference for this kind of supportive, collaborative learning relationship with others is documented by a number
of studies. These include but are not limited to research on women's
learning in study circles, business associations, therapy groups, consciousness-raising and support groups, and feminist classrooms
(Melamed, 1985; Belenky, Clinchy, Goldberger, and Tarule, 1986;
Clason-Hook, 1992; Wells, 1994). Studies from the business world
suggest that women may exhibit a preference for this type of mutually supportive learning relationship even when it is at odds with
the values of their immediate contexts. For example, Bierema (1995)
found that, despite the independent, competitive nature of the corporate environment, the use of collaborative learning was most
extensively reported by executive women, who used this type of
learning in their efforts to negotiate and influence the organizational culture. Of women's groups in general, Adrienne Rich (1979,
p. 260) writes that "one of the most powerful social and political
catalysts . . . has been the speaking of women with other women,
the telling of our secrets, the comparing of our wounds and the sharing of words."

Connected Knowing

Belenky, Clinchy, Goldberger, and Tarule (1986) have described
one kind of women's knowing and learning as connected knowing.
According to these authors, connected knowing has as its basis subjective knowing, the conviction that the most trustworthy knowledge comes from personal experience. Connected knowers learn to
understand other people's personal experience and knowledge. They
are empathetic. They take a stance of believing and trusting rather
than judging what others say. Connected knowers enjoy collaborative explorations in various kinds of groups, such as those already

mentioned. In groups, they stretch their own vision to accept others' visions, which may be quite different.

Clinchy's further work (1996) stresses that connected knowing requires sophisticated abilities. She articulates these abilities in more detail, emphasizing how connected knowers validate, understand, and trust in other knowers. Connected knowers are aware that they cannot accurately know another's world because the experiences belong to the particular person. At the same time, connected knowers use their own experiences to understand the other person. Connected knowers feel viscerally the connection with others. They seek out learning communities where they can learn in collaboration and partnership with like-minded knowers.

A few studies have researched some aspect of Belenky, Clinchy, Goldberger, and Tarule's (1986) work. I include two of them as examples. Baxter Magolda (1991), using a longitudinal study of one hundred college men and women, found that an interpersonal pattern of knowing (comparable to connected learning) was used more often by women than by men and that impersonal patterns of knowing were used more often by men than by women. Not unlike Belenky, Clinchy, Goldberger, and Tarule's more connected knowers, students who used interpersonal patterns engaged in learning with peers, valued others' ideas, approached problems from a subjective stance, and valued individual differences.

Sue Rosser (1990) studied women scientists to see if, in spite of science's attachment to separate, procedural knowing, they might use connected knowing in the practice of doing their research. She looked at all areas of doing research: types of problems chosen for study, the way hypotheses were formulated, methods of data collection and testing, conclusions and theories drawn, and the use of scientific information. The women scientists did indeed employ connected knowing as she defined it. They expanded their observations to include interactions, relationships, or events not usually observed; they accepted the personal experience of women as a valid component of experimental observation, were more likely to explore problems of social concern, investigated problems of more holistic and global scope, used more interactive data-gathering methods, were aware of potential biases (of gender, race, and class), and developed theories that were relational, interdependent, and multicausal rather than hierarchical, reductionist, and dualistic.

Other studies, although not intended to question the work of Belenky, Clinchy, Goldberger, and Tarule (1986), have findings that provide support for their concept of connected knowing and its significance for women. Helen Regan and Gwen Brooks (1995), in the study of women school leaders already discussed, named the process by which these women learned to create relational leadership as "relational knowing." This type of knowing was collaborative. The women gathered in homes, retreats, and workshops. They shared who they were, what their work was like, and what they wanted it to be like. They supported each other in their explorations. They created a synergistic environment for everyone in the group.

In one of the few discussions of the significance of race as well as gender, Patricia Hill Collins (1991) incorporates themes similar to the concept of connected learning in a discussion of Black feminist epistemology. She writes that for Black women, experience provides a criterion for judging the value of what one says. The emphasis is placed on the experiential credentials of the speaker or knower: "Individuals who have lived through experience about which they claim to be experts are more believable and credible than those who have merely read or thought about such experiences" (Collins, 1991, p. 209). The main question for them in assessing knowledge claims becomes "How do you know?" They expect narrative-style responses emphasizing personal experience. The validity of a person's knowledge is judged by the passion of her expression and her commitment to her beliefs, not solely by the internal logic of her arguments. In a Black feminist epistemology, value is placed on knowing that is based in the self, in experience, in intuition, in connection, and in embodiment. This kind of knowing is called "mother wit," or wisdom. Such knowing takes precedence over written documents because it is the product of survival in an oppressive world: "Knowledge without wisdom is an idea for the powerful, but wisdom is essential to the survival of the subordinate (Collins, 1991, p. 208).

Common Elements of Connection of Oneself with Others

Connected knowing forms the big picture for considering connection with others. Learning from personal experience is the base of connected knowing. Various other aspects include trusting, validating, trying to understand different viewpoints, not judging others, and believing that one will be treated according to the same values. Connected knowers engage in collaborative explorations of knowledge. The concept of connected learning appears frequently in the literature on women's learning, sometimes in the guise of different terms (such as *relational knowing*), yet these differing terms tend to refer to a similar cluster of attributes.

Critical Issues in Connection and Women's Learning

In this section, I consider three sets of critical issues concerning connection and women's learning. These are related to the historical construction of connection as an attribute specific to women's learning, to current constructions of women as connected knowers in various fields of study, and to questions about the importance of connection in women's learning.

Historical Construction of Women as Connected

Although this chapter has focused on more recent scholarship, the association of gender with different ways of knowing, particularly connected forms of knowing, is not new. In Western philosophy and science, women's ways of knowing typically have been seen not only as different but also as inferior to men's ways of knowing. As early as Aristotle, male philosophers claimed that women were incapable of reason or at best possessed rational faculties that were inferior to those of men (Jaggar, 1988).

Feminist scholars have pointed to eighteenth-century Enlightenment ideas about gender and knowledge as the source of beliefs that persist in modern thought. The value placed on rational thought as a way of knowing, although evident earlier, grew considerably in the Enlightenment (often called the Age of Reason). At the basis of much Enlightenment thinking was an emerging view of the physical world as governed by a few basic laws. Isaac Newton and other thinkers proposed that these laws could be discerned and understood by human beings through the use of reason, or rational, logical thinking. The belief also emerged that reason could serve as a guide to moral behavior, through individuals' ability to logically deduce ethical principles of behavior. Since all men (women were not included) were thought to possess reason, they had certain rights and the ability to participate in self-governance. Thus this perspective laid the groundwork for political change and also challenged the increasingly authoritarian and oppressive doctrine of the Christian Church (Donovan, 1987).

Enlightenment ideas might seem to be liberating, in terms of locating the source of knowledge in individuals rather than in divine authority or historical tradition. Nevertheless, as already noted, women were specifically excluded from the knowledge-creation process by their presumed lack of reason. This view of women was linked to a dualism of mind and body, and of logic and emotions, that appeared in Western philosophy as early as Plato. This dichotomy was accentuated in the Enlightenment. Reason's powers of explanation could not be applied to certain "nonrational" aspects of the human world and experience, such as emotions and intuition. Everything associated with the nonrational was devalued; thus knowledge gained through intuition was viewed with suspicion, and emotions were thought to interfere with applying logic and gaining accurate understanding. Historically, women had already been associated with the nonrational, the body, and the emotions, and in the Enlightenment such associations became even more powerful. Incapable of reason, women were also viewed as incapable of self-governance and, increasingly, of participation in the public and supposedly rational spheres of production and politics. The rise of industrialization contributed to a growing division between the public spheres and the private world of the home and domesticity. This division, and women's increasing relegation to the home, reinforced women's identification with activities, such as childrearing, that were believed to depend on nonrational, emotive types of knowledge (Donovan, 1987).

Beliefs about women's inferior capacity for rational thought, and about their "natural" bent for intuitive and affective forms of knowing, were questioned by women themselves during the Enlightenment and continue to be questioned today. Nevertheless, the influence of these beliefs is still apparent, both in women's struggles to define themselves as knowers in daily life and in "scientific" theories about women's ways of knowing. I explore these influences in the next section.

Current Constructions of Women's Learning as Connected

Scholarship in different fields has offered varied explanations for the connected nature of women's learning. These explanations are variously physiological, psychological, sociological and social-psychological, anthropological, and political.

Physiological Explanations

Some physiological approaches focus on aspects of the brain. Carl Sagan (1998) and others note that the corpus callosum, the connector between the two hemispheres of the brain, is larger in women. Currently neuroscientists believe that because of this larger connection between the two hemispheres, women use more of the brain at one time when completing a motion or engaging in solving a problem. Sagan (1998, p. C1) writes that "although there is no hard evidence, the larger connector may also account for a woman's tendency to exhibit greater intuition (the separate brain halves are more integrated)." Sagan also depicts women as "able to follow several trains of thought (or children) simultaneously," whereas men "seem more capable of focusing intensely on single topics" (p. C1). This difference is attributed to the size of the corpus callosum.

Other physiological explanations for women's learning and knowing are attributed to hormones and hormonal changes. Cases are made for the role of hormones (or, primarily, for the differential quantities of estrogen, progesterone, and testosterone in females and males) in brain development, in the maintenance of bodily tissues and organs, and in the stimulation of blood vessels to expand and allow good blood flow (thus contributing to connections between brain functioning and kinds of knowing). Naturally produced compounds, such as steroids, are related to lessened sensitivity of brain cells, stress, and problems with memory. Research on the effects that these hormones have on learning is still new, and evidence that hormonal differences contribute to a preference for connected types of learning has not yet been established. As one example, however, it can be speculated that women's lower levels of male hormones (which are typically linked to aggressiveness) may explain a preference for less competitive types of learning situations.

Psychological Explanations

An ongoing debate among psychologists is whether observed gender differences are a result of nature (biology) or nurture (primarily interactions with adult caretakers, particularly mothers; see Rosser's work, *Female-Friendly Science* [1990], for a good discussion of this debate). Judith Jordan and others' self-in-relation model of women's identity development (1991) is an example of a psychological theory about women's orientation to relationships. This model posits that gender differences are based both on body identification and on early socialization of daughters by mothers: a mother-daughter learning. The speculation is that, on the basis of gendered cultural norms and on body identification, mothers may encourage daughters to feel more connected with them and encourage differentiation with sons. Such models have been used as a basis for more specific explanations of women's orientation to connected learning. Belenky, Clinchy, Goldberger, and Tarule (1986) argue that women's experiences in the life cycle must also be taken into consideration in order to understand women's sense of connection; they point out that "for many women being a mother as well as having a woman as a mother provides a profound sense of human connection" (p. 178). This observation leads to the following perspectives, which reflect sociological and social-psychological theories of human development.

Sociological and Social-Psychological Explanations

Sociologists and social psychologists often emphasize the effects of broader gender socialization on women's learning. The Harvard Project on women's psychology and girls' development (Debold, 1996; Taylor, Gilligan, and Sullivan, 1995) has found that girls change significantly in what and how they know between the age of about eight and the time they become adolescents. Girls who have previously demonstrated complex knowledge systems appear to regress in their knowing. The researchers interpret these changes as a product of the girls' attempts to meet cultural demands to think and act as females. These demands create a rift between the self the girls know and the self society wants them to be. From this perspective, women's task as learners might be to regain a lost sense of connection with their own ways of knowing and voice, as Elisabeth Hayes discusses in Chapter Four.

Sara Ruddick (1996) provides a more positive view of how women's experience of the gender-specific role of motherhood contributes to gender-specific learning abilities. Ruddick describes "maternal thinking" in ways that are similar to descriptions of connected learning. For example, she argues that motherhood elicits concrete thinking through a mother's desire to understand the developing minds and changing behavior of her children. Mothers must be acutely sensitive to their children's needs, learning and adapting mothering strategies in response to changes in their children. Ruddick argues that maternal thinking represents a mode of thought that is just as sophisticated as more formally recognized, scientific reasoning.

Anthropological Explanations

Chapter One briefly summarized some key ideas proposed by Sandra Harding (1996) about gender and knowledge systems. Harding's work is representative of a perspective based on cultural studies in anthropology. This perspective seeks to locate the origins of gendered ways of knowing in broad social and cultural systems more so than in people's socialization into and experience of different roles. Harding (1996) talks about local knowledge systems, different standards for scientific knowledge, and ways of knowing that emerge through people's political, social, historical, and cultural knowledge-seeking projects. She proposes that there are gendered ways of knowing and learning because women and men experience "gender cultures" differently and have different interests and needs for information even when they are engaged in similar situations. Although Harding does not argue that women are more likely to exhibit characteristics of connected learning, such characteristics might be explained in terms of the gender culture that affects their experiences.

These gendered knowledge systems may differ by society, culture, ethnic background, and so on, potentially resulting in differing knowledge systems among women as well as between women and men. Such diversity may call into question the gender-specific nature of connected learning among women. For example, a study (Berner, 1994) of Native American women living on reservations in Alaska demonstrates how ethnic culture has contributed to differences among women in their orientations to learning. More specifically, the study identifies important effects of language on cognition (in this case, on connected and separate knowing and learning). Native American women who grew up speaking their indigenous language (a graphic, pictorial one) were more likely to be connected, simultaneous learners and learned better that way. Conversely, the Native American women who had grown up speaking English as their first language (an abstract, nonrepresentational language) were more likely to be separate, sequential learners and learned better that way.

There is a substantial amount of literature suggesting that certain people of color, such as Black and Hispanic people, are more likely to prefer connected forms of learning. These generalizations are typically applied to men as well as women in these racial and ethnic groups. Clearly, we need a better understanding of the intersections of race, culture, and gender (and other attributes) as they affect ways of learning.

Political Explanations

Other authors add a political dimension to the discussion of connection and women's learning. From this perspective, the relationship between knowledge and power must be acknowledged. Our knowing and knowledge systems are influenced by our positions in society. These authors suggest that particular kinds of learning for women may stem from women's subordinate position in society (Weiler, 1988). In order to negotiate a male-dominated world, women become oriented to seeking to know and understand the ideas and feelings of other people, particularly men. Such understanding may give them more power and control in relationships with others.

Furthermore, a political perspective on ways of knowing stresses that certain epistemologies are privileged. Which knowledge is canonized and seen as normative, as well as how and to whom knowledge is disseminated—these phenomena are symbolic and structural and have to do with relationships of power. For example, Aida Hurtado's work (1996) demonstrates that women's ways of knowing are enabled or restricted according to women's multiple identities (race, class, religion, and so forth) and according to whether they belong to consensually dominant social groups or consensually subordinate social groups. Therefore, women may find differential access to knowledge and to the power to create knowledge, as well as limitations on their own knowledge, not only because of gender but also because of their differing social positions, differing access to resources, and differing liabilities. Hurtado (1996) describes how women of Color use ways of knowing that are similar in some respects but different in others from White women's ways of knowing. Interestingly, in the strategies or "mechanisms" of knowledge creation—anger, silence/outspokenness, withdrawal, shifting consciousness, multiple *lenguas* (Hurtado, 1996)—the concept of connected knowing does not figure prominently.

Overall, this brief review of the varied explanations for women's orientation to "connectedness" in learning suggests that there is no definitive explanation for this orientation. Perhaps of even greater interest, however, is that this considerable body of work is based on assumptions about gender differences that are still in question. Indeed, this brief review of the historical association of women with connected forms of knowing suggests that the association may itself be socially constructed to a great extent, the product of a certain mode of social organization and of certain beliefs about human nature. In the next section, I point out some limitations of such generalizations about women's connected learning.

Importance of Connection in Women's Learning

Throughout this chapter, the nature of women's learning as connected has been assumed, implicitly if not explicitly. Nevertheless, questions remain about the extent to which connection is really important in women's learning. I would like to end this chapter by raising some challenges to the notions of connection and learning and by suggesting some cautions for educators and researchers of women's knowing and learning.

First, educators and researchers must be wary of overgeneralizing about the role of connection in women's learning. Women engage in all kinds of ways of knowing and learning that are not about connection. For example, Gilligan (1982) and Belenky, Clinchy,

Goldberger, and Tarule (1986) write about a separate way of know-ing, in which knowing is objective rather than subjective, separate from one's experiences, and impartial. Separate knowers are logical and linear; they assume a stance of doubt when first hearing new ideas. Women can and do engage in this way of knowing—perhaps not to the same extent that men do, but the extent of the differences remain unclear. Clinchy (1996) herself has written that separate knowing came easily to her, and so it took her a while to recognize that there even was a connected way of knowing. Elisabeth Hayes, my coauthor, is clearly a separate knower. I have cited several authors throughout the chapter who argue that such factors as race, class, culture, and ethnicity create considerable diversity among women in their ways of knowing and learning, but I have found few studies that attempt to tease out the intersecting influences of such factors on women's tendencies toward connected learning or any other mode of learning. Until such studies are conducted, it is important not to generalize about connection in women's learning but rather to describe clearly the particular women for whom connection seems to be important.

Second, educators and researchers alike should avoid dichoto-mizing ways of knowing and learning—by assuming, for example, that if a woman exhibits characteristics of connected knowing, she cannot also engage in procedural knowing. Indeed, readers have sometimes overlooked the constructed way of knowing described by Belenky, Clinchy, Goldberger, and Tarule (1986), which incor-porates aspects of both separate and connected knowing. Dorothy Smith (1987) describes women as more likely than men to experi-ence two modes of knowing simultaneously: one located in the body and the space it occupies, and the other passing beyond it. She writes that through their childrearing and nurturing activities, women mediate these two modes and use the concrete experiences of their daily lives to assess more abstract knowledge claims. In her more recent work, Goldberger (1996) suggests that instead of label-ing people as certain kinds of knowers (for example, labeling women individually or as a group as "connected" knowers), we might do better to see particular ways of knowing as strategies that can be acquired and used by all people.

Third, I encourage educators and researchers to move beyond assumptions that men's ways of knowing exist in opposition to women's ways of knowing and learning. Statistically, in previous research, most differences in learning style are greater within each gender than between the genders. Although gender remains a significant influence on the learning of all people, we must seek out a more complex understanding of this influence. (This issue is discussed further in Chapter Nine.)

Summary and Conclusion

This chapter has offered an initial exploration of the concept of connection in women's learning. Different meanings of connectedness have been garnered from the literature and from women's narratives. These include women's connections with/in themselves and women's connections with others. Women's connections with themselves include the concepts of global processing, subjective knowing, and intuition. My discussion of women's connections with others has addressed how women learn through interactions and relationships with others. A central focus of this discussion was Belenky, Clinchy, Goldberger, and Tarule's (1986) concept of connected knowing. The final section of the chapter has considered important issues in the discussion of women as connected knowers—namely, the historical construction of women's learning as connected, current constructions of women as connected knowers in various fields of study, and questions about the importance of connection in women's learning. What I hope most is that my efforts to differentiate among the meanings of connection will add greater richness to our understanding of women's learning, and that more work on this topic will follow.

6

Transformation

Ann K. Brooks

And of course I am afraid, because the transformation
of silence into language and action is an act of self-
revelation, and that always seems fraught with danger.
But my daughter, when I told her of our topic and my
difficulty with it, said, "Tell them about how you're
never really a whole person if you remain silent, because
there's always that one little piece inside you that wants
to be spoken out, and if you keep ignoring it, it gets
madder and madder and hotter and hotter, and if you
don't speak it out one day it will just up and punch
you in the mouth from the inside."

Audre Lorde, Sister Outsider*

T his chapter explores the idea that language and story are at the
heart of women's transformative learning. Although only a few
studies have focused specifically on women's transformative learning,
these studies and the research on women's development suggest that
many women may not experience transformative learning as the
existing theories suggest. Therefore, in this chapter, I rethink transformative learning in light of what we know about women's development and learning.

---

*Used with permission. See page vi.

Transformative learning, simply put, is learning that leads to some type of fundamental change in the learners' sense of themselves, their worldviews, their understanding of their pasts, and their orientation to the future. As Carolyn Clark (1993) explains, "Transformational learning produces more far-reaching changes in the learners than does learning in general, and these changes have a significant impact on the learners' subsequent experiences. In short, the transformational learning *shapes* people; they are different afterward, in ways that both they and others can recognize" (p. 47). This type of learning can take place gradually over time, or it can happen as a result of a particularly significant and dramatic experience.

The idea of story or narrative as central to transformative learning grew from my participation in several collaborative inquiry groups. These were groups of women who came together to research their own lives through sharing experiences and developing new ways of interpreting these experiences. In those groups I felt and witnessed the potential power of storytelling to change women's lives.

Here, I briefly review the major research and theory on transformative learning and on women's development. Next, I review some of the research that specifically addresses women's transformative learning. I dwell particularly on the collaborative inquiry project on voice and silence that I conducted together with a group of women doctoral students (Voices Group, 1996). Finally, I explore the idea of narrative and make the argument for conceptualizing women's transformative learning as a narrative process.

Transformative Learning

Since the appearance of Jack Mezirow's theory of perspective transformation, in 1978, the concept of transformative learning has become increasingly important to the field of adult education. The notion of transformation implies a metamorphosis into an entirely new form, as opposed to a simple adaptation of the existing form. Adult educators have conceptualized transformation as a learning process in three basic ways: as emancipatory learning (Freire, 1971, 1972), as a dialogue with the unconscious (Boyd and Myers, 1988), and as cognitive restructuring (Mezirow, 1995). The definition of transformative learning most familiar to adult educators probably is that of Mezirow. Central to his idea are the concepts of meaning perspectives and meaning schemes, which he defines as "generalized subtexts which we have assimilated from our narrative interaction with our culture and parents" (Mezirow, 1995, p. 44). He defines meaning perspectives as abstract and paradigmatic. They "are not simply categories for understanding; they also significantly influence and delimit the horizons of our expectations" (p. 43). Meaning schemes are the "specific set of beliefs, knowledge, judgment, attitude, and feeling which shape a particular interpretation" (p. 43). The process of transformative learning is one of transforming the "structures of meaning" (p. 45). The goal of transformative learning is the reconstitution of the structures of meaning so that they are developmentally better in that they are more "inclusive and discriminating" (p. 45).

Many adult educators have researched and critiqued Mezirow's theory of transformation. In particular, researchers have identified several weaknesses in the model: the idea that the catalyst for transformative learning is always a disorienting dilemma; the omission of historical and sociocultural context as important; the valuing of critical reflection as the most significant learning experience for adults; and the overemphasis on rationality as a way of knowing (Taylor, 1997). Although many of these criticisms have come from women researchers or from research on women, they cannot be considered a critique of the theory as it applies particularly to women's experience of transformative learning. Nevertheless, a look at some of the major research and theory coming out of women's psychology may help to make these criticisms more relevant to our understanding of women and their experience of transformative learning.

Women's Development and Transformative Learning

Almost twenty years ago, Carol Gilligan (1982), through a series of studies using a contextualized research methodology and drawing on an all-female sample, challenged the overgeneralization of Western

White male experience to other populations. The result of her work has been a small explosion of studies that have begun to tell us something about women's unique experiences of living and learning.

Women's Development

Research tells us that the lives of women generally seem to have unique characteristics that make women's lives distinct from those of men. In particular, women traditionally have lacked control over their lives in ways that have not been true for men (Bateson, 1990). The metaphor of journey that has been used in the past to describe many men's lives fails to characterize the discontinuity and multiple roles of women's lives. Some researchers and theorists (for example, Josselson, 1987; Chodorow, 1974) have noted the centrality of relational connections in women's lives (see Chapter Three for further discussion of women's identity development as relationship-oriented). Jean Miller (1986) has gone so far as to say that women tend to place the needs of others before themselves. Expanding on the same idea, Gilligan (1982) has distinguished women's moral development as centered on a movement toward increasing responsibility to and caring for others. Noting the conflict that women may encounter in developing their identities, Ruth Josselson (1996) has pointed out that women create their identities at the intersection of competence and connection. Finally, specifically addressing women's development as learners, Mary Belenky, Blythe Clinchy, Nancy Goldberger, and Jill Tarule (1986) have theorized that women move from silence to a form of constructed knowing that includes both connected and separate knowing.

Some evidence seems to be accruing that the importance of relationship extends beyond the predominantly White and affluent women and girls on whom the first studies were based. For example, Victor Turner (1997) notes that the relational approach validates important parts of Black women's maturation process: racial oppression and the requirement to be bicultural in the United States increase the value of and opportunities for relationships among women of Color, and these experiences often enhance a sense of connection to people belonging to other marginalized groups.

It is also important to note that the view of women as relational and caring is not without critics of its own. For example, theorists critical of this view have pointed out that women's acceptance of themselves as predominantly relational leaves them unprepared to compete or protect themselves in the larger society, and a study of Black women managers supports this view (Edmondson and Nkomo, 1998). These authors believe that the armoring process is a critical part of a Black woman's development and provides a self-protective buffer against racism. The armor allows a Black girl to develop and maintain a sense of self-worth, dignity, and beauty in the face of social standards that clearly send a different signal. Finally, the challenges of our postmodern era, with its explosions of technology and information, suggest that we look carefully at the difficulties adolescent girls face in forming confident, powerful adult identities. Inequities in social and economic status, negative body images, the pervasive effects of the mass media, and the declining influence of family and community are all threats to a girl's and, ultimately, a woman's developing identity.

In considering this literature in the context of women's transformative learning, I want to emphasize that none of the cited theorists claim that the qualities they identify are unique to women or that they are solely a result of either nature or socialization. What is important about these theories is that they are based on an increased awareness that the developmental experiences of men cannot necessarily be generalized to women. Similarly, the experiences of the dominant European American population cannot be used as a normative standard for other cultural and racial groups.

Women's Transformative Learning

Recently, several adult educators have consciously taken women's experiences into account in their research. In a study of the development of transformative leaders, Kathleen Loughlin (1990) theorizes that transformative learning for the women she interviewed involved the movement from alienation to agency, and from inauthenticity to being true to oneself. On the same topic, Dean Elias (1991) concludes that the baseline catalyst for women's development of a new perspective is the experience of confronting authority, whereas for men it is becoming more aware of their feelings; thus women often describe their personal transformations in terms of coming to understand the limitations on their lives that are structured into institutions and cultures, and as they develop increasing awareness, they begin not only to author their own lives but also to act in order to change society. Mechthild Hart (1985, 1990), on the basis of a study of women's consciousness-raising groups, suggests that the process of identifying the ways in which our marginality is culturally, historically, and politically structured is at the heart of the transformation that occurs in women's consciousness-raising groups. Finally, Susan Pope (1996), having studied a group of ethnically diverse working-class women who were the first in their families to graduate from college, concludes that perspective transformation for these women was not triggered by a disorienting dilemma but instead occurred over time and involved the development of personal power in the context of supportive relationships, particularly family relationships.

Research specifically intended to address women's transformative learning, as opposed to a more generalized understanding of transformative learning, was begun in 1989 at Teachers College of Columbia University by the Group for Collaborative Inquiry (1993) and was also conducted later at the University of Texas at Austin (Brooks and Edwards, 1997). Both groups of researchers drew on feminist critiques of conventional research (Harding, 1987; Lather, 1988; Reinharz, 1992) in order to develop forms of collaborative inquiry, with the purpose of democratizing the research relationship in a way that they believed would be more consonant with the population with whom adult education traditionally works (Group for Collaborative Inquiry, 1993). On the basis of its research, the Group for Collaborative Inquiry (1994) also identified boundary permeability (flexibility in concepts and thinking), holistic learning (including cognitive, affective, and embodied knowing), interconnectedness (among people and among ideas), and mutability (capacity for change) as central to women's transformative learning. In a collaborative inquiry on women's sexuality, Ann Brooks and Kathy Edwards (1997) began to conceptualize narrative as the link between individual and social transformation; the following section describes this project in more detail.

The Voices Group

Large research universities can be lonely. The culture promotes autonomy, competition, isolation, and strong egos. Although men and women alike face this environment, those who traditionally have not had open access to universities, particularly women and members of certain racial and ethnic groups, can find the university environment cold, indecipherable, and alien.

The Voices Group was formed as a collaborative inquiry group of eight doctoral students and one faculty member (myself) researching the topic of women gaining voice in academia. For me, it began when a woman about forty years old caught me in the hall.

"I don't know what to do," she said. "I've just been to see my dissertation chair, and he's making me collect my data all over again. I don't know what he wants. This is the second time this has happened. You're the only woman in the department. Can you help me?"

The primary data of the Voices Group were to be our own educational life histories (all the quotations that follow are taken from unpublished transcripts of oral narratives; the names are pseudonyms). What began as separate stories began, over time, to form a narrative plot of fighting for an education, and the individual stories became both the substance of and variations on the central plot.

For several of the researchers, the early school years were filled with shame and psychological abuse. Angela, for example, said, "He held a mirror up to my face, and I was crying, and makeup was streaming down my face, because I wore lots of eye makeup in those days, and he said, 'Look at yourself. Your face is the mirror of your soul.'" Angela also told about how hard she had struggled as a native speaker of Spanish in an English-dominant school: "I thought I was dumb until the fourth grade. I see now I wasn't dumb, I just spoke Spanish." Olivia, another participant, recalled, "She told me I looked cheap and that I wouldn't be allowed to wear those clothes to school anymore. My mother had made them for me."

Later, most of the women had struggled to push their way into college. Olivia described how she had been discouraged from pursuing her dreams: "He said I would never get into any of the really good universities—I should just be grateful for what I could get, and go to one of the local colleges."

Now, as doctoral students, they spoke of fear and voicelessness. As Ellen recalled, "Each one of us in that class had tried to assert our voice, but then we would be passed over or shot down or devalued by the professor in some way. We thought, I'm never going to say another word. Anyway, he never learned our names, so it never affected our grades." Gina commented, "And all of us in the classroom were silent. We had already learned the lesson: not to speak." Anika observed, "It seems I stopped myself from speaking before anyone else had a chance to stop me."

The inquiry group provided a way for the researchers to articulate and dignify their personal experiences as a legitimate subject of inquiry. Voicing these experiences brought us into close relationship and enabled us to develop a socially shared narrative within which each of us could place our own narratives. This was the first time that most of the group members had seen their experiences validated in the stories of others. The transformation was from silence to language and action, and from isolation to connection. Jane offered these reflections on the process: "When I was sharing my story, what actually happened was that I had a great revelation of a reframing of my past, and I believe it was because I was forced to think about it and analyze it, and then I heard everybody's reaction to it, which helped me to see a reframe." Karen observed, "When I felt myself most engaged was when we began talking about connections in our lives in different settings. It made me realize that I'm not alone."

Through the inquiry group, the women found new ways to express themselves. Calista provided a good description of this change: "I think there's power in the connection itself. From the first time we met, I've carried the power of the group with me, just in terms of feeling stronger, safer. One of the things I struggle with is this tension between my scholarship and my sexuality. But in a class this spring I said something like, 'There were three gay people here, and nobody talked about that.' And two of the members of this group were in that room. I don't think I would have had the stuff to talk about that without the power I've gotten from this group."

Jane offered another example of changes in how she now expressed herself: "In my interviewing and job search, at first professors told me not to be true to myself and my voice: Don't use any ism's. But as the semester went along, I thought, Do I say what I want to say and be who I want to be in this situation, or do I try to play the game? In my very last interview, I just threw everything to the winds, and it was just me. And I thought, Oh, great—I was too radical; nothing like what they would want. And they ended up offering me the job. There are times when you are who you are, and you can still win."

The Voices Group went on to share the story of women's marginalization in education through conference presentations. What is important in the group's story is that the move to language and connection did not stop with the inquiry group but extended into the public domain. Whenever subordinate knowledge is claimed and voiced within the public domain, the hegemony of mainstream knowledge is challenged, and public space is claimed for an additional voice. (This is an example of the collective voice of power, as described in Chapter Four.) This process is transformative of both individuals and society.

Implications

The research on women's development suggests that women are more relational than men. From this perspective, the developmental challenge for women is to integrate their inclination toward relatedness with a need for separateness and competence so that they won't totally subsume their own sense of identity and power. Another theme is the impact of institutionally structured power inequities on how women perceive themselves. The literature on transformative learning echoes these themes but also addresses the move from silence to voice, from domination to emancipation, and from inaction to action. The affective, spiritual, and embodied nature of learning for women also comes out in the research on women and transformative learning. The Voices Group in particular suggests the potentially powerful role of narrative in transformative learning for women.

Narrative

In the next sections, I explore current theories of narrative and discuss my own perspective on its significance for transformative learning. Existing theories of transformative learning, more specifically Mezirow's theory, have been the object of considerable debate and criticism. In my discussion here, I have chosen not to engage in such an oppositional dialogue or to focus on the flaws in current theories. Instead, I want to suggest that when we think about transformative learning, our task is not to use critiques as a way to make our understanding of it smaller; rather, our task is to expand the stories we can tell about it in a way that extends and makes our understanding more complex.

Narrative Conceptions of Self and Society

For Westerners, the folk psychology about the self is that it resides somewhere within the body, that it begins with some inherited predilections, and that it develops as one grows older and life experiences accrue. Donald Spence (1984) opens the door to a more complex understanding of self when he asks whether the client in psychoanalysis actually recovers the past through releasing repressed material in the unconscious or through developing a new narrative, or story, to reconstruct the self. Building on the same point, Donald Polkinghorne (1988, p. 150) writes that self is "not a static thing or a substance, but a configuring of personal events into an historical unity which includes not only what one has been but also anticipations of what one will become." This "configuring of personal events" is, simply put, a narrative or story with a sense of a past, a present, and a future that are connected in meaningful ways. Michael White and David Epston (1990) write that none of us can tell the whole of our lives; we necessarily weave in some experiences and exclude others, and in describing this process, they write (p. 12), "The structuring of narrative requires recourse to a selective process in which we prune, from our experience, those events that do not fit with the dominant evolving stories that we and others have about us. Thus, over time and of necessity, much of our stock of lived experience goes unstoried and is never 'told' or expressed. It remains amorphous, without organization and without shape."

Knowledge that remains unstoried frequently represents unarticulated pieces of our lives, just beyond our conscious awareness. Edward Bruner (1986, pp. 6–7) writes, "Some experiences are inchoate, in that we simply do not understand what we are experiencing, either because the experiences are not storyable, or because we lack the performative and narrative resources, or because vocabulary is lacking." The women who conducted the Voices Group brought language to this kind of knowledge.

Michel Foucault (1980) tells us that the process by which we select the experiences we tell is saturated with socially structured power relations. Our unstoried knowledge is subjugated in that it has been erased or silenced as a result of the domination of a language that provides ways of naming only the experiences and knowledge of dominant groups in the culture. Foucault tells us that subjugated knowledge is the knowledge that has been written out of history, such as the ideas and knowledge of women and other marginalized groups. As Teresa de Lauretis (1984) points out, we take social stories and mistakenly understand them as personal, using them to story our lives; therefore, we are not free to narrate our lives in any way we wish: our choices are limited by the language and narratives available within our culture and society, and each of us finds a way of telling our own story so that it conforms to the narratives that dominate our own culture and society.

Bruner (1986) describes the creation of narratives at the societal and cultural levels as an intersubjective process involving the re-creation of shared meanings among groups of people. For example, he writes that in the 1930s and 1940s, the dominant story about Native American tribes was that their present is disorganized, their past was glorious, and their future is assimilation, but that the current story about Native American tribes is that their present is a resistance movement, their past was exploitation, and their future is an ethnic resurgence.

Bruner explains that there were always expressions of resistance in Native American experience but that the new narratives became a part of the dominant discourse only with the formation in 1961 of the National Indian Youth Council and the American Indian Chicago Conference, the publication of the *Indian Historian* in 1964, the establishment of the American Indian Movement in 1968, and the publication of Vine Deloria's *Custer Died for Your Sins* in 1969. The resistance stories became transformative only in their performance.

What is important about performance is that it implies going public. For subjugated groups that are only newly articulating their knowledge, the movement from inchoate, deeply private, silenced knowledge to public performance is an act of great courage. The issues at stake are not just those of multiplicity; they are issues of power. White and Epston (1990, p. 19) write that "dominant narratives are units of power as well as of meaning. The ability to tell one's story has a political component; indeed, one measure of the dominance of a narrative is the place allocated to it in the discourse. Alternative, competing stories are generally not allocated space in establishment channels and must seek expression in underground media and dissident groupings."

Narrative Understanding of Transformative Learning

The work of Jerome Bruner (1985) is particularly helpful as a basis for understanding the role of narrative in transformative learning. Bruner distinguishes between paradigmatic and narrative cognition. Paradigmatic cognition operates through recognition of elements as members of a category; narrative cognition operates through the combining of elements into an emplotted story. The meaning structures to which Mezirow refers in his conceptualization of transformative learning are paradigmatic structures. They are rational and abstract and can be transformed through a process of ideal discourse. Drawing on Bruner's work, Polkinghorne (1995, pp. 10–11) writes that paradigmatic reasoning is a primary method by which humans constitute their experience as ordered and consistent.

With a familiar and decontextualized knowledge of the world, we can manage the uniqueness and diversity of each experience as if it were the same as previous experiences. We are able to learn a repertoire of responses to be applied in each conceptually identified situation. Narrative cognition, by contrast, focuses on understanding human action (Bruner, 1985). Narrative reasoning can account for the differences in people's behavior, the contextual and temporal variables, and the unique interactions that make any one situation unique. Narrative cognition selects diverse parts of a specific action and works them into a coherent whole. Stories move us emotionally. Stories justify people's actions and so have a moral dimension to them. Narrative reasoning works by analogy, moving from story to story instead of from the specific to the general. New stories are seen as similar to earlier stories but not identical to them.

Transformation through a process of narrative thinking has several distinct qualities:

1. It occurs interactively on personal and social levels.

2. It occurs as a by-product of personal story sharing.

3. It requires that the learner think both generatively and critically.

4. It requires the sharing of particular experiences and the collaborative development of abstract concepts.

5. It includes a moral dimension as the narrator weaves a criticism of the past and implies an idea of a better future.

6. This transformative process engages us not only mentally, but emotionally, spiritually, and physically.

Women's Transformative Learning as a Narrative Process

An understanding of transformative learning as a narrative process can be very useful in theorizing about the transformative learning process experienced by many women. In this type of transformative learning, personal storytelling functions as a way of establishing relational intimacy. Creatively integrating discrete bits of data into a meaningful story requires a keen sense of context and audience as well as a sense of self-competence. The integration of relational skills with other kinds of competence is a developmental goal for many women. Furthermore, all women, regardless of social position or ability to acknowledge it, are victims of institutionalized sexism. Emancipating themselves from this sexism is a process of gaining voice and taking action. The intimate sharing of stories, usually with other women in a safe context, is a time-honored way in which many women have first claimed their own voices. These new stories justify actions and implicitly make statements about what is moral and what is not. In the process of developing their relational skills, women have frequently become attuned to their embodiment of not just cognition but also emotion and spirituality. Narrative allows all these aspects of human existence to be woven meaningfully together.

Conclusion

In this chapter, I have attempted to expand how we think about transformative learning so as to include the particular experiences of women. Although most research so far has focused on relatively affluent White women, sufficient evidence exists to suggest that the importance of relationships, the integration of mind, body, and emotion, and the experience of institutionalized forms of discrimination are themes that extend across the differences among women. Transformative learning can occur and be understood in many ways, but transformation through narrative is a way that seems distinctly suited to the ways in which women think about themselves and interact with others. Transformation through narrative requires that the narrator position herself in relationship to others. Good narrative demands that she justify her actions, in terms of either a stereotypical narrative or a new narrative. Whether stereotypical or new, narratives always carry with them an implicit statement about what is considered right and good. When women get together to tell stories, they can either reinforce the existing stereotypes, which no longer fit, or they can try to touch those places that are closer to the soul and be caught up in a narrative process of transformative learning.

One additional point remains to be made: narrative transformative learning need not apply solely to women's transformative learning. All human beings create and re-create their lives through stories. All of us, men and women alike, have places within ourselves that remain unnarrated. All of us carry within us institutionalized sexism or racism. Few of us would even know how to articulate these aspects of ourselves. If we are educated, we usually find these parts of ourselves repugnant and unacceptable. We have as little language with which to describe our internalized and unconscious racism and sexism as members of subordinate groups have to describe the experience of subordination. In that sense, all of us are victims of silence, regardless of our gender, race, or social class.

7

Feminist Pedagogies

Elizabeth J. Tisdell

Feminist pedagogy is about women as learners. It is about women as knowers, teachers, actors in the world. It is also about stories— about sharing stories, feeling stories, analyzing stories, theorizing stories, reframing them in some sort of educational space, and encouraging new action in light of our educational re-storying experience together. As Ann K. Brooks describes in Chapter Six, such storytelling can be transformative. The word *pedagogy* refers to the processes of teaching and learning, whereas *feminist* focuses on women. Thus *feminist pedagogy* refers to the interactive processes of teaching and learning, particularly in relation to what facilitates women's learning. It is about recognizing the gendered nature of human experience in stories, both in personal narratives (women's and men's) and in public stories (as in history books or academic curricula). Feminist pedagogy encourages personal transformation of individual knowers by attempting to expand consciousness, capacity for voice, and self-esteem as knowers construct and express new knowledge and become more fully authors of their own lives. It encourages social transformation by inviting knowers to be actors in the world through participation in social change movements and public policy discussions that keep the interests of women in mind.

Feminist pedagogy is about women's education. It is aimed primarily, although not exclusively, at their educational needs, and it assumes that the traditional educational system has focused on the needs of men from privileged race and class groups. After all, most of the history and English books we were required to read in school were primarily by male authors, and focused on what (White) men did. Educators making use of feminist pedagogy attempt to create curricula that include authors and course content by, about, and for women as learners, and that are intended to increase women's status and opportunity in society. In addition, feminist educators try to conduct learning activities that encourage connection and relationship, and that take affective as well as rational and cognitive modes of learning into account. But what makes such an approach "feminist"? Doesn't it just make educational sense to create curricula and conduct learning activities that take into account the needs of a given audience—that encourage participants to be authors of their own lives and active in public policymaking activities of society? The answer to this question is a resounding yes, but such an approach is also feminist in that the primary audience is female and the primary concern is the education of women, an education that increases their self-esteem, knowledge, capacity for voice, and status in society. It more specifically attempts to address the educational needs of women, although many men will also benefit from such approaches. Because feminist educational approaches do target the needs of women as learners, many authors (both male and female) who discuss women's education often discuss "feminist pedagogy." Such approaches are obviously applicable to formal educational situations, as in higher education, but they are also applicable to nonformal educational situations, as in business and industry, adult basic education, and grassroots emancipatory education (Razack, 1993; Walters and Manicom, 1996).

There are many versions of feminist pedagogy, each guided by different theoretical underpinnings. All versions are concerned about increasing women's choices and status in society, and all note the importance of connection, relationship, and the role of affectivity in learning. All versions, building on and reframing the work of Frances Maher and Mary Kay Tetreault (1994), to some extent include five interrelated themes:

1. How knowledge is constructed

2. Voice

3. Authority

4. Identity as shifting

5. Positionality, or dealing with differences based on the social structures of race, class, and sexuality

My intent in this chapter is to discuss three primary strands of feminist pedagogy: the psychological models of feminist pedagogy, the structural models, and poststructural feminist pedagogies. The theoretical perspectives associated with these forms of feminist pedagogy were briefly introduced in Chapter One and will be elaborated in this chapter as they relate specifically to pedagogy. The psychological models tend to focus on women's psychological development as learners, whereas the structural models tend to focus on confronting social structures of gender, race, class privilege, and oppression as they affect women's learning. The poststructural models tend to focus on how social structures of gender, race, and class inform our individual identity and development and on how these can be analyzed and reframed in educational settings to facilitate working for social change. I have discussed elsewhere how these three strands relate to the adult education literature (Tisdell, 1995; 1998); it is my intent here to examine how the three strands play out in feminist educational practice.

Again, feminist pedagogy, in the broad sense, is about stories, both personal narratives and public stories, and their use in education. Stories give context, provide examples, touch our hearts, and put a human face on the rational world of ideas. Therefore, before discussing the three strands of feminist pedagogy, I will contextualize my own perspective for the reader by sharing relevant aspects of my own story as a feminist educator. In so doing, I will introduce some concepts, particularly around the five themes of feminist pedagogy, that provide some examples and a context for a deeper examination of the three main strands of feminist pedagogy.

Becoming a Feminist Educator

My development as a feminist educator cannot be separated from my own understanding of the development of my feminist consciousness. This has been a very gradual process that is ongoing, changing, shifting, on the move, like all of life. It is grounded in my own learning through life experience, in my socialization, and in my formal education from grade school to graduate school. It is both affective and cognitive. In what follows, I will examine how these learning experiences have contributed to shaping my consciousness and life as a feminist educator.

Gender Socialization Through Family, Church, and Formal Education

Growing up as a White middle-class Catholic girl in the late 1950s, 1960s, and 1970s, I was always aware of my gender. The things expected of me and my sister were different from the things expected of my brothers. These expectations came partly from our parents but were especially reinforced through the school system and the larger culture. I knew something about my identity as female because I was different from males, and difference is likely to make us think about our identity around that category of difference. Yet I was never consciously aware of gender privilege or gender oppression until I was in high school and involved with the Catholic Youth Organization. It came time for elections, and one of my girlfriends was going to run for president, but we were told that the president had to be a boy. This was my first recognized experience of sexism. We were not happy about this and saw it as unfair, although we didn't put up much of a fight to change it. We gave voice to it by mostly complaining about it to each other. It was 1971. But it was that initial giving voice among each other, or dialogue, in the context of our own connectedness and relationship, that helped to sow the seeds of our developing consciousness about sexism.

I went off to college in 1973. I had no real consciousness of my "middle-class with educated parents" privilege, but I had always assumed that I would go to college, like other members of my family. I majored in math, primarily because I had been good at it in high school. But in college I had only one female professor, and no professors of Color from the United States. The only female author I specifically recall reading was Margaret Mead, in an anthropology class. If you had asked me about it at the time, I wouldn't have noticed. My feminist consciousness had not been raised enough to see that the official knowledge base (what was required in the curriculum) had been constructed almost entirely by males.

Because of my interconnecting interests in social issues and what gives people meaning, I pursued a master's degree in religion and completed it in 1979. To some extent, this was an effort to resolve my ambivalent relationship with the Catholic Church. I was drawn to it because of the church's involvement in many social issues and because of my strong attention to the powerful ways, inherent in Catholicism, in which people construct knowledge and meaning through symbol and liturgy. But I also was rejecting of it because of my strong disagreement with the church on a multitude of issues that affect women. It was probably through grappling with these tensions in my M.A. program in religion, and through my exposure to feminist theology, that I began to define myself as a feminist. It is ironic to many that in the late 1970s I was introduced to feminist thinking as an academic subject at a Catholic, Jesuit institution.

Feminist Education Through Relationships

Much of my feminist education has been through life experience in the world of relationships, both in the workplace and through personal relationships with significant others. The social construction of gender and gender relations is perhaps most obvious in our personal relationships, where our unconscious expectations and beliefs about "appropriate" gender-based behavior are often played out. This initially became most obvious to me in a long-term relationship with a man that developed in and extended beyond my college days. In getting pressure from my family and the larger culture to get married, I eventually had to grapple with my own unconscious beliefs about what constituted gender-appropriate behavior for myself and others in relationships with both men and women. As a female, I had been socialized to be "nice," to be "good," and to attend to other people's needs. Thus, in the context of this long-term relationship (and in others over the years), I began to examine and alter some of the ways that I had been socialized. I tried to develop relationships with men and women that were not based on such traditional gender expectations, where some affective needs could be met by women while some of my needs for a deep personal understanding could be satisfied by men. I asked men out on dates and also learned to define what I wanted in my relationships rather than just attending to what they wanted. I also fell in love with a woman, and it threw me for a loop. I wondered if I were heterosexual; I wondered if I were homosexual. I seem to be both. I have had two great loves in my life, very long-term relationships, one with a man, one with a woman. If I have other great loves, I'm not sure if they will be with men or women, for I fall in love with a person, not a gender. But it is from my relationships with these great loves of my life that I have learned the most about gender relations.

My feminist education through life experience has also been a result of relationships with people I have known in the workplace. After I completed my master's degree, I worked for the Catholic Church as a campus minister for ten years, and it was in those years that I probably began to see myself as a feminist educator. I heard many young women's stories (stories not unlike my own): stories of a search for a woman-positive self-identity, of concerns with sexuality-related issues, of trying to develop a holistic view of life or a spirituality that fit who they were becoming. I worked with male and female colleagues who were concerned about the place of women on campus and in the curriculum. We looked at salary differentials between men and women and at issues of university policy. We were instrumental in developing a campus sexual harassment policy and in advocating for a campus childcare center. It was through our connection and relationships, through our dialogue, that we not only increased our consciousness but also implemented policy change. We moved from consciousness to action.

Becoming Aware of My "Positionality"

Over time, I began to understand gender as a social structure. But I had little awareness of other aspects of my positionality that gave me, as Peggy McIntosh (1988) notes, a knapsack of unearned privileges, such as my white skin privilege and my class privilege that had made it easy for me to go to college. This began to change in 1986, when a Black woman student, to whom I was quite close, asked me what it meant to be White. I simply had never thought about this. But she could easily say what it meant to be Black. It was then that I begin to grapple with what whiteness as privilege means. My identity shifted again, and although my being White didn't change, my understanding of my positionality as a White person began, and it continues to change. My learning here has come primarily through relationships with women of Color, who have been great feminist educators for me.

It was because of these insights into positionality, developed through relationships with other adult learners, particularly those who are different from me, that I chose to pursue a doctoral degree in adult education, with an emphasis in women's studies and in multicultural adult education. My years of doctoral study saw the continued development of the academic part of my feminist consciousness as well as of my understanding about the important intersections of gender with other structural systems of privilege and oppression (such as race, class, sexual orientation, and ableness). Since completing the degree, in 1992, I have worked as a faculty member in the context of higher education. Much of my teaching (and learning) centers on the issues that I have already mentioned: "crossing borders" of gender, race, class, sexual orientation, and ableness. I always try to use some type of feminist pedagogical approach that makes visible not only gender but also other systems of privilege and oppression that inform our lives. It takes the life experiences of the participants, stories and narratives similar to my own, into account in the learning environment. The positionality of myself and the learners, and where the learners are in relations to various aspects of their own shifting identities, is very important to how the classroom dynamics unfold and to how the participants construct knowledge. These are issues that have been central to my own educational theorizing and practice as well as to feminist pedagogy.

Feminist pedagogy, as it is discussed in the literature, has a history, and the three primary strands—the psychological, structural, and poststructural models—build on and are influenced by earlier strands. In many ways, the development of the literature in feminist pedagogy parallels my own development as a feminist thinker. As already mentioned, the earliest development of my feminist consciousness came about as a result of my being aware of differences in gender socialization and of how it affected my psychological development. This is the focus of the psychological models: women's consciousness raising and development at the psychological level. I also became aware of gender as a social structure, and as a system that privileges one group over another. I became aware as well of the significance of other social structural systems of privilege and oppression (race, social class, and sexual orientation, for example). This is the focus of the structural models. From my teaching experiences, I discovered the significance of the fact that I teach not only as a woman but as a middle-class White women. The intersecting systems of privilege and oppression that inform my constantly shifting identity also affect what I, as a teacher, see, construct, and validate as knowledge. My whiteness and my class background are as significant to this process as my femaleness is. These aspects of my own shifting identity and the identities of the learners—our races, our classes, our genders, and our consciousness of these aspects of who we are—affect our teaching and learning together in the ways we construct knowledge, come to voice, and deal with authority in the learning environment and in the world. This is the focus of the poststructural models. It is to a discussion of these three models that I now turn.

Psychological Models

There were discussions of feminist pedagogy with the proliferation of women's studies programs in the 1970s and 1980s, but there is probably no single book that has affected the development of feminist pedagogy more than Mary Belenky, Blythe Clinchy, Nancy Goldberger, and Jill Tarule's *Women's Ways of Knowing* (1986). It is not specifically about feminist pedagogy per se but is more about how women come to know and learn. The insights into teaching that are implied in this study epitomize the psychological models of feminist pedagogy, but the impact of this study on all versions of feminist pedagogy is noteworthy. Virtually all authors who write in the realm of feminist pedagogy, even those who are writing more from structural or poststructural perspectives, cite this landmark publication in relation to women's teaching and learning. Discussions of feminist pedagogy and women's learning based primarily on *Women's Ways of Knowing* are concerned with women's emancipation or liberation primarily from the perspective of what facilitates women's personal development on the psychological level. But these models are not emancipatory in the sense of having a primary concern with collective social change. They do not emphasize or really examine power relations in the larger social structure and their effects on education; rather, they focus on the needs of women as individuals.

Four of the five recurrent themes of feminist pedagogy—how knowledge is constructed, voice, authority, and identity as shifting— are evident in Belenky, Clinchy, Goldberger, and Tarule's discussion (1986). Their work focuses on how women construct knowledge and shift their identities as individuals in a small community of support where relationships are valued; it does not focus on the larger social and political mechanisms that affect what kind of knowledge is recognized as official, and how such knowledge is produced and disseminated. Certainly, their discussion of the development of voice is focused more at the individual level as well, and the discussion of authority focuses on the sharing of the authority of the teacher-facilitator with learners. Differences among women are dealt with more at the individual level, too, in this work's discussion of the five categories of knowers in a sample of 135 women. What is emphasized is the similarities among the women, in addition to the fact that most of the women learned best in situations that emphasized connection, relationship, and affectivity as well as rationality. Differences among the women, particularly around such structural issues as race and class, are not dealt with.

A critique of the psychological models has been that issues for women of Color, working-class women, and lesbian or bisexual women tend to remain mostly invisible. This is often cited as a criticism of *Women's Ways of Knowing* and is an issue that was taken up by many of the contributors to a more recent book by these authors (Goldberger, Tarule, Clinchy, and Belenky, 1996).

Structural Models

In the winter of 1990, I was a student in an adult learning class. There were eighteen of us, thirteen women and five men. Our task one night was to break into four small groups, discuss a particular adult learning theory, and then create a skit about it. There was one man in each group, although there were two men in one of the groups of five. My group was to deal with Albert Bandura's social learning theory, which focuses in part on the role of modeling in adult learning. It didn't take us long to plan our skit—we were intent on our task. We decided that Paul, one of the participants in our group, would be the narrator, and the rest of us would act out what he, as narrator, explained. In light of Bandura's theory, he would be the role model, and we would model what he said. As each group did its presentation, we were amazed by the creativity of our peers and by what we had learned about the various theories of adult learning. But, when all was said and done, the not so readily apparent dynamics were, to me, far more interesting. Each group had done what we had done: chosen the one man in the group (or one of the two men, in one case) to be in the lead role. Such a decision on the part of each group was more than likely an unconscious one. Probably all four groups operated in a manner similar to the group I was in. We were intent on our task, and so we didn't consciously think about putting a man in a leadership role. Rather, we were thinking about our presentation. But, one might wonder, why did every group put the man in a leadership role, when there were nearly three times as many women in each group? Was this merely coincidental, or was there something more going on here than met the eye?

If one were interpreting these classroom dynamics from the perspective of student-centered teaching approaches informed by humanistic psychology—which, by definition, focuses on the psychological needs and traits of individual learners—one would attribute the leadership of the males in this situation to their individual personality traits. Therefore, one might suggest that their leadership in this situation was indeed coincidental, or due only to personal charm or other such personal characteristics of these particular men. If one were operating from a psychologically oriented feminist pedagogy, one could have a similar interpretation, which would focus more on the individual personality differences between the men and the women, and on the levels at which the individual women felt "empowered" in the situation. A psychologically oriented feminist pedagogy might also suggest that the activity should be restructured to make more obvious use of connected forms of knowing (see Chapter Five), whereby the women would claim more of their own voices and thus be more likely to actively claim overt leadership roles.

But someone operating from a structurally oriented feminist pedagogy would have a different interpretation of and response to this situation. Structural feminist theorists argue that our behavior is influenced by the structural systems of power, privilege, and oppression that inform our lives. Gender, race, and class are examples of these social structures. Therefore, those operating from a structurally oriented feminist pedagogy would argue that situations like this one, in which men are more likely to be chosen for and to take on leadership positions, are not merely coincidental. Because males' greater power and privilege are structured into the very fabric of society, we are used to having men in leadership positions in all places in society. Therefore, the placement of (mostly White) men into formal or informal leadership positions is the result of an unconscious process on the part of men and women alike whereby we continue, unconsciously, to play out what is familiar. According to structural models of feminist pedagogy, power relations based on gender, race, and class should be analyzed or confronted quite proactively by the instructor as they are manifested in the classroom. This does not mean publicly embarrassing anyone, but rather calling attention to and analyzing such dynamics as they arise, to make what is unconscious more conscious. After all, we have much more power to do something about what is conscious; it is nearly impossible to actively change what is unconscious.

Structuralist models of feminist pedagogy have been strongly influenced not only by structural feminist theorists but also by the work of the Brazilian activist and educator Paulo Freire (1971), who saw the purpose of education as social change. The Black feminist writer bell hooks, who herself has been strongly influenced by Freire and by structural feminist theories, writes as follows about her (structural) feminist pedagogy:

> It is a model of pedagogy that is based on the assumption that many students will take courses from me who are afraid to assert themselves as critical thinkers, who are afraid to speak (especially students from oppressed and exploited groups). The revolutionary hope that I bring

to the classroom is that it will become a space where they can come to voice. Unlike the stereotypical model that suggests women best come to voice in an atmosphere of safety (one in which we are all going to be kind and nurturing), I encourage students to work at coming to voice in an atmosphere where they may be afraid or see themselves at risk [hooks, 1989, p. 53].

The reference that hooks makes here to "the stereotypical model" is more than likely a reference to the psychological models of feminist pedagogy that focus on the nurturing, "safe" learning environment. She wants students to come to voice, even though the classroom may never be entirely "safe," for, as Audre Lorde (1984) notes, silence, in the long run, will not necessarily protect those who have been marginalized.

All five of the recurrent themes of feminist pedagogy— how knowledge is constructed, voice, authority, identity as shifting, and dealing with difference—are central to these structural models. In hooks's words, we see evidence that a primary focus of these models is differences among women and among learners, differences based on race and class as well as on gender. The structural models emphasize what the psychological models downplay: the theme of difference and how to deal with it. There is also an emphasis on the theme of voice, on students coming to voice as critical thinkers, thereby shifting their identity (reflecting both the "voice as identity" and "voice as power" metaphors described in Chapter Four). The point is to create a space where those who have been marginalized because of gender, race, class, sexual orientation, or their intersections can come to voice and construct new knowledge. There is an emphasis on examining the political and social mechanisms that have controlled the knowledge-production process and have marginalized (or left out) the contributions of women and people of Color in what is passed on through the official curriculum. The issue of authority is discussed in these models, but there is a recognition that, although authority can be shared, it is impossible to do away completely with the authority of the instructor. The emphasis is more on appropriate uses of authority, as opposed to an emphasis on the instructor as midwife, as in the psychological models.

Like the psychological models of feminist pedagogy, the structural models emerged in a historical context. They began developing around the same time as the psychological models, in the early 1980s to early 1990s, but have different theoretical underpinnings. As noted, they are influenced both by structural feminist theorists and by such critical educators as Freire and those who rely on his work, who are concerned with structural forms of oppression and privilege of all types as they affect education. A strength of these models is attention to social structures, but some suggest that the needs of individual learners can get lost in these models.

Poststructural Models

In the fall of 1994, I was teaching a master's-level course in adult development. Students were to do a final paper on a topic of their choice related to the themes of the course. Midway through the course, when students were discussing topics for the final paper, a Black woman announced that she wanted to do hers on Black women's hair in relation to adult development. As the instructor (and as a White woman), I didn't see what hair had to do with adult development. I questioned it. The student defended her topic. Another Black woman supported her. In a ten-minute exchange, they explained to me the ritual and symbol of racial and gendered identity in Black women's care, style, and rituals around their hair. The woman interested in doing the paper explained that she wanted to focus on how these issues around Black women's hair represented their racial and gendered identities, how this had changed through history, and how it is reflective of Black women's adult development through the years—historically, socioculturally, and individually. Ultimately, she did a fascinating paper on this topic.

It was through this experience that I began thinking about how my own positionality—where I am positioned as a White middle-class woman relative to the dominant culture, and my consciousness of it as the instructor—affected what happens in the classroom. In every class I teach, I am not only female, I am also a White, middle-class female. As the instructor, I am the one in the learning environment with institutional authority and therefore have the power to determine what would be an acceptable paper for a particular course. In the scenario just described, not only did I initially not understand what this Black woman wanted to do, my initial reaction was that this was not "relevant knowledge." Had I been a Black woman myself, I probably would have understood the relevance of the topic to Black women's development. I probably would have asked some clarifying questions and emphasized the connection to adult development, but I wouldn't have so strongly questioned the student. My whiteness informed what I initially saw as valid or relevant knowledge. In this instance, although I was the instructor and thus the official teacher, both the Black women were the real teachers, and I was the learner about my own identity construction as a White woman and about the culture and ways of manifesting identity development of Black women.

At this juncture in history, there is a good deal of overlap between the structural and poststructural models of feminist pedagogy, particularly in more recent publications. The psychological and structural models of feminist pedagogy had already informed my teaching, but insights from feminist poststructural thought, in addition to the multicultural education literature that moves beyond psychological and structural models, were what contributed to the development of what I am calling "poststructural feminist pedagogies" and are what continue to offer me direction in my own teaching. These pedagogies, which highlight positionality of students but especially of instructors, offer both theoretical and practical direction to those trying to implement an emancipatory feminist approach in their own teaching. A deeper discussion of these poststructural feminist pedagogies around the five themes will make more sense after an overview of poststructural feminist thought.

There are many versions of postmodernism and poststructuralism. (Technically, there are some differences between poststructuralism and postmodernism, but for the purposes of this introductory discussion, the terms can be used interchangeably.) All versions deal in some way with the notion of deconstruction—that is, taking apart or examining how each of us has been at least partially "constructed" through our socialization, particularly around specific aspects of our identity, such as our gender, race, or class. All versions of it call into question the black-and-white notion of categories, suggesting that most of the world really exists in various shades of gray. Some versions (often called "ludic" postmodernism) focus almost exclusively on deconstruction and seem to be playing word games that are accessible to almost no one except elite academics; other versions (usually called "resistance" postmodernism) focus more on the resistance of particular marginalized groups while remaining mindful of the danger of absolutizing any category (as in such statements as "women are this, men are that"; see Lather, 1991; Sleeter, 1996). In discussing feminist poststructuralism, I am referring specifically to the ways in which marginalized groups (particularly women) challenge power relations based on gender, race, and class. Therefore, my thinking here is informed by poststructural feminist perspectives and resistance postmodernism. In light of these remarks, four primary elements of poststructural feminist thought are particularly relevant to poststructural feminist pedagogies.

First, all feminist poststructural discussions (as the term *poststructural* implies) build on and critique the structural feminist theories. They argue for the significance of gender along with other structural systems of privilege and oppression, such as race, class, and sexual orientation, but note the limitations of focusing only on social structures. The intersections of gender with other systems of oppression and privilege are key to the construction of the self in feminist poststructuralism. This is where issues of positionality are emphasized. Furthermore, the primary units of analysis in these post-structural feminist pedagogies could be conceived as the connections between the individual and the intersecting structural systems of privilege and oppression that affect how participants construct knowledge.

Second, all poststructural theories question the notion of a single truth and suggest that people come to their own versions of truth and reality in light of their life experiences and positionality.

Third, they also highlight the notion of constantly shifting identity (see Chapter Four for a discussion of this perspective in relationship to voice). It is the connection between one's individual, constantly shifting identity and social structures that is of importance here, especially in regard to how this affects positionality in the learning environment. As learners examine how social systems of privilege and oppression have affected their own identity, including their beliefs and values, their understanding and thus their identity begins to change. They also increase their capacity for agency—the capacity to have more control over their own lives. For example, if one has embraced societal prescriptions for particular gender roles (or race roles, or sexual roles that are exclusively heterosexual), and if one becomes conscious of and examines the social construction of such roles, one's identity is likely to shift, and one may develop new ways of acting in the world.

Fourth, poststructuralism calls categories and binary opposites into question. Given the importance of affectivity, connection, and relationship, emphasized in much of the literature about women's learning, it is important to consider a feminist poststructuralist deconstruction of the rational/affective dichotomy. Such a deconstruction bears in mind both the rational or cognitive aspects of affectivity and the affective components of rationality. Poststructuralists ask what the connection is between our feelings and emotions and how they relate to what we can rationally know about the world. If an idea is too contrary to one's belief system, to the way one has lived out one's social roles, it may be too scary even to consider.

Thus the emotion of fear may not allow one to consider an alternative idea to what one has held as truth. Conversely, the truth of a new idea may so resonate with us at the emotional level that it is just what we need to propel us forward into new ways of thinking and being in the world. Rationality and affectivity are not really such dichotomous categories, especially in a (feminist) poststructural understanding of the world.

Focus on Positionality, and Identity as Shifting

The tenets of feminist poststructural thought just discussed are germane to the five interrelated themes of poststructural feminist pedagogies and how they are implemented. The issues of positionality and of identity as shifting are particularly central here and affect the other three themes.

Positionality of the Educator

Clearly, the race, gender, class, or sexual orientation of the instructor has an influence on teaching and learning, on the instructor's and students' construction of knowledge, and on classroom dynamics in any adult education situation. The positionality of the educator (and the participants) always affects what goes on in adult learning activities, but the conditions under which educators will directly discuss their own positionality will vary according to the context. Under what circumstances should a Black woman instructor discuss being Black or female, or a gay White male discuss his whiteness, maleness, or sexual orientation? One might answer these questions by considering the circumstances, such as whether it seems relevant to the course content, what one's position is in the institution offering the learning activity, whether one is tenured, and who the participants are in the learning group. Of course, directly problematizing one's identity can be risky, and a significant factor to consider is who the educator is in terms of these configurations. In a higher education setting, a White, tenured male professor who is married can quite safely problematize his identity; he probably can also champion women's rights, or affirmative action, or even gay and lesbian rights and in so doing will often even be seen as a hero. If a Black woman brings up her own identity or champions women's rights, or race rights, she may be seen as pushing her own agenda. In short, who the messenger is and who the hearers are will be a large factor in determining how the message is received.

In the vignette already described about the exchange in my adult development class, I didn't initially discuss, the day that it happened, my whiteness with the participants as affecting my own construction of knowledge. But after reflecting on it, in a later class session I did use this as an example of how our positionality (and, in this case, my own) affects what we see, and how in that particular instance my "whiteness" related to what I initially considered relevant to adult development. I used this as an example and as a partial explanation of why there is a relative absence of theories about human development, or even women's development, that are very representative of women of Color. Because most published authors are White, they have in part determined by the social construction of their whiteness what is to be considered relevant. In this instance, my positionality as a White woman was directly dealt with and tied in with the themes of the course. How the positionality of students and teachers affects learning is always a consideration for poststructural feminist educators but may be dealt with more indirectly in some circumstances.

Positionality of the Learners

If the positionality of the educator has an effect on classroom dynamics and on students' learning, so do the interacting positionalities of the participants, and the systems of privilege and oppression that inform their lives are always present in classroom dynamics. As in the realm of structural feminist pedagogical approaches, writers in the realm of poststructural feminist pedagogies would suggest that educators be proactive in challenging or dealing with structured power relations in the classroom in attempting to teach for social change. Whether or not one should directly discuss issues of students' positionality depends on the context and on whether doing so is directly relevant to the themes of a particular learning activity. But power relations are present everywhere, whether or not one directly discusses positionality or gender, race, and class.

Sometimes issues can be confronted indirectly and reframed in a way that helps participants construct new knowledge and doesn't polarize a class. For example, one morning about halfway through one of my courses the class as a group got into a discussion of leadership issues in distance education. Two of the more privileged White women, who had particular technological sophistication and had more prestigious professional positions as well, said that virtually all educational institutions need to be using computers and other technology in education because in the Information Age computers are the wave of the future. A Black woman raised the issue of accessibility, asking who had access to such technology, and for what kinds of learning. The two White women replied that if students were not taught with these forms of technology or were not taught how to use them, then they would be in an educationally disadvantaged position. The Black woman raised the issue of accessibility again and was supported by a Native American woman. The Black woman also raised the issue of the significance and importance of relationship (with a flesh-and-blood facilitator and other learners) in learning, a point that several of the other women and one of the men vocally supported. The two White women espoused the merits of the Internet and e-mail in meeting relational needs. The exchange continued in a similar vein for another minute or so, and then the Native American woman, who appeared to be getting a bit exasperated, told the story of efforts being made on one of the reservations in the area to install a computer lab, but with very little attention to the cultural needs of the community. At the end of her story, she said emphatically, "And the Native American students aren't going to use it."

It is not merely coincidental that the more privileged members of the class, by virtue of their class, race, and professional status, were advocates for the importance of technology, nor is it surprising that the two women of Color raised the issues of accessibility and the learning needs of particular communities or questioned whose interests were being served by technology. Nobody talked directly about the positionality of the students, or about how their comments were related to their positionality as women or members of particular racial groups, and it would have been tangential to this particular course for me to get into this issue. But as a poststructural feminist educator I did feel that it was important to reframe the discussion in a way that made some of the issues more visible, even though they had come up somewhat indirectly. Therefore, I suggested that the question of whether to use educational technology is not an either/or consideration but rather a both/and issue: how to use it, and how to consider the often unaddressed issues that need to be attended to in making decisions in this regard. I went on to discuss how one might consider using technology in situations and communities like the ones under discussion, how these questions are related to class and access, and how to incorporate relational aspects of learning into educational technology. Clearly, this would not have been the only way to handle this situation, but I did want to attempt to validate all the positions of participants in the class and to point out the very salient issues of culture, gender, and race that were implicit in the discussion and were being brought up somewhat indirectly by the women of Color. These issues would probably not have been brought up by the other students (who were all White) in this particular discussion. Obviously, participants' comments are usually related to their life experiences, and everyone's life experience is gendered and related to his or her membership in a cultural group. In short, everyone's experience is in some way reflective of positionality.

Dealing with Differences and Similarities

Because dealing with the positionality of educators as well as learners is central to poststructural feminist pedagogies, it can seem that the emphasis falls on differences among participants (as in the structural models of feminist pedagogy) rather than on their similarities as women (as in the psychological models). But poststructural feminist educators deal both with similarities among the participants (including themselves) in the learning environment and with differences based on factors of gender, race or ethnicity, social class, sexual orientation, and so on. Difference and similarity can be dealt with in part through using portions of participants' autobiographical and life experience that are relevant both to the topic and to the various categories of positionality. The interweaving of activities throughout a course that get at the sharing of relevant life experience (whereby aspects of the participants' positionality will inevitably come up) can contribute to group bonding and group understanding. It can also help participants see things in a new way around these various sociostructural categories in relation to individuals' identity development.

Construction of Knowledge and Giving Voice

In discussing the five themes and how they are played out in poststructural feminist pedagogies, it is difficult to separate one from another because all five are so interrelated. The positionality and the constantly shifting identities of both the educator and the learners affect both how participants construct knowledge and how they come to voice. One of the professors in Maher and Tetreault's study of feminist classrooms described her style of feminist pedagogy as helping students to "see with a third eye," which makes the interconnection of the construction of knowledge with positionality particularly salient: "The 'third eye' is a form of theorizing, but rather than reflecting either a universalized mode of thought, . . . or one that is personal or psychological, . . . this way of knowing [has] a positional cast" (Maher and Tetreault, 1994, p. 202). To see with the third eye is to recognize that the self, or the author, constructs knowledge in relation to others, and that both the self and others are situated and positioned within social structures where they are simultaneously privileged and oppressed. These social structures and power relations affect not only how knowledge has been produced and disseminated in the society but also how what has counted as knowledge has been determined, and by whom.

In poststructural feminist classrooms, the interconnection of the themes of positionality, shifting identity, knowledge construction, and coming to voice, and the connection between the individual and the social context, are often apparent in students' work and in their lives. For example (see Tisdell, 1996), Nicole, a Taiwanese woman who was in one of my feminist theory classes, discussed the interconnection of these issues in her own life. The first day of class, she mentioned her need to overcome her fear of speaking in class (she is not a native speaker of English). She literally needed to "come to voice" (see Chapter Four) in spite of her fear. Later, in one of her papers, she wrote:

> I believe that there are some women [who], like me, cannot concretely distinguish what [they]/I really want to be from what my own culture wants me to be, because I have grown up under cultural expectations and internalized the cultural values as parts of my self-image. I believe . . . sharing personal experience is a good way to radicalize consciousness. Listening to the experience of others, I feel that I am not the only one who suffers [this] anxiety and threat when I am trying to confront myself and reconstruct myself. I spend more time inward-looking in order to figure out [my] real inner voice.

Clearly, Nicole is speaking directly about the connections between who she is as an individual and her own cultural identity. She is also talking about trying to determine some of her own beliefs and values rather than just uncritically accepting the values she was taught through her family, culture, religion, and so on. In so doing, she recognizes her own identity as shifting in her remark about reconstructing herself. Further, she refers to both her own experience and the scholarly reading that she has done in the class (both the affective and cognitive realms) as helping her do this.

The critical examination and naming of these connections is part of the strategy for giving voice and for working for social change and emancipation. The point is not merely to recognize these connections between our (partially) constructed identity and the social structures of privilege and oppression that inform our lives; it is also to actively work to change such conditions. Nicole also discusses the importance of moving to action, and she deals with how she can reframe what she is learning in light of her own positionality and apply to her own culture what she is learning in a class in the United States. In particular, she writes about the importance of an appreciation of her own standpoint as a Taiwanese woman in a class with Western feminists:

> Absorbing the experience of Western women, I have to [be] concerned with my standpoint in order to come to a more appropriate way to educate my people. . . . The way I want to do it is to encourage and support Chinese women to radicalize their consciousness. . . . Sharing experience is a good way to understand women's oppression.

Nicole implies in what she says here that she plans on going back to Taiwan to apply to teaching in her own culture what she has learned about "radicalizing" consciousness by discussing personal experience. This is how she is moving to action.

A heterosexual male student in a different class used similar techniques to move to action by taking a public stand and encouraging others to do so against heterosexist and homophobic remarks coming across his company's e-mail system. There are myriad ways for people to move from consciousness to action around any of these issues, but the point in poststructural feminist pedagogies is not only to help students deal with the connections but also to encourage them (and ourselves) to move to action.

The theme of voice is central to poststructural feminist pedagogies, as it is to all the models of feminist pedagogy. Yet, given that feminist poststructuralism also focuses on the deconstruction of binary opposites, the voice/silence dichotomy would also be deconstructed here. Much of the feminist literature, such as *Women's Ways of Knowing* (Belenky, Clinchy, Goldberger, and Tarule, 1986), associates voice with knowledge, empowerment, and the active claiming of a transformed identity. Silence implicitly seems to connote the converse. As Nancy Goldberger (1996) suggests on the basis of her study of bicultural women, silence is sometimes resistance, power, and the active construction of knowledge. Sometimes voice screams through silence, through artwork, dance, gesture, and other forms of nonverbal expression. Silence may indeed be a lack of voice or a lack of power, but it is often not that, especially for those cultural groups that have an appreciation of silence that White Western cultures lack. Those adult educators using poststructural feminist pedagogies, then, would foreground issues of positionality and the voices of those who have not been represented in the curriculum and the classroom, but they would not assume that silence means lack of voice; rather, they would ask questions about what is "underneath silence" (Goldberger, 1996, p. 343).

Feminist Authority: Limitations and Possibilities

In light of this discussion highlighting positionality (especially of the educator), knowledge construction, and voice, what is the role of the adult educator in poststructural feminist pedagogies, and how is the issue of authority conceptualized and implemented in practice?

First, the role of the educator is to help adult learners examine the connections in the ways already noted.

Second, poststructural feminist educators maintain a proactive role as challengers of unequal power relations and are proactive in working for social change, which is neither comfortable nor easy. They have an overt political agenda in attempting, as hooks (1994) suggests, to "educate for the practice of freedom." Like Freire, they see themselves as radical educators who challenge the status quo, as opposed to facilitators who may allow learners to center only on what they want to learn, which may inadvertently maintain the status quo. Furthermore, an assumption underlying poststructural feminist pedagogies is that usually those with the greatest racial, sex, and class privilege are more often recognized or given more status in (mostly unconscious) ways in the classroom by teachers and other participants. Thus, poststructural feminist educators more directly seek out and validate the contributions of those who have been more marginalized by systems of oppression. At the same time, they recognize that because identity is constantly shifting, these categories of identity do not always remain stable, nor do they always determine who, typically, has status or is marginalized in a particular learning environment.

Third, poststructural feminist educators make use of what hooks (1994) describes as "engaged pedagogy," which takes into account people's emotions as well as critical-thinking skills in learning and working for social change. This is especially important in classes that are specifically about issues of gender, race, class, sexual orientation, and/or ableness, which are extremely emotional issues for people. In my first attempt at teaching a course on diversity and equity in education, I made the mistake of trying to keep the lid on emotions, which had the paradoxical effect of having emotions erupt in less than helpful ways. Since then, my teaching partner and I have specifically created activities that are likely to access people's emotions. Examples include the use of films, and the writing and sharing of each participant's cultural story around awareness of race, gender, ableness, and/or sexual orientation in the class itself. Paradoxically, allowing for such expression of personal experience and emotion not only make visible everyone's positionality early on but also allows space for the discharge of emotion, and this gives participants more intellectual energy to deal with the cognitive and/or theoretical material in the course.

Fourth, in poststructural feminist pedagogy educators directly consider how their own gender, race, or class might affect the way learners deal with them as authority figures. There are many writers and educators following structural models, both feminist and otherwise, who attempt to teach for social change by encouraging students to examine structural power relations that affect their lives and have affected their access to education. But, as Sue Middleton (1993, p. 131) notes, most educators (and writers) do not discuss the ways they had access to or "have been empowered and politicized by means of their own education." By attending to their positionality, poststructural feminist educators ask not only what their positionality has to do with how they have come to construct knowledge and to be educators but also how it affects their own teaching (and learning) around issues of authority, knowledge construction, identity as shifting, and dealing with "others."

Fifth, although poststructural feminist educators have an agenda for social change and emancipation, they more directly discuss the limitations of their own capacity to facilitate social action or emancipatory activities. Poststructural feminist educators problematize the conditions that have informed their own lives, and they examine and acknowledge the limitations and possibilities of their positionality for their own teaching and learning. Elizabeth Ellsworth (1989) calls this "the pedagogy of the unknowable," referring to the limitations of what educators can know at any time because of their unconsciousness of their own positionality. There are also limitations posed by institutional constraints, such as those that require educators to be in an evaluative role and to satisfy the demands of the institution (Gore, 1993). Through examining, problematizing, and owning one's positional limitations and possibilities, as well as the institutional constraints in which the learning activity is conducted, the possibility for emancipatory education becomes greater than if one had ignored dealing with these issues.

Conclusion

Feminist pedagogy is about stories, especially about women's stories. It is about using stories and examples from real life in educational situations to facilitate both women's development and structural social change for women. It challenges us to think about our gender socialization and our socialization around race, class, and sexual orientation. But using feminist pedagogy in educational situations is not just about expanding our thinking. It is also about facilitating action and behavioral change. To be sure, the manifestation of action or behavioral change as a result of our constantly shifting identity, and of our teaching and learning together, is often beyond the scope of a particular educational activity. Often it takes time to integrate new modes of thinking and being, and the behavioral change, action, or social action can be manifested only after there has been enough integration time.

Feminist pedagogy can be used in many educational situations. Although many of the stories and examples that I have used in this chapter are based on my own experiences as a teacher and a learner in higher education classrooms, its use is by no means confined to these settings. There are many who apply discussions of women's learning and feminist pedagogy to classes in English as a second language and to literacy education, health education, human resources development, counseling, and community-based education (Hayes and Colin, 1994; Walters and Manicom, 1996). Broadly speaking, feminist pedagogy is about women's education, on behalf of making structural change for women. Typically, there is someone who is identified as the educator, but feminist pedagogy doesn't always require that a particular person be in a formal educator role. There are situations where women get together, engage in self-education activities, and organize for change on their own behalf, such as when women organize and create policy change with regard to pay-equity disputes on college campuses and in organizations across the country.

To be sure, each of the three models of feminist pedagogy has a different emphasis. They are not equally applicable to all educational contexts. But I do believe that the poststructural feminist pedagogies now offer something different from what the other models do, and that they offer the most potential for working toward social change for women. Poststructural feminist thought itself is not uncomplicated in its theoretical underpinnings. Nevertheless, in making use of stories and of some themes of poststructural feminist pedagogies, it becomes possible to unite affective and cognitive forms of knowing to help participants not only understand complex theoretical material but also put it into practice.

One of the participants in my feminist theory class, reflecting on the relationship between affective and rational forms of knowledge and what she had learned in the class, said:

> I can say that I learned the theories. I know the difference between liberal feminism, Marxist feminism, [and] postmodern feminism. I know the difference between the arguments of Nancy Chodorow, Jane Flax, bell hooks, Patricia Hill Collins, and Judith Butler [all feminist theorists]. I now know a lot about feminist theory based on my experience and the reading I did in . . . class, and many of these ideas are fascinating and useful for me. But what I will always remember from this class are the stories.

The stories, critical reflection on them, and the context of the experience are often what promotes learning and change. The stories touch our hearts; they embody and put a human face on the abstract world of ideas. They move our spirits. It is through the interaction of our hearts, minds, and spirits that we eventually move to action. It is this interaction that promotes women's learning, at least the learning that is most significant.

8

Perspectives on Practice

Jane M. Hugo

There are many pragmatic reasons to heed what researchers are saying about women's and girls' learning. Women are the numerical majority in the United States. They continue to increase their participation in the paid labor force, staying longer than in the earlier part of the twentieth century and dominating not only the service sector but also the contingency-worker sector—two of the new realities of work in this postindustrial era. Women are more often the victims of violence than are men. Women who are single heads of households and their children are among the poorest in the country who would benefit most from education's implicit promise of an improved living standard. Women are increasingly victims of heart disease and breast cancer, and yet they still have a longer life expectancy than men, living well past the childbearing years that bracketed their lives a century ago. Not only do women do the majority of home care, they also do a tremendous amount of community caretaking through their volunteer work. They are the next generation's "first teachers."

Each of these aspects of American women's current social situation is a site for adult education. Workplace training, higher education, professional development, adult basic education, health education, consumer education, volunteer development, community advocacy, and leisure education will all be more effective if features of women's lives and learning are integral to their design.

The value of understanding women's learning comes from how practitioners take and use this knowledge in service of their visions of adult education. Educational visions—whether an individual's or an agency's—constitute one of the frames of reference through which we see problems, formulate questions, generate conversation, highlight patterns, and craft new learning environments.

To re-vision our commitment to women learners means to look again, to see anew. It means to step back from our practice in order to pay closer attention to the broader elements that shape our perspectives. It also means to move in closer to our own work with women learners in order to see where, specifically, we might do the work differently.

Formal adult education can be as disparate as graduate education, museum docent training, union organizing, employee training at a utility company, adult basic skills education in a grassroots organization, preventive health work with older adults, maintenance training in the military, and formation work for lay ministers in a church. Because of this variety of contexts, all of which are important to the women who want to learn in them, this discussion of the implications of insights into women's learning will center on practitioners. They are, in most instances, the ones who often organize the formal learning. It is the practitioner's commitment to his or her work that is a powerful transformational force in adult education, even in contexts that would have it be otherwise.

To explore the implications of the women-centered knowledge brought together in this book, I have divided this chapter into four parts. First, I list the general implications I draw from the case built by the other authors. Second, I ask practitioners to think about what happens in adult education when women enter a context as learners. To do this, I take readers through a problem-posing exercise and consider a story about people living along a river, and I offer glimpses of how one group of adult educators might respond to the exercise. Third, I look at the different implications practitioners might choose to act on, given their commitment to teaching. Fourth, I close with a set of recommendations for what more might be done to permeate the adult education field with an understanding of women as learners. Threaded throughout these discussions will be observations on what else we need to know and on challenges we face in providing women learners with the best learning experiences we know how to design.

General Implications

This book presents a feminist interpretation of a wide array of research on women as learners. If I were to prepare a list of relevant action items, the list would look like this:

- Respect women as thinking and feeling people; design learning for women as whole people

- Respond to women learners as women from specific social contexts

- Become aware of and list your organization's assumptions about women learners; check them out by attending to women's feedback

- Trace the lines of power and privilege holding the educational status quo in place; find out how women figure into who benefits and how

- Acknowledge that race, class, and gender affect you, too; reflect often on how they do

- Question how instructional and administrative processes affect women learners

- Create spaces for women learners to talk, question, be in charge, work together, and succeed

- Understand that resistance from some women learners may be in their best interest; try to understand why

- Read and talk more about the interplay of race, class, and gender in your work with women learners

- Make the invisible visible, and create a richer, more complex picture of women as learners

- Be open to changing your mind and the way you do things in light of what you learn

Each of these items would generate fruitful discussion with colleagues. Each would also suggest different things to be done, according to the work context.

Gaining Perspective

Acknowledging that there is still much to research about women as learners, I think it is fair to say that adult education has been slow to integrate the feminist research of the last twenty-five years. As professionals, we have a problem knowing how best to respond to the diversity of women who are learners in our contexts. We need to understand how broader structural factors constrain some kinds of change and encourage others. One of the strongest implications of this volume is that adult educators need to understand better their own locations within their social worlds in order to recognize and negotiate the individual or collective issues women bring as learners.

Those interested in popular or critical education often use "codes," or problem-posing exercises, as a way to increase understanding of an issue needing some resolution. Codes are simplified pictures or stories that encapsulate the tensions and contradictions that exist in a situation. Because a code is often a stylized or metaphorical version of a problem, it creates a certain distance on an issue, affording those close to the problem a new perspective from which to discuss it. A problem-posing activity is often accompanied by a set of structured questions to guide a group as it names issues, explores root causes, and identifies possible solutions for the problems illustrated by a code.

A code came to mind as I reflected on the knowledge about women's learning set forth in this book. The code is the story of how a village located on a riverbank noticed and responded to a class of people. As you read the story, picture the scene and its action. Imagine yourself in the story. At the end of the story, you'll find a set of questions to facilitate your analysis of it.

The people who lived in a village next to a river often walked along the banks of the river. One day, a group of women and men were shocked to find a baby girl adrift on the river and rapidly being swept to her death. Someone managed to get a boat out into the swift current and caught the baby.

There was a meeting of the leaders of the village to discuss whose child she was. Because the child didn't belong to anyone in the village, someone stepped forward and offered to raise the infant. The village was pleased with itself.

The next day, another baby girl was seen out on the river. Because the first rescue had been dangerous for the villager going after the baby, someone had the idea of tying a rope to the rescue boat as it went out onto the river. People joined together to do this. A second baby girl was saved and cared for.

More baby girls appeared on the river. The village came together to organize a better system for rescuing the babies. From time to time, the government of the country in which the town was situated rewarded the villagers for their efforts by giving them money to feed and house the babies. At other times, the villagers had to raise the money themselves.

Before long, a whole industry grew up around saving the "river girls." There were new jobs in designing rescue equipment, training, and fundraising. New village departments formed to handle adoption requests, government payments, and home visits. Scholars followed the growth and development of the children, occasionally even talking with the river girls. Studies showed the river girls lagged behind the boys in key areas.

At a community meeting on system improvements, a handful of villagers came forward and wondered aloud if someone shouldn't go upriver and find out where the babies were coming from and why they were appearing. The suggestion caused a stir. Another group asked, "What about our boy children? Shouldn't we be concerned about them, too?" A cacophony of opinions arose about how to proceed.

Use the story to uncover your understanding of adult educators' responses to women as learners. The following questions will help you start with the story, shift to your own experiences, and, finally, move on to thinking about the broader field:

1. What do you see happening in this story? Who are the people you see? Which people don't you see?

2. What are the different people in the story doing? thinking? feeling?

3. Why did the suggestion at the meeting cause a stir?

4. Whom do you identify with in the story? Why?

5. Where have you seen the characters' actions and attitudes mirrored in adult educators' responses to women as learners?

6. What are the consequences of the situation you have just described above?

7. What can we do to reverse the negative consequences and strengthen the positive consequences?

The success of women learners is a core concern of my own and of many of the adult literacy practitioners with whom I work.

My primary adult education work is as a member of the national field service staff of Laubach Literacy, the nation's largest nonprofit, volunteer-based adult literacy organization. I am responsible for coordinating national office efforts to support staff- and volunteer-development activities in the area of basic literacy instruction. Most of the volunteers and staff in the Laubach membership network are women. Another part of my work is to coordinate the United States component of a global women's literacy initiative. This project works to enable low-income women to use basic education as a tool for personal and community problem solving. Laubach does this by giving grants to nonprofit, community-based organizations that link instruction in literacy or in English as a second language with women's concerns and with social change.

I can imagine myself sitting with a group of adult basic education teachers or volunteers and trying to uncover the meaning of this code for ourselves. At first, we'd want to jump right to a description of how this situation is just like many programs we know—for example, like the welfare-to-work programs that "rescued" poor women from dependence, but without much thought about their educational needs. Another woman might laugh about the unevenness of funding for women's concerns: she can get a grant if she includes a few units on women's health in her curriculum, but she cannot get money to fund a video project that the women in her class want to do on their neighborhood's history.

The group leader would slow us down and get us to go back and deal with the questions in order. We would fill in the imagined details about the rescuers and about how a small rescue project grew into a bigger project that eventually had its own momentum, sustained by the well-intentioned people living in the village. Maybe we'd explore what it feels like for the river girls to feel safe at last. Or maybe we would think about how unsettling and downright nervy it feels when people challenge what's working well, or at least well enough.

Having stepped back into the story more carefully, we would be ready to step back away from it to think about what happens in our own practice. We know many adult female students who make their way "downstream" from traditional K–12 schooling or from cultures that barely allow girls enough access to education to survive life's currents. Some of us would acknowledge how we make our living rescuing women who don't have the literacy skills to survive in our world. And, yes, we feel good helping them, but what would it mean for us to go beyond rescuing?

Another practitioner would redirect the conversation to something she'd read by a Ph.D. about women learners—and she would share her frustration that it was too theoretical. She would remind us that she's held accountable for the pass rate in her classroom on the high school equivalency examination: students want to master the skills needed to pass the test, and so she doesn't feel that she has the luxury to discuss (for example) power relations with her students. Besides, that's not what the women say they want; they want to get good jobs or be of more help to their kids. But, she might say, she does want to do a little more with project-based learning: she's noticed the female students helping each other at break; maybe a small group of women working together could help more women deal with the "setback issues," such as unpredictable childcare or a partner's jealousy. Those of us who had read anything good about project-based learning would pass on our suggestions for her to continue her thinking.

If we encourage it, the discussion would generate more questions about larger issues. Our experiences are so different from those of our students; where do we find common ground? Why don't they grab hold when we reach out? Literacy education for "quick workforce attachment" and education for children's literacy seem like the only goals that public funders are backing these days. How will women's other goals be met? Will we throw women back into the river because they don't meet our funding criteria? What are the economics of adult literacy education today? Is work on one part of the river more valued than work on another?

This imagined dialogue about the river story, and many of the stories shared in this volume, remind us to look at ourselves in rela-

tion to broader social contexts. Adult educators who exempt themselves from this analysis seriously limit their ability to recognize the
lines of power and privilege that affect women as learners. We can use
problem-posing scenarios, practitioner inquiry groups, and critical-
incident descriptions to uncover themes of gender, difference, economics, status, power, voice, and silence in our lives and in our work.

The authors whose work appears in this volume push us to revise
our views on women's learning and human development. In addition, however, they want us to open our eyes to women learners' lives
as they are embedded in race, class, and gender arrangements in our
culture and in multiple subcultures. All this is highly contested ter-
rain. It is often very politically and personally charged work. Much
of the feminist research on women's learning challenges deeply held
beliefs that are reinforced by social institutions, public policies, cultural or community mores, and religious traditions. These institutions exert a strong organizing effect on women's (and men's) formal
learning and on our practice, much as the riverbanks in the code
give shape and direction to the river's course. But we can be agents of
change; the questions are where and how to begin.

Deepening Practitioners' Commitment
to Women as Learners

Anne Lamott (1994, p. 19) tells a story that gives me fortitude about
beginning. Thirty years ago, her brother, who was ten at the time,
was trying to write a report on birds, a report that had been assigned
three months before. It was due the next day. She writes that her
family members "were out at our . . . cabin in Bolinas, and he was
at the kitchen table close to tears, surrounded by binder paper and
pencils and unopened books on birds, immobilized by the hugeness
of the task ahead. Then my father sat down beside him, put his arm
around my brother's shoulder and said, 'Bird by bird, buddy. Just take
it bird by bird.'" One place adult educators can start re-visioning
our commitment to women as learners is in our individual practice,
grounded as it is in our perspectives on teaching and learning.

Teacher by teacher and administrator by administrator, we can take the insights offered in this book and enhance women's learning experiences.

Each adult educator has a role to play in improving women's education, but we don't all have the same point of entry into the work. To suggest ways individual teachers might use the women-centered knowledge on learning presented in previous chapters, I've chosen to build my discussion around a taxonomy of teaching perspectives or commitments outlined by Daniel Pratt and Associates (1998), which asserts that teaching perspectives are linked to complex, interrelated belief structures about knowledge and learning. My goal is to point out the utility of these insights, and some of their challenges, to the maximum range of adult educators who work with female learners. These beliefs help establish what knowledge, and whose knowledge, is considered valid, as well as the degree to which learning is about acquisition of knowledge or about making meaning from internal and external realities. Pratt (1998c, p. 280) recognizes the emotional-cognitive link in the teaching-learning transaction when he notes that teaching is "visceral." The belief structures supporting this transaction encompass orientations to learning, knowledge, roles, responsibilities, control, authority, and relationships. Pratt notes five commitments or perspectives to teaching among the 250 practitioners involved in his research. The five commitments were to (1) effective delivery of content (transmission perspective), (2) modeling ways of being (apprenticeship perspective), (3) cultivating ways of thinking (developmental perspective), (4) facilitating self-efficacy (nurturing perspective), and (5) seeking a better society (social reform perspective). These five perspectives have points of overlap. Pratt admits that instructors can hold more than one perspective, but he also says his research suggests that "one perspective is usually more dominant while the others act as auxiliary or backup perspectives. That is, there is usually something about one perspective that is more central to people's values and personal philosophies than other perspectives" (Pratt, 1998a, p. 204).

Pratt and Associates (1998c), some of whom are women, do not position their work as feminist. Their goal is to have readers reflect on and appreciate the "legitimacy of multiple perspectives" (p. 280) on teaching. They attend to the dynamics of teaching and learning with an eye to beliefs, goals, roles, responsibilities, commitment, difficulties, contexts, and power issues. Nevertheless, they do this without explicit reference to the influence of gender, race, or class. This gap in the discussion is an opportunity to show how attention to these invisible aspects can help practitioners better fulfill their commitment to adult education. The next part of this chapter keys the implications for research on women as learners to the core concerns of adult educators who, Pratt argues, already hold certain intellectual and emotional positions in their work. Pratt and his colleagues talk about "learners," without ever distinguishing them by sex. I have been more explicit at times in my discussion of their ideas, in order to underscore the connection between a perspective's operation and women learners.

Commitment to Effective Delivery of Content

Adult educators working from this first perspective have an abiding respect for their subject matter, be it wire splicing, computer software, developmental psychology, or personal finance. They're enthusiastic, want to convey the content accurately, and want students to be interested in it, too. The central belief operating in this perspective is that there is a "relatively stable body of knowledge and/or procedures that must be reproduced by female learners. The instructional process is shaped and guided by the content, and it is the teacher's job to accurately represent that content and productively manage learning" (Pratt, 1998b, p. 218).

I believe such practitioners would want to deepen their expertise in women's motivations to learn, barriers to women's learning, and women's experiences in specific content areas. They look to authoritative sources to stay current in their content areas. Knowledge about women's ways of knowing, self-esteem issues, and identity formation need to be integrated into the knowledge bases that these teachers and administrators respect (see, for example, Caffarella, 1996, for application to the staff development field). The information gatekeepers in specialty areas need to use their positions to disseminate this knowledge through textbooks, journal articles, conference programs, Web pages and links, bibliographies, and collection development in corporate libraries as well as in academic libraries.

Becoming familiar with stories of women's experiences in specific content areas gives these teachers gender-specific and -relevant examples to reinforce or illustrate content application. For example, Susan Eisenberg (1998) enables teachers in the construction trades to bring women's experiences into discussions of apprenticeships or crew relationships. Wendy Luttrell's *Schoolsmart and Motherwise: Working-Class Women's Identity and Schooling* (1997) would alert adult literacy teachers to the conflicted experiences of White and Black mothers who feel they must set themselves and their own education aside while working and raising their families.

Because educators coming from this perspective are rooted in a commitment to the effective transmission of knowledge and to skill acquisition, they want to organize the presentation, review, and application of their content areas in ways that facilitate that transmission and mastery (Boldt, 1998, p. 79). When working with women learners, these teachers should consider a strategic use of student talk to facilitate the successful transmission of content to female learners.

The discussion in Chapter Four of voice as talk (either "report talk" or "rapport talk"; see Tannen, 1994) could help adult educators think about how they make space for and guide women's talk. How could they provide multiple avenues for women to voice understanding and uncertainty? The activities that they could incorporate into their classroom management and instructional strategies include all-female work teams, presentations, debates, conferencing, papers, application problems grounded in women's experiences, and computer-mediated communication. In addition, these teachers could set ground rules for classroom discussions in order to minimize negative stereotypes around gender, race, and class that can interfere with women's mastery of subject matter.

If the workplace is the instructional context, an instructor in charge of teaching women a job (like carpentry or asbestos removal) that has not been a traditional one for women should at least acknowledge the structural barriers women will face in those occupations and the gendered aspects of many women's level of confidence. As a result of such awareness, instructors could build in more frequent review points and set up a buddy system for women, to ensure knowledge transfer once they are out on actual worksites.

Commitment to Modeling Ways of Being

Apprenticeship, or the modeling of ways of being, is the second perspective that will benefit from attention to women as learners. Practitioners working from this perspective are mentors or coaches. They see to it that learners move toward mastery of craft knowledge and toward membership in a community of practice. These practitioners believe that learning is best done in "social contexts of application and practice" (Pratt, 1998b, p. 227).

To these adult educators, "knowledge, role (identity), and context are inseparably entwined" (Pratt, 1998b, p. 227). Women learners are expected to observe, work alongside, and interact with expert practitioners, who model and make visible the knowledge embedded in such real-world settings as hospitals, personnel departments, and university classrooms. These practitioners see their work as the "enculturation of novices" (Pratt, 1998a, p. 228) into various communities of practice and into specialized kinds of knowledge. According to Pratt's research, they expect students "not just to learn about something but to learn to be something" (Pratt, 1998b, p. 228). As role model or coach, this type of practitioner makes sure that novices have a wide enough range of experiences to learn not only the domain content but also the tacit knowledge. Janice Johnson and Daniel Pratt (1998) point out that the hidden curriculum includes learning how and when to talk and be silent as mature practitioners do.

Seasoned practitioners coming from this perspective could enhance their practice by integrating knowledge about women's identity formation and the gendered nature of learning/teaching contexts. Because identify formation is so central to this teaching perspective, the idea that women's learning is influenced by their identity issues has implications for practitioners committed to modeling ways of being. Chapter Three, for example, discusses multiple approaches to women's identify formation. Practitioners who coach women learners should weigh the value of the autonomy models, the relational approaches, and the social interaction approaches to their work with female novices. Research cited in this volume has shown the gendered aspects of women's identity formation (behaviors and feelings such as women's self-doubt and their expectations that others will do things for them) and an internalized evaluation system that privileges male performance in the learning context as the measure of success. Practitioners committed to women learners joining their communities of practice need to examine how the experiences they give women learners are either going to exacerbate these gendered identity issues (should they exist) or counteract them. Human resource development practitioners looking for examples of how these concerns show themselves in business settings, for instance, should read Laura Bierema's (1999) research on executive women's learning and development in the context of corporate organizational cultures.

Practitioners committed to apprenticing women learners in authentic contexts of practice will be more effective if they analyze the barriers women face as learners in those contexts. How does the community of practice stigmatize aspects of women's identities in ways that deny them access to its tacit knowledge and power? For example, how might a trainer of emergency medical technicians in an urban fire department modify his or her coaching when faced with such diverse female candidates as a working-class Hispanic woman who grew up in public housing and was associated with a gang, a college-educated White woman who is a feminist, and a

Black woman who is a mother and a lesbian? Each aspect of these women's multiple identities will have a positive or negative valence in the context of firefighter culture. To be the most effective coach, this practitioner would need to have sufficient awareness of patriarchy's organization to recognize barriers or borders that channel or divert power in the site of the learning. This volume suggests that educators holding the apprenticeship perspective would need to model or coach "border crossing" skills if each of these women were to be successful in the firefighter culture. The literature on women as learners gives the practitioner conceptual frameworks and language to help female novice practitioners name the issues they encounter as they try on the new ways of being, tailoring them to themselves and the unique demands of their practice.

Women's differing views of knowledge authorities and the central role of relationships also have implications for practitioners situated in the apprenticeship perspective. They believe that content and skill mastery are best demonstrated through a growing independence in "knowing-in-practice" and an ability to generalize skills to new problems (Johnson and Pratt, 1998, p. 93). The practitioner's expectation is that the novice will, through the apprenticeship relationship, become an expert. Women learners have to negotiate achieving both relationships and autonomy. The literature on women's ways of knowing and the role of relationships in women's learning give adult educators a deeper understanding of the tensions that can exist for women in an apprenticeship relationship. The relationship-building phase of learning may go smoothly, but female novices may hit a rough patch when the community of practice expects them to leave collaborative learning behind and act more autonomously. Failure to do so could cost women acceptance, but success in achieving independent application of knowledge may sever relationships that have come to be meaningful in themselves and to be sources of identity or self-esteem. Practitioners could make this tension a point of conversation with women learners and with colleagues in the fields of practice.

Practitioners operating from this apprenticeship perspective will confront places, perhaps even in their own thinking, where women's experience and needs as learners are at odds with the standards of a community of practice. As gatekeepers to that community, they will need to grapple with how to respond. I'm reminded of an example from my own graduate studies. I became vocal about the importance of gender issues in adult education in the mid-1980s. A White male faculty member who sincerely saw his role as coach and mentor seemed conflicted over the socialization paths down which he wanted to escort me, and about my questioning of those very routes to "equality" within the professoriate. I felt that my emerging identity as a feminist challenged too many of his notions of the field's focus, its accepted methodologies, and, ultimately, his privileged position. My need to exercise a new "voice" (the talk, identity, and power of which are discussed in Chapter Four) violated some of the tacit understandings of when to talk and when to be silent. The result was frustration on his part and mine. His not grasping what I, as a woman, wanted that was different from what he (and the field he represented) was offering got in the way of his being able to mentor me, and it also got in the way of my learning as much as I might have learned from him. Had he been grounded in a feminist literature on women as learners, perhaps he would have taken a very different approach with me.

In writing this chapter on the implications of an increased understanding of women as learners, I've found myself imagining an audience of male readers. Maybe the greater impact of this knowledge will be on female practitioners. The feminization of the adult education professoriate is under way. Selected parts of the field, such as adult literacy, are already dominated by women. There is a need for more research on how female novice practitioners and mature female practitioners "unpack" or analyze the gender constructs that they think they share and, furthermore, on how they navigate the mentoring relationship in light of differences in class, race, sexual orientation, and ethnicity.

Commitment to Cultivating Ways of Thinking

Adult educators committed to developing learners' ways of think-ing are a third group for whom the content of this volume has important implications. Within this perspective, the most valued outcomes are for a teacher to assist a learner in developing "increas-ingly complex and sophisticated forms of thought related to one's content, discipline, or practice. The key to learning (and teaching) lies in finding effective 'bridges' between present and desired ways of thinking" (Pratt, 1998b, p. 234). A teacher coming from this per-spective, say Ric Arseneau and Dirk Rodenburg (1998), bases her teaching and learning on cognitive principles that stress the role of a student's prior knowledge, the importance of building new learn-ing from prior knowledge, the woman's active role in constructing meaning, and the role of intrinsic and extrinsic motivation in sup-porting either sophisticated or superficial approaches to learning. In this view of teaching and learning, the teacher needs to understand the context in which new knowledge will be used and to be adept at helping women learners better transfer new knowledge from one context to another. According to Arseneau and Rodenburg (1998, p. 122), "the idea is to have learners 'reach across contexts' to make links and understand new concepts in light of what they already understand (i.e., recontextualize information)."

Pratt (1998b, p. 234) describes this sort of teacher as a "guide." As such, the teacher knows the end point of this developmental process and thus can, through knowledge of the student's starting points, artfully design learning opportunities and question strate-gies that build the necessary cognitive bridges each female learner requires.

Finally, teachers who have this commitment believe that learn-ers need to develop not only their critical intellectual abilities but also more autonomy with respect to the teacher. Women learners need to believe in their own abilities. The teacher lays the ground for this developing autonomy by helping female students develop a sense of personal control, gain access to learning resources, and develop the skills needed to take control of their learning (Arseneau and Rodenburg, 1998, p. 132).

What are the implications of this volume for adult educators committed to this orientation? The foremost implication is that feminist research and analysis offer these educators new ways of recognizing the gendered nature of human experience. This assertion alone has implications for the ways in which they go about helping women learners know themselves, value the knowledge they bring to a discipline or practice, and cross the bridges "between present and desired ways of thinking" (Pratt, 1998b, p. 234). Pratt notes that these teachers are committed to encouraging learners to think about familiar concepts in new ways. In order to do this more effectively, these practitioners have a dual task: first, they need to re-vision the desired ways of thinking for their disciplines or areas of practice in light of feminist analyses of dominant practices and their effects on women; and, second, they must think about how best to build on the diverse experiences of each female learner.

Adult educators will be better guides if they understand women learners' perceptions of their own starting points in any given learning context. Chapter Four provides a lens with which to evaluate how program designs or instructional activities invite female learners to explore and explain their starting points. For example, a career counselor working with displaced female workers might have as goals teaching them to think about work and career in certain ways, to explore career options, to translate skill sets across work contexts, and to present themselves to potential employers in such a way as to underscore the contributions they would make to those employers' goals. To begin developing these ways of thinking, the career counselor would want to guide women in activities that make visible their thinking and their feelings about themselves and their experiences with work. Such talk would begin to make women's experience central to all the learning that would happen from that point on. It would also give the teacher an opportunity to acknowledge the differences and similarities among women's experiences in the class. With such a window into their thinking, the counselor could see how to foster the inside-out learning process that could build on and deepen their personal ways of thinking about work and about themselves as workers.

These teachers' beliefs point to a readiness to incorporate individually focused knowledge about women's psychological and cognitive development. On the whole, I think it would be a comfortable move for these practitioners to refine their approaches and recast them in terms of the feminist psychological theories described in Chapters One and Seven. This re-visioning would encourage them to temper their emphasis on thinking by attending to women's affective learning as well. Following the beacons set out by Carol Gilligan (1982) and Mary Belenky, Blythe Clinchy, Nancy Goldberger, and Jill Tarule (1986), we would see more effort made to use connected teaching and learning, more foregrounding of women's experience, more confirmation of women as knowers in learning communities, and more of an emphasis on women "coming to voice"—that is, women recognizing their role in the construction of knowledge.

These practitioners would factor the impacts of race, class, sexual orientation, and ability into their understanding of each woman learner, but I don't think they would include an ongoing analysis of these systems of privilege and oppression unless the specific content area demanded it. For example, feminist theory classes in higher education, and staff development courses in total quality management for military personnel, could be taught by practitioners from this perspective. These educators would want women learners to develop a sophisticated understanding of these content areas. Using the concepts of voice, power, positionality, and interlocking oppressions, women would learn to theorize their experience in the feminist theory course. In the staff development class, women would learn to think about the principles of continuous improvement in the military context, perhaps applying them to diverse cases, but the educator's commitment would be to challenging the women to shift their thinking about management strategies. This educator's understanding of the concepts drawn from research related to women as learners would be a tool for guiding students toward the desired ways of management thinking; it would not be used to challenge the way of thinking itself.

Questions rather than answers are critical to this cadre of practitioners. Questions are the bridges to new ways of thinking. The feminist research about women as learners provides questioning heuristics for practitioners. One of the goals of this volume is to get adult educators to take a fresh look at what is most familiar to us: learners and learning. It might be an interesting exercise for practitioners to go through this text and make a list of the questions central to it. These questions could help them reframe their own question-posing strategies. Questions make misconceptions visible but simultaneously, as Pratt says, build cognitive connections.

A common difficulty faced by teachers rooted in the beliefs of this perspective is giving up the role of expert; there are also attendant power issues related to assessment of prior knowledge and ways of knowing (Pratt, 1998b, p. 235). Some teachers are likely to be challenged by women learners who experience voice as power, be they loud (in attitude and gesture if not in voice) women of Color or young, old, or experienced women. Others may resist the silence that women learners use to create a sense of safety. The discussion in Chapter Four of women's talk and silence offers those of us operating from this and other perspectives important insights into the source of our own resistance to certain types of women learners.

Commitment to Self-Efficacy

The growing knowledge about women as learners can help in re-visioning the fourth cluster of beliefs, which Pratt calls the nurturing perspective. This perspective has much in common with the commitment to developing ways of thinking. It is rooted in the belief that there is a critical relationship between a learner's self-concept and learning (Pratt, 1998b, 239). The teacher is a facilitator and friend, one who is respectful of and empathetic to the learner's needs. Such a teacher designs instruction in ways that build and support female learners' trust and self-confidence and a sense of personal growth stemming from their achievements. Teachers operating out of this perspective value intellectual development, according to Pratt, but they take a more holistic view of learners and thus work with the emotional sensibilities learners bring. As a result, these teachers are committed to nurturing female and male learners' feeling of or belief in their own power and capacity to learn. No matter what the content, it is critical that learners "be in a position from which learning is possible" (T'Kenye, 1998, p. 155).

Pratt (1998b, p. 240) notes that "more than any other perspective, [this one] resembles the andragogical image of an adult educator as portrayed in North America by Malcolm Knowles." My coauthors in this volume challenge those of us who share this learner-centered perspective to approach female students with an awareness of the impact of sociocultural influences on each woman and on groups of women.

Feminist researchers strongly urge practitioners to think anew about what a woman's "self" is and what shapes it. If we believe that our work is to cultivate female learners' self-efficacy, then we must pay attention to the many ways in which feminist researchers have called into question the dominant model of the separate, unitary, or autonomous self. Women's development, as we are coming to understand it and as Chapter Six describes it, is a mix of dominant narratives and counternarratives drawn from the connections between and among individual women and their cultural and historical situations. Not only does the knowledge about women as learners ask us to rethink the reductionist characterizations that the field promulgates about "adult learners," it also asks us to recognize the power and potential of differences among women. Teachers committed to self-efficacy would find that the qualitative research done on how women experience learning, and on the obstacles they face, confirms intuitions on which they may already be acting. Additional insights into women's similarities and differences would give these educators the courage to risk building the kind of environment in which bonding, conflict, and working through conflict are part of women reaching greater safety.

Nevertheless, feminist theories of knowledge construction and production, particularly the poststructural theories, also underscore the role in the learning equation of the teacher's identity. To revision their power as teachers, practitioners with a commitment to learners' self-efficacy need to analyze their power not only as authority figures in formal educational settings but also as people who draw on privileged sources of authority in our society.

The nurturing perspective, in Caddie T'Kenye's words (1998, p. 151), "recognizes the potential for either wounding or nurturing that comes with the role of the teacher." Teachers operating out of this perspective strive for power with rather than power over women learners. The same feminist research that may affirm practitioners' intuited notions of women's differences or individual, gendered needs may also be disconcerting if these teachers examine their caring and nurturing understanding through the additional lens of positionality. For example, Frances Maher and Mary Kay Tetreault, authors of The Feminist Classroom (1994), came to realize that in their research they had not fully interrogated the privileged social position assumed in their whiteness; as a result, they revisited their data analysis and found the "well-marked path" of their own White privilege, which normalized White frames of reference and set out terms of "the other." They came to a new understanding of how "in the dark" they had been as White feminist theorists and practitioners, even as they had been advocating that women learners "see with a third eye" and "first [know] the place where [they] were]" (Maher and Tetreault, 1994, p. 202). Their reexamination of their caring, challenging stance is an informative lesson for teachers who share a commitment to the development of women's self-efficacy as learners.

Commitment to Seeking a Better Society

The fifth and final teaching perspective to benefit from knowledge about women as learners is what Pratt calls the social reform perspective. Teachers committed to seeking a better society have an "explicit, well-articulated ideal" that informs and dominates their teaching; this central ideal might be a "social, political, or moral imperative," but the teacher believes that it applies to all, and that it is necessary to bring about a better society (Pratt, 1998b, pp. 246–247). Furthermore, teachers with this orientation have a strong sense that they need to advocate for their ideals. As a result, says Pratt, these instructors focus on "collective social change rather than individual learning" (p. 247). These teachers don't disregard individual learning, but they make this ideal or ideology an explicit organizing principle in their work. The content they teach is presented in the context of this ideal. Tom Nesbit (1998) gives a fuller account of this perspective as he writes about radical education in mathematics. His discussion of the socially constructed nature of mathematics (for example, the presumptions of textbooks, the location of math inadequacies in individuals, the influence of rational and objective views of reality, and the distancing of math from other social or economic issues) illustrates the ways in which teachers in this belief perspective can help learners use a critical ideology to deconstruct the dominant view of mathematical knowledge or learning.

The instructor's primary responsibilities within this perspective are threefold: to demonstrate the relationship and connection between the ideal and the content area, to move individual learners to "commitment and action," and to live the ideal in both words and actions (Pratt, 1998b, p. 247). Pratt points out that teachers operating out of fidelity to these responsibilities will have problems with women students who "enrolled for 'content,'" or who disagree with the ideal or feel pressure to conform to the ideal.

Practitioners who locate themselves in the social reform perspective have beliefs that draw them to the larger sociopolitical and socioeconomic interpretations of women's educational experiences, particularly analyses of the interlocking systems of oppression marked by class, race, gender, and sexual orientation. They make space for women learners' narratives and life experiences in order to distill the themes and tensions that form the heart of their problem-posing methodology. Using knowledge about women learners, they could create new codes about women's voice, power, authority, and relationships with men or other women. These practitioners would not be as eager to settle for the more individually focused, psychologically based knowledge about women's learning (as in the women's developmental literature or the literature on women's cognitive development). In fact, these approaches would be problematized by such adult educators. As in the story of the river girls, these educators would be taking students to the headwaters of the river to discover and stop the root causes of the female children's being put at such risk.

Teachers and students who come from the social reform perspective have had its boundaries outlined by theorists like Paulo Freire, Henry Giroux, Antonio Gramsci, Michel Foucault, Jacques Derrida, and Karl Marx (Wink, 1997). From the work of these men and that of many others have arisen critical theory and critical pedagogy. Nevertheless, their theories have glossed over gender as a unit of analysis and do not present women as embedded differently from men in social power relations.

Adult educators committed to seeking a better society have a chance to re-vision their commitment in light of structural and poststructural feminist pedagogies, which have borrowed from and transformed critical theory and pedagogy. The concepts of authority, voice, context, identity, resistance, and the social construction of knowledge are found in both feminist and critical theories and pedagogies. By considering information on women as learners, social reform practitioners could turn the kaleidoscope, tumbling accepted ideas into new arrays. Women's experiences refract these critical concepts in different ways.

As Sharan Merriam and Rosemary Caffarella (1999, p. 363) point out, critical theory rarely offers guidance on how to "manage the teaching and learning encounter to effect the theory's desired ends (emancipation through rational discourse)." The literature on feminist pedagogy, by contrast, does elaborate the theory-to-practice connection; Merriam and Caffarella cite Elizabeth Tisdell's contributions in particular. In the knowledge base on women as learners presented here and beyond in women's studies and queer studies, social reform practitioners can find over twenty years of classroom and community applications of feminist pedagogy.

The knowledge about women that is now available to practitioners committed to creating a better society could help them take informed action. They would know the reasons for challenging colleagues to ask, "How does what we're doing affect women learners?" They could lobby professional associations to support more research on women's learning and to make race, class, and gender power analyses a core element of professional and volunteer development. They could power the engines of community action to reshape public policies (such as the federal welfare legislation) that severely limit the access of low-income women to educational opportunities.

Unfortunately, the language used by many feminist and critical theorists to discuss women's experiences of power, oppression, and emancipation has often been exclusionary. Practitioners wanting to deepen their ability to, in bell hooks's words (1994), "teach to transgress" have to expend a fair bit of energy simply decoding the ideas about women's narratives, positionality, collective identities, and poststructuralism. Some might argue that it is in the interests of privileged academic theorists, feminist or otherwise, to maintain the linguistic divide between theorists and female students in order to preserve the teacher's place in the academy.

In parallel with Lisa Delpit's argument (1995) concerning the education of children of Color, others might be concerned that social reform educators' ideology will drive the implications of this knowledge base, at the expense of women learners. If women are to realize the benefits that they want from their educational efforts, social reform educators must help them develop the ability to function in the dominant discourses in their respective areas of practice. As Delpit suggests, teachers committed to a better society must allow discussions of oppression and privilege to become a part of instruction. They must acknowledge the "unfair 'discourse-stacking' that our society engages in" against people of Color, for example (Delpit, 1995, p. 165). But, along with this acknowledgment, teachers need to teach women the discourse "which would otherwise be used to exclude them from participating in and transforming the mainstream" (Delpit, 1995, p. 165). In my own area of practice, this would mean that it's not enough if I teach a group of Black women literacy students to do a power analysis of their lack of rural ambulance services; I must also teach them the reading and writing skills that will give them greater access to mainstream power.

For social reform educators, learning means the critical examination of the norms and practices of a particular role, group, setting, and set of relationships (Pratt, 1998b). The more this new knowledge about women's learning clarifies and extends educators' critical vision, the more likely they are to be able to enter the lives of women learners at "the nexus of injustice" (Pratt, 1998b, p. 250) and work for social change for all.

Recommendations for Future Work

I've explored some of the ways individual adult educators might re-vision their practices on the basis of core commitments to their work. The question of implications for the field as a whole remains. The village in the riverbank story could represent the adult education field itself. From a constellation of beliefs, from lines of power and privilege, from economics, and from socially constructed notions of race, class, gender, and sexual orientation, the practitioners respond to women who want to learn from and with them. Any re-visioning of women's learning opportunities is going to happen in response to the multitude of contexts in which that learning takes place. One thing is certain: there is plenty more to do. Here are four recommendations for continuing the field's re-visioning of its commitment to women learners.

Increasing the Visibility of Women as Learners

Some of the knowledge about women as learners has already been incorporated into the adult education field. The results from psychological and cognitive research on women seem to have been the easiest to integrate. For example, it is heartening to see how much Merriam and Caffarella (1999) now include on women learners. This visibility is the direct result of over a decade's worth of work on the part of a small but gutsy cadre of graduate faculty, students, and community practitioners in the field. But is a handful of publications sufficient? No. The information gatekeepers in adult education need to do more if what is known now and what is to come is to permeate the work of the field and not just be a selective graft here and there. Publishers, journal editors, conference program chairs, journal reviewers, faculty, Web "masters," librarians, discussion-list moderators, trainers, and consultants can all play a role in making this growing body of knowledge more visible and in suggesting new questions for research.

Putting Knowledge into Practice

We need to recognize that it's easier to think about women as learners than to do something with our knowledge. Earlier in this chapter, I wrote that paying attention to the gendered lives of women is personally charged work. It puts you in the path of controversy. It touches individual as well as social beliefs and behaviors woven into the fabric of our work as adult educators.

Two recent literacy-related studies reinforced for me the start we have made, as well as the distance we still have to go before gender-, race-, class-, or ability-based oppression and privilege will no longer organize the education of women and girls. One of these studies (Commeyras, 1999) looked at how interested a random sample of United States K–12 educators, administrators, and teacher educators in reading/language arts were in gender issues. The results of this study suggest that most respondents were interested in knowing about gender issues in literacy education. In addition, they were willing to consider teaching suggestions that addressed gender issues in literacy. Nevertheless, far fewer were willing to consider teaching scenarios where sexism was explicitly addressed. Michelle Commeyras (p. 361) says this finding "indicates their awareness that it is difficult to teach in ways that invite challenges to something controversial like gender roles, relations, and regimes." The other study (Purcell-Gates, Degener, and Jacobson, 1998), of 271 adult literacy programs in the United States, examines the relevance of materials and activities that are described as being either "life-contextualized" or "life-decontextualized," and it looks at who controls decisions in classrooms, which in turn are described as being either "monologic" or "dialogic." Of the programs studied, 73 percent are classified as life-decontextualized/monologic; only 8 percent are described as life-contextualized/dialogic. According to these researchers, the results are not particularly surprising because the model of literacy instruction that emphasizes teacher control and skills-based, decontextualized materials "is an old and deeply embedded one in this country" (p. 13). The research team also notes that "most programs clustered around the middle of [a] two-dimensional grid of characteristics," a fact suggesting that teachers and programs feel pulled toward the ends of these continua. Even so, 20 percent of the programs are judged to be highly life-decontextualized and highly monologic, whereas only 1 percent are judged to be both highly life-contextualized and highly dialogic.

Several of my coauthors in this volume have pointed out that many women learn better and feel better about themselves as learners when the learning is relevant to their lives and when they are respected as active partners in the learning process. They have also argued for new approaches to instruction that are based on an understanding of gender issues. The two studies just described suggest to me that emancipatory or transformational learning opportunities for women in organized adult education settings will not be the norm anytime soon. The hopeful interpretation is that there are cracks in the middle ground that may also be receptive to new views of women as learners.

Providing Staff Development on Women as Learners

We want more practitioners to go beyond thinking about women as learners and to become actively engaged with women's gender issues. To accomplish this, the field needs to offer more examples of this work where it happens—in businesses, community organizations, government training facilities, schools, and virtual spaces like the Internet. We need more modeling of the processes involved. Many adult educators have come through educational programs that reflect the dominant social arrangements. Practitioners need staff development opportunities in which they can experience the kinds of teaching environments that research is telling us are effective for women. Practitioners need more stories from colleagues who have put into practice the pedagogical skills and analytical strategies that enable them to foreground women's similarities and differences as well as the connections (among race, class, gender, ability, and sexual orientation) that this volume has highlighted.

Broadening Contributions to the Knowledge Base

The riverbank story talks about the industry that grew up around the rescuing of baby girls. Adult educators are part of a culture that manages what the river brings them, and they may even manipulate their particular points of the river in order to get the most out of it. Women learners and the knowledge that is constructed about them are commodities, and they have been for much of this century.

We live in an emerging global information society. A process of re-visioning our commitments to women's learning will have to deal with the commodification of knowledge and its function as cultural capital. The feminist discussions of women's learning that have migrated into adult education, or that have been created by adult educators, have not sufficiently turned our attention to economic understanding. We are still predominantly focused on interpersonal and intrapsychic issues that are influenced by biological and cultural factors. Even the use of the term *class*, and of class as a concept, is more an identity marker than an analytical tool.

The accumulated knowledge about women's learning draws our attention to many more pieces in the kaleidoscope that are or have been women's experience as learners. Adult educators need to hear the voices of theorists and practitioners exploring the economic or class issues at play in women's formal and nonformal knowledge construction, in women's schooling, and in the social policies regulating the education of low-income women. Socialist feminism and materialist feminism seem to offer further insights into women's issues of voice, identity, power, and self. According to Rosemary Hennessy and Chrys Ingraham (1997, p. 2), "if feminism is to maintain its viability as a political movement aimed at redressing women's oppression and exploitation worldwide, the theory that underlies feminist practice cannot eclipse the material realities that bind race, gender, sexuality, and rationality to labor." Carol Stabile (1997, p. 396), another feminist concerned with postmodernism's message and prominence in higher education, writes:

> A grim irony inheres in the fact that as capitalism's attacks on the working class, the poor, and social programs intensify, at a time when the division of wealth is deepening, intellectuals discover that identity is actually fluid and discursive, that the economy is actually discursively constructed, and that class position no longer matters. Why, at this point in history, did postmodernist social theory become popular within the academy? Why did arguments against class as a category of analysis emerge at a point when class divisions were growing?

In addition to a feminist class analysis, a more thorough historical analysis of women's learning efforts might shed light on the changing nature of connections and on the many stories of women's learning that have been silenced or muffled by the dominant historical educational narratives.

Conclusion

My vision of women's learning is pushed forward by an experience I had team-teaching a graduate class in the late 1980s with my coauthor Elisabeth Hayes. The course was on feminism and adult education. As an opening icebreaker we asked the students, all women, to describe images that captured how they felt about themselves as learners. The one answer I remember, more than a decade later, came from a woman who said that she thought of herself as a Jaguar up on blocks. That image of a finely crafted, powerful vehicle going nowhere was disturbing. Adult education needs to be a source of better images for women as learners.

9

Creating Knowledge About Women's Learning

Elisabeth Hayes

As stated in Chapter One, the formal knowledge base that we had to draw on as source material for this book was much more limited than we anticipated. That had some positive effects: it prompted us to draw on women's stories and other nonacademic sources, perhaps more so than if the formal scholarship had been more extensive. But it also meant that we now can point more to questions or issues that have been raised than to a coherent, well-developed body of knowledge about any facet of women's learning. Yet perhaps that is not such a bad thing. Our rapidly changing social context and its effects on gendered norms and women's lives, combined with new developments in feminist theory, make any claims to definitive knowledge about women's learning seem suspect. Instead, what is necessary is an ongoing, evolving process of questioning old beliefs and assumptions and building new knowledge about women's learning, both for ourselves individually and, in a broader sense, as part of formal scholarship. We hope that the ideas in this book can stimulate further interest and commitment on the part of more people to women's learning as a focus for formal research as well as more informed practice and personal insights.

In the next sections, I will address a number of broad issues applicable to building knowledge about women's learning: the value of a focus on women's learning; the need for gendered analyses of women's learning; reconceptualizing adult learning theory in light of women's learning; accounting for diversity among women; developing concepts derived from women's learning; more holistic perspectives on learning; understanding learning in the context of women's changing conceptions of self; and broadening the knowledge about women's learning that informs our teaching.

Why Women's Learning?

As discussed in Chapter One, the decision to write a book on women's learning was in many ways a political decision. It was political in that we wanted to give more visibility and credibility to women's learning in its own right, not in comparison with men's learning. Some people question the value of research on women's learning, asking how we can know if what we find is really unique to women. What they are implying is that studying women's learning is not important unless one can draw conclusions about how women differ from men. Such people have missed the point entirely, and such an argument subtly reinforces the hierarchy of male privilege. Why is women's learning important only as it relates to men's learning? The purpose of research on women's learning is to explore women's learning as important in its own right.

Nevertheless, there are some potential dangers in studying women's learning. One danger is that such work can lead to assertions that certain attributes or qualities of women's learning are innate, fixed, and uniform across situations ("essential" attributes of women) rather than integrally connected to a particular set of situational, social, and historical circumstances, and thus changeable as those circumstances change. This essentialism is most often apparent in scholarship that remains at a purely descriptive level, making broad generalizations about how women prefer to learn or their learning behavior, without putting their learning into context or probing more deeply into why women might express such preferences or act in such ways. To make that point a little more concretely, I'll use the example of connected learning (see Chapter

Five). Much of the literature describes connected learning as a seemingly innate preference of women, without consideration of why women might tend to prefer such a learning mode. Much research on women as connected learners has been done in the context of traditionally competitive and frequently impersonal classes in higher education. Women's preference for noncompetitive, connected forms of learning may be linked to self-doubt about their ability to succeed in such environments rather than to more intrinsic learning styles. Such preferences may not be as strong in other contexts. Nevertheless, often such findings based on women in higher education settings are generalized to women's learning in all settings.

A second danger of research on women's learning is that it can unintentionally reinforce oppositional categories of women versus men. Simply by studying "women's learning," we implicitly set up women's learning as different from, or in opposition to, men's learning. Mary Belenky, Blythe Clinchy, Nancy Goldberger, and Jill Tarule (1986) provide a cautionary example of this danger, stating that they chose to include only women in their study so that they could identify patterns of thought and knowledge more reflective of women's voices and experiences. Unfortunately, in their discussion they contrast their findings with those from the research of William Perry. This is problematic because Perry studied a very selective group of men (undergraduates at Harvard) in contrast to the more diverse group of women studied by Belenky, Clinchy, Goldberger, and Tarule. The differences between the groups in age, educational background, and socioeconomic levels make the comparisons invalid to begin with. Even though the authors acknowledge the need for caution in making comparisons, they fall into the trap of making generalizations about differences between men and women. The many similarities among women and men's ways of knowing become obscured—for example, Belenky, Clinchy, Goldberger, and Tarule's overall scheme of ways of knowing is remarkably similar to Perry's. Perhaps it is not surprising, then, that readers of Belenky, Clinchy, Goldberger, and Tarule (1986) tend to be even more extreme in interpreting the findings as "women are this way, so men must be the opposite." For example, when Belenky, Clinchy, Goldberger, and Tarule state that connected knowing comes more easily to many women than separate knowing, many readers seem to interpret this as "all women are connected knowers and all men are separate knowers." Caution is needed on the part of readers as well as researchers to avoid leaping to such conclusions.

I would like to point out, too, that overgeneralization about differences between women and men is a very common pitfall even when researchers actually collect comparative data. Mary Crawford (1995), citing Janet Hyde (1990), has pointed out how sex differences in mathematics ability have been exaggerated and distorted in scholarship and the popular media. Although there is actually more overlap than difference in boys' and girls' test scores, and although factors other than sex, such as age and race, have a significant impact, the "superior" mathematics ability of males has been widely acclaimed and even attributed to genetics or hormones.

Some scholars have argued that, by its nature, sex/gender "difference" research will lead to an exaggeration of differences and, further, to judgments of women's differences from men as deficiencies. Crawford (1995) suggests an alternative to sex/gender difference research that tends to treat gender as an attribute of individuals. She argues that gender differences, our conceptions of masculinity and femininity, are the products of socially and culturally determined belief systems rather than purely biological factors. These beliefs create different expectations and norms for people of each sex. We experience considerable social pressure to conform to gendered norms, although we each choose to conform or not in different ways, so that there is considerable variation, for example, in how different women might adopt certain kinds of "feminine" behavior in different situations.

In the broadest sense, this perspective leads us to ask how societal and cultural belief systems about gender shape women's learning. Such a perspective allows for the possibility that women and men may think, act, and learn in overtly similar ways, without draw-ing the conclusion that gender is irrelevant. Instead, this perspective encourages us to probe more deeply into the gendered origins and meanings of these apparent similarities. Using the example of learn-ing styles, although some women as well as some men may exhibit overtly similar preferences for abstract thought, these preferences may not have the same meanings and consequences for them. If engaging in abstract thinking is a masculine trait, according to dominant belief systems, then women with this preference may experience internal and external conflicts that men do not. They may be judged nega-tively by other people who view them as "unfeminine." In some sit-uations, this lack of conformity may be a benefit, if the masculine trait is more valued. As an example, when I was in high school, and as an undergraduate in college, I often tried to conceal my "smart-ness" in social situations because it seemed to make me less attractive to men. In the classroom, however, I found it was to my advantage to impress my teachers and fellow students with my capacity for ana-lytical thought and logic. Indeed, I think that in some cases I stood out even more than men with similar abilities because I contra-dicted the assumptions people had made about me as a diminutive, feminine-looking woman. As my example suggests, this perspective on gender can help us see and better understand how women's self-image and behavior may change across situations. It also encour-ages us to explore diversity among women as learners, which is the last concern that I will point out.

A final danger of research on women's learning is the creation of a generic category of women that can render invisible the consider-able diversity among women as learners. Some scholars would argue that it is impossible to truly capture diversity among women if we insist on using women as a category of analysis. Nevertheless, I think we have the potential to build knowledge about women's learning more generally that also helps us understand diversity among women. I'll return to this concern as a separate point because it emerged as a major issue in scholarship and stories of women's learning. First, however, I will discuss how a gendered analysis can contribute to a richer understanding of women's learning.

The Need for Gendered Analysis

A major limitation of many studies that we reviewed on women's learning is the lack of what I would describe as a gendered analysis of women's learning experiences. The researchers provide rich descriptive information and themes concerning women's learning but typically do not interpret these findings in terms of the influence of gender.

A study of women in higher education can serve as an example of this purely descriptive, gender-free approach. This study (Rountree and Lambert, 1992) focuses on adult women students in two higher education institutions. The researchers provide a context for their study by describing the growing numbers of women in the workforce and as students in higher education. They state, "Adult women are a special population with unique problems" (Rountree and Lambert, 1992, p. 87), but, unfortunately, the authors do not explain how women are "special" or suggest any reasons why they might have "unique problems," particularly as connected to gender. Using a questionnaire, the researchers collected information about the learning objectives, preferred learning methods, and self-perceived personal traits of 145 adult women learners in two-year higher education programs. Some of their findings are really quite interesting because they challenge some dominant stereotypes about women learners. Overall, the respondents seemed to have high self-esteem, exhibit a wide variety of motivations for learning, and find a variety of learning methods helpful. Unfortunately, the authors provide almost no interpretation of their findings, nor do they point out how their findings differ from beliefs about women learners in other literature. From a gendered perspective, we might have referred to the literature suggesting that women prefer learning methods that allow them to connect with other learners, the instructor, and the subject matter (see Chapter Five) and contrasted this perspective with the findings in this study that lectures (typically considered to be "unconnected" learning) and small-group discussion (typically considered to be "connected" learning) were indicated as helpful by equal proportions of women. We might also have pointed out that considerably more than half the women (68 percent) found it helpful to critique books or writings, something that is often thought to be at odds with women's learning preferences. Readers are left with many questions about the presumed significance of gender in women's learning preferences, which the authors do not even begin to address.

Also of interest in the study was that many women gave themselves relatively high ratings on a list of personal traits typically associated with academic success. Half the women rated themselves as above average in academic ability, and 65 percent indicated that they were above average in their ability to do independent work. This contrasts quite a bit with the dominant image of the insecure adult woman student who needs extra support to succeed academically. Nevertheless, the authors do not point out that women tended to rate themselves much lower on certain traits. For example, 60 percent rated themselves as average or below in mathematical ability, and 59 percent as average or below in assertiveness.

Although I am wary of the dangers of overgeneralization about women, from a gendered perspective such trends deserve more scrutiny. For example, what is the significance of gender in women's self-evaluations of their assertiveness? Assertiveness typically is considered to be a more "masculine" trait. Were the women less likely to see themselves as assertive because that conflicts with appropriate female behavior? How does this affect their academic success? Of interest as well is that 41 percent of the women had quite positive perceptions of their assertiveness, seeing themselves as above average on this trait. How do we explain this finding in light of the general tendency for assertiveness to be considered unfeminine? Of course, some of these questions could not be answered, given the nature of the study and the data that were collected. In fact, the potential for doing a gendered analysis depends on framing the study in a certain way, and I will illustrate that point later on with another study.

What, then, is a gendered analysis? At the most general level, doing a gendered analysis of women's learning means looking for the influence of gender on whatever aspect of women's learning is being studied. Why is such an analysis important? My argument for gendered analysis is based on the assumption that, by studying women's learning in particular, one is asserting that gender makes a difference in learning. Otherwise, one would simply be studying "people's" learning, or learning in general. That's not an approach I would advocate, but I see the world through a gendered lens that makes gender stand out for me as a primary focus of concern in a study of women's learning.

To illustrate one approach to a gendered analysis, I'll use Rosalind Edwards's study (1993) of adult women undergraduate students. I referred to her study in Chapter Two in my discussion of how women handle the conflicts and intersections of learning in different contexts. I'll point out several elements of her study that reflect a gendered analysis of women's learning. The focus of this study is interactions between family and education in the lives of adult women undergraduate students. She begins the report of her research by discussing some key feminist concepts that informed her work. She critiques theories of women's identity development that emphasize the connection of women's identities to their role as caregivers in the private sphere. Edwards argues that the dichotomies of public/private and of male/female identity are simplistic and not factual, but they do represent dominant belief systems that shape how people see the world, and themselves in it. These concepts, by providing an explicit perspective about the significance of gender in women's lives, lay the foundation for the questions that were central to the study. Edwards set out to explore how women perceived and negotiated the public/private dichotomy of family and school, looking at how they attempted to connect or separate these presumably separate spheres and at the tensions that they experienced as a result.

The gendered, or feminist, theoretical framework provides an explicit way to bring gender into the analysis of the findings. Edwards found that the women in her study varied considerably in the extent to which they attempted to separate or connect family and educational experiences, and that they used different means of separating and connecting these experiences. Edwards moves, however, from a description of what the women did to an analysis of why they held certain beliefs about family and school and engaged in certain actions. Many of the women, as well as their partners, relatives, and friends, believed that the women's pursuit of education should not interfere with their caring for their families. Edwards attributes this belief to the broader social construct of the separation of private and public spheres and to the dominant belief system that suggests women's primary responsibilities lie in the private sphere. She argues that the women who tried to keep their educational activities separate from family life were those who were most accepting of this belief system. The women who attempted to make more connections often encountered resistance and even ended relationships with their partners because of the conflicts this generated. Edwards explains this conflict in terms of male-female power relationships: the women's entrance into the "public" sphere of education took time and attention away from their partners and enabled them to develop knowledge that might give them more equality and status.

Doing a gendered analysis does not mean applying existing concepts about gender in an uncritical manner. In her analysis, Edwards questions the presumed dichotomy of a male emphasis on separation and a female emphasis on connection by pointing out that the women in her study varied considerably in the extent to which they valued and attempted to make connections among the various aspects of their lives. Some of the women quite enjoyed, for example, the opportunity for independence and individuality that higher education offered them and in fact were willing to sacrifice their relationships for it. Thus Edwards's study illustrates another aspect of a gendered analysis of women's learning: it can contribute to the development of feminist theory itself, as well as to more particular knowledge of different aspects of women's learning.

To summarize, a gendered analysis of women's learning would include an explicit theoretical stance toward gender, questions framed in light of this stance, interpretation of findings in relation to this gendered perspective, and potential contributions to feminist theory as well as to knowledge of women's learning. The specific nature of the gendered analysis will vary according to the feminist theoretical perspective that one adopts. For example, each of the three frameworks discussed in Chapter One would offer a different explanation for women's math anxiety, but each would be a gendered analysis.

Reconceptualizing Adult Learning Theory

Feminist scholarship has been instrumental in identifying the biases and limitations of dominant theories and concepts that have been derived primarily from the experiences and perspectives of privileged White men. Such challenges have been rare in scholarship on adult learning, with the exception of Belenky, Clinchy, Goldberger, and Tarule (1986). Nevertheless, as Daniele Flannery (1994) and Joyce Stalker (1996) have pointed out, adult learning theory is permeated by sexist and racist assumptions that marginalize and devalue the experiences of women and people of Color. A significant task for future scholarship on women's learning is to use women's experiences and perspectives to expose these biases and reconceptualize dominant adult learning theories.

Stalker (1994) provides one example of such scholarship in her discussion of women mentors in higher education. Stalker argues that traditional conceptions of mentoring reflect a bias toward male experience and do not adequately portray women's experience of mentoring. For example, she points out that mentoring is typically portrayed as a supportive relationship of mutual benefit for mentor and mentee. She notes, however, that this view ignores the potential for oppression and exploitation in mentoring relationships, dimensions that are particularly apparent in the problems associated with men mentoring women. Stalker also points out the limitations of a view of mentoring that assumes mentors are firmly established and comfortable with the academic culture and seek to socialize mentees into this culture. This view, she states, does not take account of the position of women mentors, who may feel themselves to be simultaneously outsiders and insiders in academe because of its patriarchal structure, which continues to marginalize women. Women mentors may support women mentees in resisting and transforming these oppressive structures rather than simply encouraging them to conform and accept them. Thus, Stalker argues, conceptions of mentoring should be based on a more dynamic view of power that takes into account the position of the mentor in structural power relationships and allows for the possibility of mentoring as a means of structural change.

Ann Brooks, in Chapter Six, provides another good example of reconceptualizing adult learning theory. In Brooks's work, as in Stalker's (1994), we can see the importance of close attention to women's experiences as a key factor in their challenges to adult learning theory. Rather than trying to fit women's experiences into existing frameworks, they use the contradictions between women's experience and theory to open up new visions and possibilities. They do not treat women's experiences as deviant or problematic. For example, Stalker might have described the resistance of some women mentors to the academic culture as examples of poor adjustment and failed mentoring, but instead she uses it to achieve a new understanding of power in both the process and the goals of mentoring. Brooks might have characterized the importance of personal relationships in women's transformative learning as an indicator of excessive dependence on others, but instead she uses it to question the centrality of independence and autonomy in transformative learning theory. Although each author grounds her work in women's experiences, each also draws on theories outside adult education in generating new perspectives. Stalker draws on structural feminist theories for the concepts of patriarchy, structural power relations, and individual resistance, which helped her re-vision the nature of mentoring. Brooks uses narrative theory, not a specifically feminist theory, although that is popular among certain feminist scholars as an approach to studying and understanding women's experiences. Indeed, one reason for the persistence of androcentric biases in adult learning theory is that it continues to be uninformed by other theoretical perspectives that better account for gender and are more inclusive of diverse people's experiences.

In reconceptualizing adult learning theory, we should be wary of replacing one set of presumably universal truths about adult learning with yet another. Our goal should be to develop more inclusive understandings of adult learning that, as Flannery (1994) suggests, allow for differences to exist and that are explicitly contextualized. By *contextualized*, I mean that we identify whose experiences served as the basis for our theories—and whose experiences are not represented—and that we strive to be increasingly aware of and explicit about how our own standpoints and values have shaped our theories.

Diversity Among Women

There are two ways in which we might give more attention to diversity in future research on women's learning: by overcoming White, middle-class biases while being more inclusive of currently underrepresented groups of women; and by developing theory, methods of analysis, and interpretations that help us see and understand diversity as well as similarities among women.

Overcoming Biases

Much of the published research we located on women's learning focuses on the experiences of White, highly educated, economically advantaged women. This is perhaps not surprising because much of the research was on women learners in higher education programs, who tend to fit this profile. When women of Color were included, most often they were Black, and so we are left with an even greater dearth of knowledge about women of different races, cultures, and ethnicities. Lesbian women, women with disabilities, women over the age of sixty-five—the list of marginalized groups is quite extensive. A goal for future research should be to bring these women into the story so that we have a more inclusive understanding of women's learning.

Being inclusive means more than simply doing research on special groups of women, such as doing research on lesbian women's ways of knowing or Mexican women's development of voice. It can be all too easy to apply concepts derived from White women's experience to women of Color, creating a bias similar to the bias that results from applying concepts derived from male experience to women. Earlier in this book, we pointed out that dominant conceptualizations of women's ways of knowing and voice have suffered from exactly these kinds of biases. Each of us must approach research on women's learning with a sensitivity to our own potential biases and an openness to challenging our assumptions and perspectives. Developing this more inclusive understanding in the academic world is a particular challenge because the majority of researchers studying women's learning are White women (male researchers of women's learning are definitely in the minority).

A study of Navajo women by Donna Deyhle and Frank Margonis (1995) provides a good example of how researchers were able to identify and challenge concepts in feminist theory that are based on White, middle-class women's experiences. The researchers' goal in this study was to provide a better understanding of Navajo women's relationships to schools, and in so doing they exposed a number of biases in educational theory. As Deyhle and Margonis describe, a large proportion of Navajo women do not complete high school, and very few go on to postsecondary education. There is a high teenage-pregnancy rate among Navajo women, which is a major factor contributing to their high dropout rates. Using concepts from feminist reproduction theory (a type of structural feminist theory, as described in Chapter One), these high pregnancy and dropout rates would be explained in terms of the reproduction of women's roles in the private or domestic sphere. According to this theory, society exerts pressure on women to choose the private sphere over success in the public sphere of school and to work through a belief system that idealizes romance and domesticity. From this perspective, Navajo women's school-leaving behavior would be explained as an acceptance of these idealized notions of women's roles in the home and acceptance of a subordinate position in relation to men. Deyhle and Margonis argue, however, that in Navajo culture there is not the same split between the public sphere (as the realm of income-generating work) and the private sphere (as the realm of caretaking and domesticity). The Navajos engage in primarily home-based economic activities, such as farming and crafts; accordingly, the private sphere is a locus of value and achievement. The Navajo culture is matriarchal: women have considerable status, and mothers wield great influence over their daughters' life choices. For Navajo women, a choice of family over school or outside employment is not based on a romantic ideal of devotion to husband and children. To them, family is a wide network of kin, and their school-leaving behavior represents a commitment to community and a participation in their matriarchical lineage. Education and outside employment are based on values of individual achievement that are at odds with the Navajo values of interdependence and community. School often becomes irrelevant to Navajo women because it does not assist them in assuming their roles in the community. Deyhle and Margonis point out that, among its other limitations, feminist reproduction theory is based on an implicit assumption of individualism that is at odds with Navajo culture. In feminist reproduction theory, women's choices between achievement in education and work or in domestic roles within the nuclear family are viewed as based on their personal interests or ambitions, not as choices made to support the general good of the community.

Acquiring sensitivity to another culture, as Deyhle and Margonis (1995) have done, is not easy. An endnote to their article states that Deyhle, the primary author, conducted ethnographic fieldwork on a Navajo reservation for ten years, work that included participating in many community events, attending classes and extracurricular events with high school students, and otherwise immersing herself in Navajo culture. Vanessa Bing and Pamela Reid (1996) suggest that, in addition to cultural sensitivity, White women need to become aware of their own White privilege and of how it affects their values, beliefs, and actions. In general, whiteness has remained an invisible yet central aspect of White women's identities and experiences. Until White women become more aware of White privilege and how it affects their choices of what to study and the methods they use to study it, our knowledge of women's diversity will remain limited.

Our knowledge can be considerably enhanced by the work and perspectives of women scholars from more diverse racial and cultural backgrounds. The work of feminists of Color in other disciplines has yielded significant new insights into women's diversity. We need to make greater efforts to develop a more diverse group of women scholars pursuing research on women's learning.

In this discussion, I have primarily used examples of biases related to race and culture because these have been given the most attention in the feminist literature, largely because of critiques by women of Color. Nevertheless, we should not ignore the need for greater sensitivity to the experiences of women of different sexual orientations, physically challenged women, and other groups. Achieving this sensitivity depends first on a philosophy that values diversity as well as similarity and, second, on the continued development of theoretical frameworks that enable researchers to choose research topics and interpret findings adequately.

Theoretical Frameworks for Understanding Diversity

Developing a more inclusive understanding of women's learning means more than simply adding more diverse women to the pot and stirring. Just as our theoretical frameworks are important for a gendered analysis of women's learning, these frameworks also determine how we approach the study of diversity among women and how we make meaning of our findings. In our review of scholarship, we found few examples of the application of well-developed theoretical frameworks that account for diversity to the study of women's learning. One notable exception was Wendy Luttrell's study (1989) of working-class women's ways of knowing. I referred to her study in Chapter One as an example of scholarship reflecting a structural feminist orientation. Luttrell was trained as a sociologist, and her work is rooted in feminist theories that draw on sociological perspectives on class-based power relations as well as those based on race and gender. The use of such frameworks has been rare in the literature on women's learning, perhaps because much of this literature has been grounded in psychology rather than sociology. Bing and Reid (1996) observe that psychological research rarely even reports the class status of research participants and even less frequently makes it an explicit focus of study. We may need to turn to the sociological literature for the development of theories that better account for class differences among women learners.

Work by Black feminists and other feminists of Color is another source of theoretical perspectives on diversity. In general, these perspectives are particularly helpful in illuminating the significance of race as it intersects with gender and class in shaping women's experiences and consciousness. Typically, these perspectives offer a positive image of the strengths of women of Color and of their resistance to dominant societal structures that marginalize and oppress them. The concept of multiple or shifting consciousness (Hurtado, 1996) is often a part of these perspectives. This concept reflects women of Color's identification with multiple stigmatized groups and their awareness of multiple forms of oppression. Some of this work gives attention to diversity within racial groups and to intraracial discrimination (for example, the hierarchy based on skin color that can exist among Black women).

Another potential source of theoretical perspectives is the growing body of scholarship on lesbianism and women's sexual orientations. This literature has broad implications for understanding women's diversity as it relates to learning. For example, Chapter Three describes a perspective on lesbian identity development that can broaden our understanding of women's identity-related learning. Ann Brooks, in her earlier work with Kathleen Edwards (Brooks and Edwards, 1997), draws on this literature in her reworking of transformative learning theory. A particularly intriguing aspect of this work is the fluid nature of sexual identity described by the women in this study, suggesting the need to challenge the dichotomy of heterosexuality/homosexuality and to open up new understandings of shared as well as diverse aspects of women's experiences.

Poststructural feminist thought offers an additional theoretical lens through which to conceptualize further research on women's learning. The poststructural emphasis is less a delineation of general influences from such formations as race, gender, and class (as in structural feminist theories), or of the experiences and consciousness of a particular oppressed group (such as Black women), than an examination of the dynamics of identity formation. It is less a delineation of differences among groups than an analysis of how women experience and express shifting identities that reflect multiple social influences. The concept of positionality is central to poststructural feminist work and has only begun to be used in studies of women's learning. Frances Maher and Mary Kay Tetreault (1996) observe that positionality, and poststructural feminist thought more broadly, have the potential to allow us to see how diversity itself is constructed and constantly changing. It emphasizes understanding how we construct the meaning of gender, race, and other positions in particular situations, influenced but not controlled by dominant cultural meanings.

Developing New Concepts of Women's Learning

Grounding our understanding of adult learning in women's experiences has given a more central role to such concepts as voice and connection in learning, and it has opened up new perspectives on existing concepts, such as identity and transformation. Nevertheless, as we have shown in previous chapters, the use of these concepts has become problematic; they have become generic labels applied to diverse phenomena. This rather indiscriminate use of concepts makes it difficult to be sure what is actually being discussed in the literature or in our conversations with each other. In some cases, it has led to the conflation of one meaning with another—for example, in terms of voice, equating talk with power. In future scholarship, we need to be more careful in distinguishing among the different meanings of such concepts as voice and connection. We hope that the frameworks we have provided here will serve as a useful starting point for greater conceptual clarity.

Another issue for future scholarship is the development of a more sophisticated understanding of the concepts we have begun to identify as central to women's learning. Frequently we have found in the literature that these concepts are treated in rather superficial ways. For example, connected learning is sometimes equated simply to learning with other people rather than to learning in a particular way with other people (trying to understand their perspectives, building on their ideas, and so forth). Such superficial treatment adds little to our understanding, and it can actually do more harm than good by perpetuating vague generalizations about women's learning. Recently some scholars have begun to explore the depth and complexity of concepts such as connected learning, and their work is suggestive of the kind of careful analysis that needs to be done. Blythe Clinchy's analysis (1996) of connected and separate knowing is one informative example. She argues that connected learning has been falsely equated with an uncritical acceptance of other people's perspectives, and she goes on to provide a detailed discussion of the rigorous procedures involved in connected knowing, including rather sophisticated abilities for empathy. Further work like hers needs to be done, not only with connected learning but also with voice, identity, transformation, and other concepts that will emerge from our continued exploration of women's learning.

An additional direction for future scholarship is to investigate the meanings of these concepts for more diverse groups of women. Once again, the concept of voice provides an useful example. Voice as talk, as an expression of identity, or as an expression of power can have different meanings for women of different cultures and classes. As Patrocinio Schweickart (1996) has pointed out, in some cultures silence is valued just as much as if not more than speech, and women who are silent are not necessarily voiceless or powerless. Aida Hurtado (1996) suggests that gaining a voice, for many women of Color, is not a matter of asserting an individual identity but rather a struggle to express and represent identities connected to groups and communities.

Feminist scholars writing from poststructuralist perspectives stress the importance of close attention to the language that we use in naming our experiences, encouraging us to continuously deconstruct concepts to reveal their implicit meanings and assumptions. We must continue to be self-reflective about how our language, our naming of experience, both opens up or expands and closes down or limits our understanding of women's learning and adult learning in general. For example, the concept of connection in learning helps us see the importance of relatedness in learning, unsettling the primacy of the autonomy and individuality so often touted in adult learning theory. But does viewing learning as connected lead us to ignore the value of solitude in women's learning, the importance of withdrawal as well as connection in learning? Although voice gives us a more active, expressive conception of acquiring knowledge than the more passive metaphor of vision, how does voice also restrict our understanding? For example, do both voice and vision place too much emphasis on the role of language in knowing? What about knowledge that is embodied, that cannot be expressed or understood as voice? A poststructural perspective reminds us that all concepts are social constructions, limited by our own positions and social contexts as researchers. From this perspective, the goal is not to achieve absolute truth, a single valid theory about women's learning, or any other phenomenon, but rather to become more able to interpret the truth and reality from multiple perspectives that allow us to grasp the complex, dynamic, and often contradictory nature of human experience.

More Holistic Perspectives on Learning

One of the themes that cuts across the chapters in this book is the need for a more holistic understanding of women's learning. By *holistic*, I mean two things: learning as a process that involves not only cognitive but also emotional, spiritual, and embodied dimensions; and learning as a process that occurs not only in formal educational settings but also, and integrally, in the workplace, the home, the family, and the community.

For many years, feminist scholars have challenged the value and primacy given to cognitive, intellectual ways of knowing in formal education. Women's personal accounts of their learning often vividly convey the emotional, bodily, and spiritual dimensions associated with learning. Nevertheless, apart from recognizing the existence of an emotional dimension of learning and validating it (rather than suggesting that emotions are barriers and should be weeded out of the learning process), the literature on women's learning offers only limited insights into the role of emotions, and still fewer into the role of the body and the spirit. Current feminist scholarship suggests that we should question the very split between thought and feeling, mind and body, body and spirit. Such dichotomies are rooted in a historical Euro-American conception of knowledge and human nature that has divorced reason from all other human attributes and privileged it as the source of true knowledge. These dichotomies have been gendered and power-laden in the association of women's knowledge with inferior realms, such as the emotions and the body. A more integrated perspective on human nature suggests that we should strive to understand learning as it reflects the whole person, not ignoring or subordinating any dimension of experience. As yet, however, we have few examples of this more integrated perspective in the published literature on women's learning. A potential barrier to such work is that the dominant culture has reinforced the split to such a great extent that we often do not recognize the importance of all dimensions in our own learning experiences, much less think to give them attention in our research and scholarship. Elizabeth Debold, Deborah Tolman, and Lyn Brown (1996), who argue for "bringing body back into knowledge" (p. 116), provide some intriguing examples of how young girls learn to adopt the cultural split of mind and body in their ways of knowing. Clinchy (1996) provides examples of a more integrated way of understanding thought and feeling in connected knowing. Nancy Goldberger (1996), in her interviews with people of diverse cultural backgrounds, provides some intriguing examples of body knowledge. The words of some of her interviewees are evocative of the new perspectives offered by a more holistic perspective on learning and knowing: "My gut always knows what is right"; "I listen with my skin"; "The body knows" (pp. 352–355).

To develop a more holistic understanding of women's learning, we also need to explore learning in contexts other than formal education. As noted in Chapter Two, little formal scholarship addresses these contexts. Although an emphasis on formal education caters to the interests of educators, it is doubtful that this emphasis reflects the most important learning experiences from the perspective of women learners. In fact, when I ask women and men students in my courses on adult learning to write autobiographies of their learning experiences, typically the learning that they identify as most significant has taken place outside the classroom. Because cognitive learning is typically emphasized in formal education, this focus on formal education has undoubtedly contributed to the bias toward cognitive dimensions of learning in our scholarship. Giving more attention to women's learning in diverse environments could give us more insight into noncognitive dimensions of learning because they may be more obvious and significant. Broadening our vision to these other contexts might also give us a better understanding of women's learning abilities and strengths, in situations where they are not constrained by the structures of formal education.

Learning and Women's Conceptions of Self

Thinking about learning in a more holistic manner can illuminate how learning goes beyond developing intellectual skills and involves broader changes in identity and self-worth. As described in Chapter Three, women's learning is intertwined with who we are, with our conceptions of ourselves, with our multiple identities. This theme is echoed throughout the rest of the chapters, and in particular in the chapters on voice and transformation. This perspective on learning and the self can help us understand why women may experience considerable conflict and tension as a result of their participation in learning experiences such as higher education; they are struggling with coming to know and be themselves in new ways, not just mastering a new body of knowledge. Much recent scholarship and women's own accounts present a positive image of women as active seekers and shapers of learning opportunities for personal growth rather than as passive recipients of subject matter or skills.

Although past scholarship on women's learning offers descriptive information about women's experiences of personal growth and change, the authors rarely move beyond description to a more theoretical or conceptual level of analysis. The potentially relevant body of theoretical literature on women's psychosocial development is rarely cited in studies of women's learning (Caffarella and Olson, 1993). This body of literature includes traditional theories that emphasize autonomy (theories typically based, originally, on male experience but now being extended and tested against female experience) as well as theories based specifically on female development, which emphasize relationship. On the basis of their review of this literature, Rosemary Caffarella and Sharon Olson conclude that "women's development is characterized by multiple patterns, role discontinuities, and a need to maintain a 'fluid' sense of self" (p. 143). Nevertheless, they also point out that empirical support for these conclusions and for specific theories is limited, and they identify a number of directions for further research. Chapter Three points out a number of potential limitations of theories that emphasize the attainment of autonomy and theories that emphasize relationship. Future studies of adult women's learning that are based on or seek to validate such theoretical perspectives might provide greater insight into the connections between changes in identity, learning, and education for women. They may also help to elaborate or challenge existing theories of psychosocial development.

In Chapter Three, Daniele Flannery points out that both the autonomy-oriented and relational approaches to understanding identity and development tend to be based on psychological, essentialist assumptions. She suggests a third way to understand learning and identity development: as intersecting with social, cultural, and historical influences. Structural feminist theories, for example, make issues of power, oppression, and the influence of social structures central to understanding women's identities and social worlds. Starting from such perspectives, future research might approach women's identity development not just as a psychological phenomenon but also as a process highly affected by environmental, social, and historical factors that contribute to women's experiences of oppression. The studies on women's learning that we reviewed touch only briefly on the significance of such factors.

More attention to social and historical contexts can help us better understand why and how women interpret their own experiences of personal growth in certain ways. For example, few women in the studies we reviewed spoke of the significance of social and political transformation when they described personal growth or returning to school. Similarly, in their research on women's developmental patterns, Baruch, Barnett, and Rivers (1983) found that women connected their changes in self-esteem to individual, age-related factors without identifying the influence of any broader social or political changes. As the researchers point out, the women's interpretations mirror the dominance of individualistic, age-related explanations for personal growth in our society as a whole. Future research must, as Carol Ryff (1985, p. 110) has argued, "combine questions of subjectivity, experiences, and developmental change with studies of actual events or experiences in people's lives, so as to illuminate where outside changes are producing inside changes, and alternatively, where inside changes are leading to external transitions."

Feminist poststructuralist theories offer another theoretical perspective with particular value for understanding the interrelationship of women's identity and social contexts. In particular, the poststructural concept of positionality suggests that women's identities are not fixed or unitary but are positions constructed relative to a constantly shifting pattern of relationships, ideologies, and institutions. Maher and Tetreault's research (1994) on women's studies classes provides a useful example of how the concept of positionality can be applied to understanding how students and teachers construct knowledge about their own positions relative to gender and race.

Broadening the Knowledge That Informs Our Teaching

Chapter Seven, on feminist pedagogies, makes it clear that we have a rich and multifaceted literature on teaching women. As Elizabeth Tisdell describes in that chapter, these pedagogies are largely based on theoretical perspectives and philosophical assumptions, often linked to values and behavior associated more with women than men, such as caring, nurturing, and connection. Although theory and philosophy are legitimate sources of guidance for teaching, our understanding of how to teach women could benefit from our drawing on other sources of knowledge.

Scholarship on women's learning, as reviewed in this book, offers valuable yet often neglected information to inform the design of teaching practices for women. In general, the insights gained from this scholarship suggest a need for educators to be more cautious about using common generalizations about women's learning as a basis for teaching. For example, the notion that women tend to prefer connected learning needs to be more critically assessed. As Chapter Five suggests, there is considerable diversity among women in their preferences for different modes of learning, and not all women may be responsive to a "connected" approach to teaching. Further, we should be careful in how we interpret prescriptions for practice that are based on these assumptions. For example, a common goal of feminist pedagogies is to allow women to give voice to their experiences and perspectives. Often, however, voice becomes equated with talk, and emphasis is placed on encouraging everyone to say something in class discussions. Nevertheless, as discussed in Chapter Four, not all women feel that talking in class is an empowering or desirable experience; some women may find silence a preferable mode of learning, without feeling that they are voiceless or unengaged in the learning process. In some cases, women may find silence in the classroom safer and more supportive than public exposure of their ideas and experiences.

Stories of women's experiences with feminist pedagogies and other teaching practices are an additional source of knowledge. We already have a number of teachers' thoughtful published accounts of their use of these pedagogies (see, for example, the journal *Feminist Teacher*). These accounts give us a richer understanding of how theory becomes translated into practice, and in some cases they also raise questions about the use of certain recommended teaching approaches. Teachers' stories have illustrated, among other things, the challenges of creating the safe learning environments advocated in the more psychologically oriented feminist pedagogies. These stories offer examples of how difficult it can be for learners and teachers to confront sexism and racism in the classroom and in other realms of experience. Students' stories of their experiences with these pedagogies are more rare but are equally valuable. For example, in a collaboratively written article by Saundra Gardner, Cynthia Dean, and Deo McKaig (1989), a teacher and two students describe how power differentials persisted in feminist classrooms and led to the marginalization of nonfeminist students, working-class women, and lesbians. The students were able to describe biases in interactions and dialogue that the teachers evidently did not recognize. By drawing on stories such as these, we can not only gain more concrete examples for practice but also build a more nuanced, sensitive understanding of the strengths and limitations of these practices.

Another source of enhanced knowledge is the more formal research on feminist pedagogy and on women's responses to different teaching approaches. There are a few significant studies that can serve as starting points. *The Courage to Question*, a national study of women's studies programs conducted by the Association of American Colleges and the National Women's Studies Association (Musil, 1992), offers broad information about student learning in women's studies courses, although the focus is not specifically the impact of feminist pedagogy. Maher and Tetreault's study (1994) offers more detailed descriptions of teaching and learning in women's studies courses.

Feminist pedagogy, as it has been practiced in women's studies courses in higher education, has been criticized for its emphasis on sharing experiences and promoting a supportive emotional climate, to the neglect of fostering critical-thinking skills. This criticism, to some extent, reflects a difference in the value placed on certain educational goals. Many feminist educators have pointed out the limitations of emphasizing critical thinking over other means of knowing and learning. Nevertheless, formal research does not offer enough evidence for us to draw any general conclusions one way or the other about what students really learn through feminist pedagogy. Caryn Musil (1992) identifies a number of impressive learning outcomes that are based on students' self-reports. These outcomes include students' development of more critical perspectives on the construction of knowledge. We need to follow this study up with more investigations of how feminist pedagogies affect student learning. One point made by Musil is that the content of women's studies, not just the pedagogy, is particularly influential; indeed, in feminist pedagogies, it is hard to separate content from process. Structural models, for example, presume a particular knowledge goal, which is to help students become more aware of unequal power relationships as manifested and supported by economic, political, and other societal systems. One question that arises for both research and practice is the extent to which adopting feminist pedagogy implies making changes in course content and teaching practices: Can feminist pedagogies be successful or meaningful without a particular stance toward course content?

More broadly, much theory about feminist pedagogies has been developed and put into practice in higher education, often in the context of women's studies courses where an explicit goal was to foster awareness of the significance of gender in personal experience, in knowledge building, and in society at large. How can we use feminist pedagogy in different learning contexts, with different goals and constraints? There are few published examples of how feminist pedagogy has been used in other adult education settings. How might elements of feminist pedagogy be applied, if at all, to informal learning situations as well?

A final question relates to the agenda of both social and personal change that is a goal of many feminist pedagogies. As Elizabeth Tisdell notes (Chapter Seven), currently poststructural feminists are cautious in their estimations of how feminist pedagogy might challenge social structures, and yet their goal still moves beyond the individual to some sort of collective change. Musil (1992) has found evidence that some students became more committed to and engaged in social action as a result of their participation in women's studies courses. The information that this study provides is scanty, however. We need more knowledge about the links between feminist pedagogies, individual change, and collective change.

Summary and Conclusion

Our current understanding of women's learning, although much richer and more substantial than it was even a decade ago, is still constrained by inadequate theoretical perspectives, lack of attention to diversity among women, and other limitations. In this chapter, I have outlined just a few major avenues and issues for building further knowledge about women's learning. Other issues, and more particular questions for further research, are suggested in the preceding chapters. We hope that other researchers will be inspired by ideas and issues raised in this book to pursue further investigations of women's learning that will continue to challenge old assumptions and provoke new insights. What we once assumed to be truths about women and women's learning have come to be questioned as the social context has shifted, as gender roles have changed, and as we have developed new ways of understanding gender and its significance in our lives. I can recall feminists saying in the past that the day would come when feminism would no longer be necessary because sex or gender would no longer be a determining factor in people's life choices, opportunities, social status, and so forth. I suppose the same could be said about women's learning—that one day gender will be irrelevant to an understanding of learning. Nevertheless, given the present significance of gender in people's lives, I think we have a long way to go before we can safely assume that gender does not have an important role in women's and men's learning.

Although this chapter was written primarily for researchers, I would like to end by noting that we are all creators of knowledge about women's learning, even if we are not doing formal research or publishing articles and books on the topic. Teachers create knowledge through their teaching as they interact with women and men students, see how their students respond to different learning activities, and assess their students' learning. As individuals, we create knowledge in our daily lives by reflecting on our own learning experiences, sharing stories about learning with other women (and men), reading books like this one, and comparing the ideas in books with our experiences. Ideally, by making women's learning more visible as a legitimate and important topic for understanding, we can all contribute to building new knowledge to inform our teaching, learning, and living.

Postscript

Re-Searching for Women's Learning

Daniele D. Flannery

You will see, and perhaps feel, that this postscript is very different in tone, voice, and style from the rest of the book. It is written differently because it is in part an attempt to recognize the different ways of knowing and different identities we share as women. Throughout the book we have stressed that we can come to know in different ways. We can learn and discuss our learning with varied language and images. We can respect and experiment with other ways of knowing. This postscript is intended to present ideas in a somewhat different way from the rest of the book, and to address readers on a more personal basis as learners. The postscript also reflects another side of myself as a knower and learner. Betty Hayes, Ann Brooks, Elizabeth Tisdell, Jane Hugo, and I are not just academics. We have lives outside academia (as other women do outside their work) and ways of expressing ourselves that are different from academic writing. This postscript is written as an expression of those other ways of being and knowing.

The ideas in the postscript represent a gathering together of wisdom suggested by various women after reading this book in manuscript form. The postscript offers suggestions for congratulating ourselves as women for facing society's constructions of gender in our lives and doing something about them—suggestions for learning, unlearning, and relearning.

Celebrate Your Learning and Our Learning

We are constantly learning, whether or not our learning gets written about. We are involved in day-to-day maintenance, community service, environmental issues, relationships with family, with co-workers, and so forth. Know that this is happening. Give yourself credit for your learning. Talk about it to your friends. Let girl and boy children hear about your various learnings.

Figure out your own learning, that is, your learning that is most in sync with you. This isn't necessarily a sit-down, time-consuming thing; its about being conscious of learning as you go about the everyday activities of life. It's about feeling what fits *and* what is (or has become) perceived duty. I have a friend for whom reading is an unpleasant task, and yet she is a reader. I often see her on her porch with a book. One day I finally asked her directly, "Why do you read so often when you dislike it so much?" Her response was that ever since grade school she had believed that she could not be an educated person if she did not read, and so she continued to make herself read! But the way she really loves to learn is by listening to people's passionate talk and watching movies.

Don't allow your learning to be defined only as formal learning, when most of our learning takes place in our everyday lives. As Elisabeth Hayes notes in Chapter Two, our learning takes place through information that we gain about ourselves, as well as in our homes and families, in our leisure activities, in our communities, through our volunteering, and in the settings that are specific to our racial, cultural, ethnic, and social groups. Insist that all your learning be recognized by yourself as well as by others.

Be okay with wherever you are in learning. We all come into the spirals of learning at our own particular points of entry, with our own histories, cultures, and values. Gloria Steinem refers to our stories as "mini-novels," self-contained but with learnings for everyone. Listen to the stories in Chapter Six, by Ann Brooks, about transformative learning and hear how very different women are, one from the other.

Learn wherever you learn. As I started my work on this book, my friend Ann said, "Don't forget the importance of counseling for our learning—and unlearning and relearning—as women." Lots of women learn in counseling—individual and group counseling, or sometimes in the kind of counseling that takes place over the back fence or a cup of coffee, or through the counseling available in books, tapes, talks, and so on. And some women don't learn in these ways but instead learn from the everyday surviving of life—from children, from pets, from mothers and grandmothers, from neighbors, from midwives.

Find places where you can learn in the way that you actually do learn. Don't allow your learning to be determined by social structures like schools, universities, or even churches. We can learn what we please, how we please. If a university insists on a certain mode of teaching—say, lecturing—and your learning style is collaborative, then go elsewhere, or lobby to change the university's forms of teaching, and write very specific comments on the professor's evaluation sheet, and then, if things do not change, and if you must continue in that class or school, find ways to learn with others of like preferences.

Define Yourself

Name the aspects of gender that influence your learning and knowing. Don't ignore those structures of your life that are determined by societal definitions of gender. Think of your learning, of women's learning. We women learn constantly, but this learning is devalued. Many women learn how to work in low-end jobs and how to provide for themselves and their children. That is some learning! Could we all do that? Could we pay the rent, put food on the table, see that the children are cared for on a wage of five dollars an hour, two hundred dollars a week, before taxes? And what about waitresses, who get two dollars and change per hour plus tips? Isn't making it under those conditions learning? Yet society often sees this kind of learning as dumb, and these women learners as failures. Or what about the learning that older women do to maintain themselves—to struggle with such physical aspects of aging as hair loss, wrinkles, difficulties in walking, and so forth, while still meeting society's expectations that age won't show and thus walking without the aid of a cane or a walker. That, too, is some learning! What about moms who figure out which cough syrup best fits the symptoms, and which diapers are the best deal for the money? Isn't that some learning? If we as women do not recognize and tout other women's learning, who will?

Think also about how you learn. Let's remove phrasing from our own language when it puts women's learning down—for example, the phrase (and I have used it myself) *touchy-feely*. I have come to see that this phrase can denigrate women's learning and make it less serious. When this phrase is used, it's a code phrase for what is intangible and iffy, for that "feelings stuff"—none of which, in this culture, is worthy of much attention, and all of which are denigrated by association with femaleness.

Promote other women's learning—for example, intuitive learning. This is another kind of learning, primarily but not exclusively a women's learning, that society devalues. Many women, too, have bought into dismissing women's intuition, but how much is lost to us in society when numbers of women do not use their intuition?

Break the silences that have formed some of your ways of knowing—the silences about racism, sexism, ageism; the silences about sexual harassment and sexual discrimination, about dominance and abuse of power at home, at work, at school. No more secrets! As Elisabeth Hayes notes in Chapter Four, how difficult it can be to "give voice," to name previously unarticulated experiences! Beginning may be difficult, but just as we have learned to keep silent, we can also learn to express ourselves. The beginnings don't have to be public; they can be in your own journal or diary, through a piece of art or a song. Then, gradually, you can move to tell a trusted friend or drop a hint to someone who might listen. In time, we women want to roar (I'm not there yet)—together, we hope—about the devaluing of our lives, knowing, and learning.

Work on understanding your own racism and how it affects your knowing and learning. Those of us who are White women must understand whiteness and how it shapes our knowing.

Work for social change with respect to gender prescriptions. Don't allow girls to continue to be defined by societal prescriptions and to subsume themselves in the process.

Unlearn, Learn, Relearn

Unlearn your gendered self. As Chapter Three clearly shows, many of us have to unlearn the gendered selves, and the low value we place on ourselves, that we've acquired over time. We have to work at putting the forces that have told us how to think and act in certain ways in their proper places. I don't mean for this to sound easy. I know I've worked for over ten years now in one particular life setting and still have trouble valuing myself there, according to my own criteria.

Survive.

Get up and face each day.

Examine history—family and community stories—for examples of women's lives in the past, and examine the present for new ways of thinking about your life.

Learn from women of other cultures and classes. Listen to women you know. Find women in their own neighborhoods, their own places of worship, their own health clinics. Talk to them. Share stories.

Express yourself. Explore your own creative potential.

Wail.

Draw on walls.

Write—graffiti-journals, poems, letters, short stories—any creative original work.

Draw, paint, sculpt, weave, braid, sew, tat, quilt, make cabinets, darn socks.

Read about other women's learning. Read Maya Angelou's *I Know Why the Caged Bird Sings*, Gloria Anzaldúa's *Borderlands/La Frontera*, Mary Catherine Bateson's *Peripheral Visions: Learning Along the Way*, Pearl Cleage's *Mad at Miles: A Blackwoman's Guide to Truth*, Gloria Steinem's *Revolution from Within: A Book of Self-Esteem*.

Journey into learning. Take along three sister travelers from Native American folklore as your guides. The Old Spider Woman is the Great Mother, creator, weaver, tender of the fires of life, teacher of culture. "She is the eldest God, the one who remembers and re-members" (Allen, 1989, p. 2). She weaves us together. She gives to her daughters a covering of creative wisdom attached by a thin thread to her web. The Seeker Woman is a guide for women on a journey into the unknown, into the darkness, into places where we don't want to go. Her gifts are consciousness and enlightenment, insights and intuition, and unmasking, which reveals inner truth. The Woman of Knowledge is a guide for turning things upside down on our learning journeys, for looking and listening and feeling and thinking with different eyes. Her gifts are openness, willingness to question, change, and creativity.

References

Adams, S. "Women Returners and Fractured Identities." In N. Charles and F. Hughes-Freeland (eds.), *Practicing Feminism: Identity, Difference, and Power*. London: Routledge, 1996.

Allen, P. G. (ed.) *Spider Woman's Granddaughters*. New York: Fawcett, 1989.

American Association of University Women. *The AAUW Report: How Schools Shortchange Girls*. Washington, D.C.: AAUW Educational Foundation, 1992.

Anderson, D. A., and Hayes, C. L. *Gender, Identity, and Self-Esteem*. New York: Springer, 1996.

Angelou, M. *I Know Why the Caged Bird Sings*. New York: Bantam, 1997.

Anzaldúa, G. *Borderlands/La Frontera: The New Mestiza*. San Francisco: Aunt Lute Books, 1987.

Arseneau, R., and Rodenburg, D. "The Developmental Perspective: Cultivating Ways of Thinking." In D. D. Pratt and Associates, *Five Perspectives on Teaching in Adult and Higher Education*. Malabar, Fla.: Krieger, 1998.

Association of American Colleges. *Association of American Colleges' Project Reports on the Status and Education of Women*. Washington, D.C.: Association of American Colleges, 1989.

Baber, K. M., and Allen, K. R. *Women and Families: Feminist Reconstructions*. New York: Guilford Press, 1992.

Baird, I. C. "Learning to Earn 'the Right Way': Single Welfare Mothers in Mandated Education Programs." Unpublished doctoral dissertation, Pennsylvania State University, 1994.

Bardwell, J. R., Cochran, S. W., and Walker, S. "Relationship of Parental Education, Race and Gender to Sex-Role Stereotyping in Five-Year-Old Kindergartners." *Sex Roles*, 1986, *15*, 275–281.

Baruch, G., Barnett, R., and Rivers, C. *Lifeprints: New Patterns of Love and Work for Today's Women*. New York: McGraw-Hill, 1983.

Bateson, M. C. *Composing a Life*. New York: Plume, 1990.

Bateson, M. C. *Peripheral Visions: Learning Along the Way*. New York: Harper-Collins, 1994.

Beal, C. R. *Boys and Girls: The Development of Gender Roles*. New York: McGraw-Hill, 1994.

Beausoleil, M. "Women Found Less Confident About Their Ability to Succeed." *Patriot News*, Oct. 26, 1997, p. C3.

Belenky, M. F., Bond, L. A., and Weinstock, J. S. *A Tradition That Has No Name: Nurturing the Development of People, Families, and Communities*. New York: Basic Books, 1997.

Belenky, M. F., Clinchy, B. M., Goldberger, N. R., and Tarule, J. M. *Women's Ways of Knowing: The Development of Self, Voice, and Mind*. New York: Basic Books, 1986.

Berner, B. H. "Efficiency of Information Processing as a Function of Cognitive Style and Language Dominance." Unpublished doctoral dissertation, Boston University, 1994.

Bierema, L. "How Executive Women Learn Organizational Culture." *Human Resource Development Quarterly*, 1995, *7*(2), 145–164.

Bierema, L. "A Model of Executive Women's Learning and Development." *Adult Education Quarterly*, 1999, *49*(2), 107–121.

Bing, V., and Reid, P. T. "Unknown Women and Unknowing Research: Consequences of Color and Class in Feminist Psychology." In N. R. Goldberger, J. M. Tarule, B. M. Clinchy, and M. F. Belenky (eds.), *Knowledge, Difference, and Power: Essays Inspired by Women's Ways of Knowing*. New York: Basic Books, 1996.

Bingham, M. B. "Appalachian Women Learning in Community." Unpublished doctoral dissertation, University of Tennessee, 1995.

Black, E. "Brave New World? Aspects of Office Skills Training in a College of Further Education." *Gender and Education*, 1989, *1*(2), 127–137.

Boldt, A. "The Transmission Perspective: Effective Delivery of Content." In D. D. Pratt and Associates, *Five Perspectives on Teaching in Adult and Higher Education*. Malabar, Fla.: Krieger, 1998.

Boston Women's Health Book Collective. *The New Our Bodies, Ourselves*. New York: Simon & Schuster, 1984.

Boyd, R. D., and Myers, J. G. "Transformative Education." *International Journal of Lifelong Education*, 1988, *7*(4), 261–284.

Brooks, A., and Edwards, K. "Narratives of Women's Sexual Identity Development: A Collaborative Inquiry with Implications for Rewriting Transformative Learning Theory." In R. Nolan and H. Chelesvig (eds.), *Proceedings of the 38th Annual Adult Education Research Conference.* Stillwater: Oklahoma State University, 1997.

Brown, C. E. "An Exploration of the Relationship Between Women's Orientation Towards Learning, Perceptions of Self-Efficacy, and Patterns of Involvement in the Context of Childbearing and Childbirth." Unpublished doctoral dissertation, Pennsylvania State University, 1994.

Brown-Collins, A. R., and Sussewell, D. R. "The African-American Woman's Emerging Selves." Journal of Black Psychology, 1986, *13*, 1–11.

Bruner, J. *Actual Minds, Possible Worlds.* Cambridge, Mass.: Harvard University Press, 1985.

Bruner, E. "Ethnography as Narrative." In V. W. Turner and E. M. Bruner (eds.), *The Anthropology of Experience.* Chicago: University of Illinois Press, 1986.

Caffarella, R. "What Women Have Taught Us About Teaching Adults." *Journal of Staff Development,* 1996, *17*(4), 40–45.

Caffarella, R .S., and Olson, S. K. "Psychosocial Development of Women: A Critical Review of the Literature." *Adult Education Quarterly,* 1993, *43*(3), 125–151.

Cain, M. "Adult Learning in Two Social Movement Organizations: The Role of Gender, Class, and Power." Unpublished doctoral dissertation, University of Wisconsin, 1998.

Candy, P. C. *Self-Direction for Lifelong Learning.* San Francisco: Jossey-Bass, 1991.

Castellano, O. "Canto, locura y poesía." In M. Anderson and P. H. Collins (eds.), *Race, Class, and Gender: An Anthology.* Belmont, Calif.: Wadsworth, 1992.

Charmaz, K. "Struggling for a Self: Identity Levels of the Chronically Ill." In J. Roth and P. Conrad (eds.), *Research in the Sociology of Health Care.* Vol 6: *The Experience and Management of Chronic Illness.* Greenwich, Conn.: JAI Press, 1987.

Chicago, J. *Through the Flower: My Struggle as a Woman Artist.* New York: Penguin, 1974.

Chodorow, N. "Family Structure and Feminine Personality." In M. Z. Rosaldo and L. Lamphere (eds.), *Women, Culture and Society.* Stanford, Calif.: Stanford University Press, 1974.

Clark, C. "Transformational Learning." In S. Merriam (ed.), *An Update on Adult Learning Theory.* New Directions for Adult and Continuing Education, no. 57. San Francisco: Jossey-Bass, 1993.

Clason-Hook, C. "Study Circles: Promoting Caring Learning Environments for Latina Women." Unpublished doctoral dissertation, University of Massachusetts, 1992.

Cleage, P. *Mad at Miles: A Blackwoman's Guide to Truth*. Southfield, Mich: Cleage Group, 1991.

Clinchy, B. M. "Connected and Separate Knowing: Toward a Marriage of Two Minds." In N. R. Goldberger, J. M. Tarule, B. M. Clinchy, and M. F. Belenky (eds.), *Knowledge, Difference, and Power: Essays Inspired by Women's Ways of Knowing*. New York: Basic Books, 1996.

Cohen, R. A. "Conceptual Styles, Culture, Conflict, and Nonverbal Tests of Intelligence." *American Anthropologist*, 1969, *71*, 828–856.

Collins, P. H. *Black Feminist Thought: Knowledge, Consciousness, and the Politics of Empowerment*. New York: Routledge, 1990.

Commeyras, M. "How Interested Are Literacy Educators in Gender Issues? Survey Results from the United States." *Journal of Adolescent and Adult Literacy*, 1999, *42*(5), 352–362.

Congo, M. G. "The Truth Will Set You Free, but First It Will Make You Crazy." In E. D. Gray (ed.), *Sacred Dimensions of Women's Experience*. Wellesley, Mass.: Roundtable Press, 1988.

Crawford, M. *Talking Difference: On Gender and Language*. Thousand Oaks, Calif.: Sage, 1995.

Crawford, M., and MacLeod, M. "Gender in the College Classroom: An Assessment of the 'Chilly Climate' for Women." *Sex Roles*, 1990, *23*, 101–122.

Cunningham, P. M. "The Adult Educator and Social Responsibility." In R. G. Brockett (ed.), *Ethical Issues in Adult Education*. New York: Teachers College Press, 1988.

Debold, E. "Knowing Bodies: Gender Identity, Cognitive Development and Embodiment in Early Adolescence." Unpublished doctoral dissertation, Harvard University, 1996.

Debold, E., and Brown, L. "Losing the Body of Knowledge: Conflicts Between Passion and Reason in the Intellectual Development of Adolescent Girls." In C. Gilligan, L. Brown, A. Rogers, and E. Debold (eds.), *A Selection of Working Papers Through 1991*. Cambridge, Mass.: Graduate School of Education, Harvard University, 1991.

Debold, E., Tolman, D., and Brown, L. M. "Embodied Knowledge, Knowing Desire: Authority and Split Subjectivities in Girls' Epistemological Development." In N. R. Goldberger, J. M. Tarule, B. M. Clinchy, and M. F. Belenky (eds.), *Knowledge, Difference, and Power: Essays Inspired by Women's Ways of Knowing*. New York: Basic Books, 1996.

Delany, J. "African American Women in a Predominantly Caucasian Female Profession: Learning Paths to Positions of Prominence." Unpublished document, 1999.

de Lauretis, T. *Alice Doesn't: Feminism, Semiotics, Cinema.* Bloomington: Indiana University Press, 1984.

Deloria, V. *Custer Died for Your Sins: An Indian Manifesto.* New York: Macmillan, 1969.

Delpit, L. *Other People's Children: Cultural Conflict in the Classroom.* New York: New Press, 1995.

Deyhle, D., and Margonis, F. "Navajo Mothers and Daughters: Schools, Jobs, and the Family." *Anthropology and Education Quarterly,* 1995, 26(2), 135–167.

Donovan, J. *Feminist Theory: The Intellectual Traditions of American Feminism.* New York: Ungar, 1987.

Edmondson Bell, E.L.J., and Nkomo, S. M. "Armoring: Learning to Withstand Racial Oppression." *Journal of Comparative Family Studies,* 1998, 29(2), 285–295.

Edwards, B. *Drawing on the Right Side of the Brain.* Los Angeles: Tarcher, 1989.

Edwards, R. *Mature Women Students: Separating or Connecting Family and Education.* London: Taylor and Francis, 1993.

Eichler, M. *Non-Sexist Research Methods: A Practical Guide.* Boston: Allen & Unwin, 1988.

Eisenberg, S. *We'll Call You If We Need You: Experiences of Women Working Construction.* Ithaca, N.Y.: ILR Press, 1998.

Elias, D. G. "Educating Leaders for Social Transformation." Unpublished doctoral dissertation, Columbia University, 1991.

Ellsworth, E. "Why Doesn't This Feel Empowering? Working Through the Repressive Myths of Critical Pedagogy." *Harvard Educational Review,* 1989, 59(3), 297–323.

Emmanuel, D. "A Developmental Model of Girls and Women." *Progress: Family Systems Research and Therapy,* 1992, 1, 25–39.

Erikson, E. *Identity, Youth and Crisis.* New York: Norton, 1968.

Fassinger, P. A. "Understanding Classroom Interaction: Students' and Professors' Contributions to Students' Silence." *Journal of Higher Education,* 1995, 66(1), 82–96.

Flannery, D. D. "Global and Analytical Ways of Processing Information." In D. D. Flannery (ed.), *Applying Cognitive Learning Theory to Adult Learning.* New Directions for Adult and Continuing Education, no. 59. San Francisco: Jossey-Bass, 1993.

Flannery, D. D. "Changing Dominant Understandings of Adults as Learners." In E. Hayes and S.A.J. Colin (eds.), *Confronting Racism and Sexism*. New Directions for Adult and Continuing Education, no. 61. San Francisco: Jossey-Bass, 1994.

Flannery, D. D. "Adult Education and the Politics of the Theoretical Text." In B. Kanpol and P. McLaren (eds.), *Critical Multiculturalism: Uncommon Voices in a Common Struggle*. Wilton, Conn.: Bergin & Garvey, 1995.

Flannery, D. D., and Hayes, E. "Women's Learning: A Kaleidoscope." In H. Reno and M. Witte (eds.), *Proceedings of the 37th Annual Adult Education Research Conference*. Tampa: University of South Florida, 1996.

Flax, J. "Postmodernism and Gender Relations in Feminist Theory." *Signs*, 1987, *14*, 621–643.

Foucault, M. *Power/Knowledge: Selected Interviews and Other Writings*. New York: Pantheon, 1980.

Freire, P. *Pedagogy of the Oppressed*. New York: Herder and Herder, 1971.

Freire, P. *Cultural Action for Freedom*. Harmondsworth, Engl.: Penguin, 1972.

Freysinger, V., and Flannery, D. D. "Women's Leisure: Affiliation, Self-Determination, Empowerment and Resistance." *Society and Leisure*, 1992, *15*(1), 303–322.

Furst, T. "Going Back to School: Women's Reentry Student Experiences." Unpublished doctoral dissertation, Cornell University, 1991; abstract in *Dissertation Abstracts International* 54 (1994): 1389A.

Gal, S. "Between Speech and Silence: The Problematics of Research on Language and Gender." In M. di Leonardo (ed.), *Gender at the Crossroads of Knowledge: Feminist Anthropology in the Postmodern Era*. Berkeley: University of California Press, 1991.

Gallos, J. V. "Women's Experiences and Ways of Knowing: Implications for Teaching and Learning in the Organizational Behavior Classroom." *Journal of Management Education*, 1993, *17*(1) 7–26.

Gardner, S., Dean, C., and McKaig, D. "Responding to Differences in the Classroom: The Politics of Knowledge, Class, and Sexuality." *Sociology of Education*, 1989, *62*, 64–74.

Gilligan, C. *In a Different Voice: Psychological Theory and Women's Development*. Cambridge, Mass.: Harvard University Press, 1982.

Goldberger, N. R. "Cultural Imperatives and Diversity in Ways of Knowing." In N. R. Goldberger, J. M. Tarule, B. M. Clinchy, and M. F. Belenky (eds.), *Knowledge, Difference, and Power: Essays Inspired by Women's Ways of Knowing*. New York: Basic Books, 1996.

Goldberger, N. R., Tarule, J. M., Clinchy, B. M., and Belenky, M. F. (eds.). *Knowledge, Difference, and Power: Essays Inspired by Women's Ways of Knowing.* New York: Basic Books, 1996.

Gorback, K. F. "Going Back: A Study of Women Re-entering Adult Education Through Greater Avenues for Independence." Unpublished doctoral dissertation, University of California, 1992.

Gore, J. *The Struggle for Pedagogies.* New York: Routledge, 1993.

Gowen, S. G. "Beliefs About Literacy: Measuring Women into Silence/Hearing Women into Speech." *Discourse and Society,* 1991, *2*(4), 439–450.

Gowen, S. G., and Bartlett, C. "'Friends in the Kitchen': Lessons from Survivors." In G. Hull (ed.), *Changing Work, Changing Workers: Critical Perspectives on Language, Literacy, and Skills.* Albany: State University of New York Press, 1997.

Greaves, G. "Older Widowed Women: Their Reflections on Learning to Make Decisions." Unpublished doctoral dissertation, University of Toronto, 1992.

Grodin, D. "Women Reading Self-Help: Themes of Separation and Connection." *Women's Studies in Communication,* 1995, *18*(2), 123–134.

Group for Collaborative Inquiry. "A Model for Transformative Learning: Individual Development and Social Action." In R. Brockett and C. Kasworm (eds.), *Proceedings of the 35th Annual Adult Education Research Conference.* Knoxville: University of Tennessee, 1994.

Group for Collaborative Inquiry. "The Democratization of Knowledge." *Adult Education Quarterly,* 1993, *44*(1), 43–51.

Guinier, L., Fine, M. and Balin, J. "Becoming Gentlemen: Women's Experiences at One Ivy League Law School." *University of Pennsylvania Law Review,* 1994, *143*(1), 1–10.

Hall, R., and Sandler, B. *The Classroom Climate: A Chilly One for Women.* Washington, D.C.: Association of American Colleges Project on the Status of Women in Education, 1982.

Harding, S. (ed.). *Feminism and Methodology: Social Science Issues.* Bloomington: Indiana University Press and Open University Press, 1987.

Harding, S. *Whose Science? Whose Knowledge? Thinking from Women's Lives.* Ithaca, N.Y.: Cornell University Press, 1991.

Harding, S. "Gendered Ways of Knowing and the 'Epistemological Crisis' of the West." In N. R. Goldberger, J. M. Tarule, B. M. Clinchy, and M. F. Belenky (eds.), *Knowledge, Difference, and Power: Essays Inspired by Women's Ways of Knowing.* New York: Basic Books, 1996.

Hardy, V., Hodgson, V., and McConnell, D. "Computer Conferencing: A New Medium for Investigating Issues in Gender and Learning." *Higher Education*, 1994, *28*, 403–418.

Hare-Mustin, R. T. "The Problem of Gender in Family Therapy Theory." *Family Process*, 1987, *26*, 15–27.

Haring-Hidore, M., Freeman, S. C., Phelps, S., Spann, N. G., and Wooten, H. R., Jr. "Women Administrators' Ways of Knowing." *Education and Urban Society*, 1990, *22*(2), 170–181.

Hart, M. "Thematization of Power, the Search for Common Interests, and Self-Reflection: Towards a Comprehensive Concept of Emancipatory Education." *International Journal of Lifelong Education*, 1985, *4*(2), 119–134.

Hart, M. "Liberation Through Consciousness Raising." In J. Mezirow and Associates, *Fostering Critical Reflection in Adulthood*. San Francisco: Jossey-Bass, 1990.

Hayes, E. "Students' Perceptions of Women and Men as Learners in Higher Education." *Research in Higher Education*, 1992, *33*(3), 377–393.

Hayes, E., and Colin, S. (eds.). *Confronting Racism and Sexism*. New Directions for Adult and Continuing Education, no. 61. San Francisco: Jossey-Bass, 1994.

Hayes, E., and Flannery, D. D. "Adult Women's Learning in Higher Education: A Critical Review of Scholarship." *Initiatives*, 1995, *57*(1), 29–40.

Hayes, E., and Flannery, D. D. "Narratives of Adult Women's Learning in Higher Education: Insights from Graduate Research." *Initiatives*, 1997, *58*(2), 61–80.

Hayes, E., and Smith, L. "Women in Adult Education: An Analysis of Perspectives in Major Journals." *Adult Education Quarterly*, 1994, *44*, 201–221.

Heaney, T. "Learning to Control Democratically: Ethical Questions in Situated Adult Cognition." In P. Collette, B. Einsiedel, and S. Hobden (eds.), *Proceedings of the 36th Annual Adult Education Research Conference*. Edmonton: University of Alberta, 1995.

Heilbrun, C. *Writing a Woman's Life*. New York: Ballantine, 1989.

Hennessy, R., and Ingraham, C. (eds.). *Materialist Feminism: A Reader in Class, Difference, and Women's Lives*. New York: Routledge, 1997.

Hensley, B. H. "Women as Lifelong Learners." Paper presented at the annual meeting of the American Educational Research Association, New York, 1996.

Herrmann, N. The *Creative Brain*. Lake Lure, N.C.: Brain Books, 1990.

Hewitt, J. *Self and Society*. New York: Simon & Schuster, 1992.

Hochman, T. *Black and White Styles in Conflict*. Chicago: University of Chicago Press. 1981.

Hollis, K. L. "Autobiography and Reconstructing Subjectivity at the Bryn Mawr Summer School for Women Workers, 1921–1938." *Women's Studies Quarterly,* 1995, *1/2,* 71–100.

hooks, b. *Talking Back: Thinking Feminist, Thinking Black.* Boston: South End Press, 1989.

hooks, b. *Teaching to Transgress.* New York: Routledge, 1994.

Horgan, D. D. "A Cognitive Learning Perspective on Women Becoming Expert Managers." *Journal of Business and Psychology,* 1989, *3*(3), 299–313.

Horsman, J. *Something in My Mind Besides the Everyday: Women and Literacy.* Toronto: Women's Press, 1990.

Horwitz, D. S. "Class Pictures: An Album of Stories from Reentry Women in the Community College." Unpublished doctoral dissertation, Northern Illinois University, 1994; abstract in *Dissertation Abstracts International* 55/05 (1994): 1180A.

Hotchkiss, L., and Brown, H. "Sociological Perspectives on Work and Career Development." In D. Brown, L. Brooks, and Associates, *Career Development and Choice* (3rd ed.). San Francisco: Jossey-Bass, 1996.

Hoy, J. C. "Learning in the Workplace: A Study of the Settings and Resources for the Learning of Executive Women." Unpublished doctoral dissertation, Columbia University, 1989.

Hurtado, A. "Strategic Suspensions: Feminists of Color Theorize the Production of Knowledge." In N. R. Goldberger, J. M. Tarule, B. M. Clinchy, and M. F. Belenky (eds.), *Knowledge, Difference, and Power: Essays Inspired by Women's Ways of Knowing.* New York: Basic Books, 1996.

Hyde, J. "Gender Comparisons of Mathematics Attitudes and Affect: A Meta-analysis." *Psychology of Women Quarterly,* 1990, *14*(3), 299–324.

Jaggar, A. *Feminist Politics and Human Nature.* Totowa, N.J.: Rowman and Little-field, 1988.

Johnson, J., and Pratt, D. "The Apprenticeship Perspective: Modeling Ways of Being." In D. D. Pratt and Associates, *Five Perspectives on Teaching in Adult and Higher Education.* Malabar, Fla.: Krieger, 1998.

Johnson-Bailey, J. "Making a Way out of No Way: An Analysis of the Educational Narratives of Reentry Black Women with Emphasis on Issues of Race, Gender, Class, and Color." Unpublished doctoral dissertation, University of Georgia, 1994; abstract in *Dissertation Abstracts International* 55/09 (1995): 2681A.

Jordan, J. V., Kaplan, A. G., Miller, J. B., Stiver, I. P., and Surrey, J. L. *Women's Growth in Connection: Writings from the Stone Center.* New York: Guilford Press, 1991.

Josselson, R. *Finding Herself: Pathways to Identity Development in Women*. San Francisco: Jossey-Bass, 1987.

Josselson, R. *Revisiting Herself: The Story of Women's Identity from College to Midlife*. New York: Oxford University Press, 1996.

Kazemek, F. "Women and Adult Literacy: Considering the Other Half of the House." *Lifelong Learning*, 1988, *11*(4), 15, 23–24.

Keddie, N. "Adult Education: An Ideology of Individualism." In J. L. Thompson (ed.), *Adult Education for a Change*. London: Hutchinson, 1980, pp. 45–64.

Kelly, J. "A Study of Gender-Differential Linguistic Interaction in the Adult Classroom." *Gender and Education*, 1991, *3*(2), 137–143.

Kerr, P. A. "A Conceptualization of Learning, Teaching, and Research Experiences of Women Scientists and Its Implications for Science." Unpublished doctoral dissertation, Cornell University, 1988.

Kopka, T., and Korb, R. *Women: Education and Outcomes*. Washington, D.C.: National Center for Education Statistics, U.S. Department of Education, 1996.

Lakoff, G., and Johnson, M. *Metaphors We Live By*. Chicago: University of Chicago Press, 1980.

Lakoff, R. *Language and Woman's Place*. New York: HarperCollins, 1975.

Lamott, A. *Bird by Bird: Some Instructions on Writing and Life*. New York: Doubleday, 1994.

Lather, P. "Feminist Perspectives on Empowering Research Methodologies." *Women's Studies International Forum*, 1988, *11*, 569–581.

Lather, P. *Getting Smart*. New York: Routledge, 1991.

Levy, J. "*Psychological Implications of Bilateral Asymmetry*." In S. Diamond and G. Beaumont (eds.), Hemispheric Function in the Human Brain. New York: Halstead Press, 1974.

Lewis, D. K. "The Black Family: Socialization and Sex Roles." *Phylon*, 1975, *36*(3), 221–237.

Lindsey, L. *Gender Roles: A Sociological Perspective*. Englewood Cliffs, N.J.: Prentice Hall, 1997.

Lorde, A. *Sister Outsider*. Trumansburg, N.Y.: Crossing Press, 1984.

Loughlin, K. "A Call to Action: Women's Perceptions of the Learning Experiences That Influenced Consciousness-Raising: A Retrospective Study." Unpublished doctoral dissertation, Columbia University, 1990.

Louis, B. S. "The Relationship of Learning to the Significant Life Events of Marital Separation and Divorce." Unpublished doctoral dissertation, Rutgers University, 1985.

Luke, C. "Women in the Academy: The Politics of Speech and Silence." *British Journal of Sociology of Education*, 1994, 15(2), 211–230.

Luria, A. R. *The Working Brain: An Introduction to Neuropsychology*. New York: Basic Books, 1973.

Luttrell, W. "The Getting of Knowledge: A Study of Working-Class Women and Education." Unpublished doctoral dissertation, University of California, 1984.

Luttrell, W. "Working-Class Women's Ways of Knowing: Effects of Gender, Race, and Class." *Sociology of Education*, 1989, 62, 33–46.

Luttrell, W. *Schoolsmart and Motherwise: Working-Class Women's Identity and Schooling*. New York: Basic Books, 1997.

MacKerarcher, D., and McFarland, J. "Learning Working Knowledge: Implications for Training." *Women's éducation des femmes*, 1993/1994, 10(3/4), 54–58.

Magolda, M. B. *Knowing and Reasoning in College: Gender-Related Patterns in Students' Intellectual Development*. San Francisco: Jossey-Bass, 1991.

Maher, F., and Tetreault, M. *The Feminist Classroom*. New York: Basic Books, 1994.

Maher, F., and Tetreault, M. "*Women's Ways of Knowing* in Women's Studies, Feminist Pedagogies, and Feminist Theory." In N. R. Goldberger, J. M. Tarule, B. M. Clinchy, and M. F. Belenky (eds.), *Knowledge, Difference, and Power: Essays Inspired by Women's Ways of Knowing*. New York, Basic Books, 1996.

Maher, F., and Tetreault, M. "Learning in the Dark: How Assumptions of Whiteness Shape Classroom Knowledge." In C. A. Woyshner and H. G. Gelfond (eds.), *Minding Women: Reshaping the Educational Realm*. Review Series, no. 30. Cambridge, Mass.: Harvard Educational Review, 1998.

Marcia, J. "Development and Validation of Ego-Identity Status." *Journal of Personality and Social Psychology*, 1960, 3(5), 551–558.

Martínez Alemán, A. "Girlfriends Talking." *About Campus*, Jan.–Feb. 1998, pp. 4–8.

McCarn, S. R., and Fassinger, R. E. "Revisioning Sexual Minority Identity Formation: A New Model of Lesbian Identity and Its Implications for Counseling and Research." *The Counseling Psychologist*, 1996, 24(3), 508–534.

McHale, S. M., Bartko, W. T., Crouter, A. C., and Perry-Jenkins, M. "Children's Housework and Psychological Functioning: The Mediating Effects of Parents' Sex-Role Behaviors and Attitudes." *Child Development*, 1990, 61, 1413–1426.

McIntosh, P. "White Privilege: Unpacking the Invisible Knapsack." *Peace and Freedom*, July–Aug. 1988, pp. 10–12.

Melamed, L. "Play and Playfulness in Women's Learning and Development." Unpublished doctoral dissertation, University of Toronto, 1985.

Merriam, S., and Caffarella, R. *Learning in Adulthood* (2nd ed.). San Francisco: Jossey-Bass, 1999.

Messick and Associates. *Individuality in Learning: Implications of Cognitive Styles and Creativity for Human Development*. San Francisco: Jossey-Bass, 1976.

Mezirow, J. "Transformation Theory of Adult Learning." In M. Welton (ed.), *In Defense of the Life World*. Albany, N.Y.: State University of New York Press, 1995.

Middleton, S. "A Post-Modern Pedagogy for the Sociology of Women's Education." In M. Arnot and K. Weiler (eds.), *Feminism and Social Justice in Education: International Perspectives*. London: Falmer Press, 1993.

Miller, J. B. *Toward a New Psychology of Women*. Boston: Beacon Press, 1986.

Moon, J. V. "Singing for Our Lives: Creating Home Through Singing." Unpublished master's thesis, University of Toronto, 1993.

Moraga, C. "La Güera." In C. Moraga and G. Anzaldúa (eds.), *This Bridge Called My Back: Writing by Radical Women of Color*. New York: Kitchen Table Press, 1983.

Moraga, C., and Anzaldúa, G. (eds.). *This Bridge Called My Back: Writings by Radical Women of Color*. New York: Kitchen Table Press, 1983.

Morgan, M. *Mutant Message*. New York: HarperCollins, 1994.

Morrison, M. "Part-Time: Whose Time? Women's Lives and Adult Learning." In R. Edwards, A. Hanson, and P. Raggart (eds.), *Boundaries of Adult Learning*. New York: Routledge, 1996.

Musil, C. (ed.). *The Courage to Question: Women's Studies and Student Learning*. Washington, D.C.: Association of American Colleges and National Women's Studies Association, 1992.

Nesbit, T. "The Social Reform Perspective: Seeking a Better Society." In D. D. Pratt and Associates, *Five Perspectives on Teaching in Adult and Higher Education*. Malabar, Fla.: Krieger, 1998.

Nesdoly, C. S. "Native Women's Perception of an Adult Upgrading Program." Unpublished master's thesis, University of Alberta, 1993.

Noddings, N. *Caring: A Feminist Approach to Ethics and Moral Education*. Berkeley: University of California Press, 1984.

Orenstein, P. *School Girls: Young Women, Self-Esteem and the Confidence Gap*. New York: Doubleday, 1994.

Polkinghorne, D. *Narrative Knowing and the Human Sciences*. Albany: State University of New York Press, 1988.

Polkinghorne, D. "Narrative Configuration in Qualitative Analysis." In J. A. Hatch and R. Wisniewski (eds.), *Life History and Narrative*. London: Falmer Press, 1995.

Pope, S. M. *Wanting to Be Something More: Transformations in Ethnically Diverse Working-Class Women Through the Process of Education*. Santa Barbara, Calif.: Fielding Institute, 1996.

Pratt, D. D. "Analytical Tools: Epistemic, Normative, and Procedural Beliefs." In D. D. Pratt and Associates, *Five Perspectives on Teaching in Adult and Higher Education*. Malabar, Fla.: Krieger, 1998a.

Pratt, D. D. "Analyzing Perspectives: Identifying Commitments and Belief Structures." In D. D. Pratt and Associates, *Five Perspectives on Teaching in Adult and Higher Education*. Malabar, Fla.: Krieger, 1998b.

Pratt, D. D. "Evaluating Teaching: Approaches That Are Equitable and Rigorous." In D. D. Pratt and Associates, *Five Perspectives on Teaching in Adult and Higher Education*. Malabar, Fla.: Krieger, 1998c.

Pratt, D. D., and Associates. *Five Perspectives on Teaching in Adult and Higher Education*. Malabar, Fla.: Krieger, 1998.

Purcell-Gates, V., Degener, S., and Jacobson, E. *U.S. Adult Literacy Program Practice: A Typology Across Dimensions of Life—Contextualized/Decontextualized and Dialogic/Monologic*. (NCSALL Report #2) Cambridge, Mass.: National Center for the Study of Adult Learning and Literacy, 1998.

Quigley, B. A., and Holsinger, E. "Happy Consciousness: Ideology and Hidden Curricula in Literacy Education." *Adult Education Quarterly*, 1993, *44*(1), 17–33.

Ravindran, S. "Nonformal Education Has Opened the Doors for Many Women to Increase Learning and Other Opportunities." *Knowing Women: Women and Educational Alternatives Worldwide*, 1989, *27*, pp. 7–12.

Razack, S. "Teaching Activists for Social Change: Coming to Grips with Questions of Subjectivity and Domination." *Canadian Journal for the Study of Adult Education*, 1993, *7*(2), 43–56.

Regan, H. B., and Brooks, G. H. *Out of Women's Experience: Creating Relational Leadership*. Thousand Oaks, Calif.: Corwin Press, 1995.

Reid, P. T. "Women of Color Have No Place." *Focus: Newsletter of the Psychological Study of Ethnic Minority Issues, Division 45 of the American Psychological Association*, 1995, *7*, 1–2.

Reinharz, S. *Feminist Methods in Social Research*. New York: Oxford University Press, 1992.

Reinharz, S. "Toward an Ethnography of Voice and Silence." In E. J. Trickett, R. J. Watts, and D. Birman (eds.), *Human Diversity: Perspectives on People in Context*. San Francisco: Jossey-Bass, 1994.

Resides, D. L. "The Thing Not Named: How Lesbians Experience Graduate School." Unpublished doctoral dissertation, Pennsylvania State University, 1997.

Reybold, L. "A Sociological Perspective of Knowing: A Grounded Theory of Epistemological Development of Malaysian Women." In R. Nolan and H. Chelesvig (ed.), *Proceedings of the 38th Annual Adult Education Research Conference*. Stillwater, Okla.: Oklahoma State University, 1997.

Rice, J. K., and Meyers, S. "Continuing Education for Women." In S. B. Merriam and P. M. Cunningham (eds.), *Handbook of Adult and Continuing Education*. San Francisco: Jossey-Bass, 1989.

Rich, A. *On Lies, Secrets, and Silence*. New York: Norton, 1979.

Rockhill, K. "Literacy as Threat/Desire: Longing to Be SOMEBODY." In J. Gaskell and A. McLaren (eds.), *Women and Education*. Calgary, Alberta, Canada: Detselig Enterprises, 1987.

Rogers, A. "Voice, Play, and Practice of Courage in Girls' and Women's Lives." *Harvard Educational Review*, 1993, 63(3), 265–295.

Rosser, S. V. *Female-Friendly Science: Applying Women's Studies Methods and Theories to Attract Students*. New York: Pergamon Press, 1990.

Rountree, J., and Lambert, J. "Participation in Higher Education Among Adult Women." *Community Junior College Quarterly*, 1992, 16, 85–94.

Ruddick, S. "Reason's 'Femininity': A Case for Connected Knowing." In N. R. Goldberger, J. M. Tarule, B. M. Clinchy, and M. F. Belenky (eds.), *Knowledge, Difference, and Power: Essays Inspired by Women's Ways of Knowing*. New York: Basic Books, 1996.

Ryff, C.D. "The Subjective Experience of Life-Span Transitions." In A. Rossi (ed.), *Gender and the Life Course*. Hawthorne, N.Y.: Aldine, 1985.

Sadker, M., Sadker, D., and Klein, S. "The Issue of Gender in Elementary and Secondary Schools." In G. Grant (ed.), *Review of Research in Education*, no. 17. Washington, D.C.: American Educational Research Association, 1991.

Safman, P. "Women from Special Populations: The Challenge of Reentry." In L. Lewis (ed.), *Addressing the Needs of Returning Women*. New Directions for Continuing Education, no. 39. San Francisco, Jossey-Bass, 1988.

Sagan, C. "Science of the Sexes." *Baltimore Sun*, Oct. 25, 1998, pp. C1, C6.

Saltonstall J. F. "Learning About Learning: A Study of Women's Ways of Learning and Being in a Formal Educational Environment." Unpublished doctoral dissertation, Harvard University, 1989; abstract in *Dissertation Abstracts International* 50/07 (1990): 1902A.

Schmitt-Boshnick, M. "Spaces for Democracy: Researching the Social Learning Process." In P. Collette, B. Einsiedel, and S. Hobden (eds.), *Proceedings of the 36th Annual Adult Education Research Conference*. Edmonton: University of Alberta, 1995.

Schroeder, D. and Mynatt, C. "Female Graduate Students' Perceptions of their Interactions with Male and Female Major Professors." *Journal of Higher Education*, 1993, 64(5), 555–573.

Schultz, L. M. *Awakening Intuition*. New York: Harmony Books, 1998.

Schweickart, P. "Speech Is Silver, Silence Is Golden: The Asymmetrical Intersubjectivity of Communication Action." In N. R. Goldberger, J. M. Tarule, B. M. Clinchy, and M. F. Belenky (eds.), *Knowledge, Difference, and Power: Essays Inspired by Women's Ways of Knowing*. New York: Basic Books, 1996.

Scott, K. Y. *The Habit of Surviving: Black Women's Strategies for Life*. New Brunswick, N.J.: Rutgers University Press, 1991.

Sleeter, C. *Multicultural Education as Social Action*. Albany: State University of New York Press, 1996.

Smith, D. *The Everyday World as Problematic*. Boston: Northeastern University Press, 1987.

Solsken, J. W. *Literacy, Gender, and Work in Families and in School*. Norwood, N.J.: Ablex, 1993.

Spence, D. *Narrative Truth and Historical Truth*. New York: Norton, 1984.

Spender, D. *Man Made Language*. New York: Routledge, 1980.

Stabile, C. A. "Feminism and the Ends of Postmodernism." In R. Hennessy and C. Ingraham (eds.), *Materialist Feminism: A Reader in Class, Difference, and Women's Lives*. New York: Routledge, 1997.

Stalker, J. "Athene in Academe: Women Mentoring Women in the Academy." *International Journal of Lifelong Education*, 1994, 13(5), 361–372.

Stalker, J. "Women and Adult Education: Rethinking Androcentric Research." *Adult Education Quarterly*, 1996, 46(2), 98–113.

Steinem, G. *Revolution from Within: A Book of Self-Esteem*. Boston: Little, Brown, 1993.

Steinhauer, J. "For Women in Medicine, a Road to Compromise, Not Perks." *New York Times*, March 1, 1999, pp. A1, A21.

Stern, D. N. *The Interpersonal World of the Infant*. New York: Basic Books, 1985.

Tannen, D. *Talking from 9 to 5*. New York: Avon, 1994.

Tarule, J. M. "Voices of Returning Women: Ways of Knowing." In. L. H. Lewis (ed.), *Addressing the Needs of Returning Women*. New Directions for Continuing Education, no. 39. San Francisco: Jossey-Bass, 1988.

Taylor, E. "Building Upon the Theoretical Debate: A Critical Review of the Empirical Studies of Mezirow's Transformative Learning Theory." *Adult Education Quarterly*, 1997, 48(1), 34–59.

Taylor, J. M., Gilligan, C., and Sullivan, A. M. *Between Voice and Silence: Women, Girls, Race and Relationship*. Cambridge, Mass.: Harvard University Press, 1995.

Thornborrow, N., and Sheldon, M. "Women in the Labor Force." In J. Freeman (ed.), *Women: A Feminist Perspective*. Mountain View, Calif.: Mayfield, 1995.

Tisdell, E. "Interlocking Systems of Power, Privilege, and Oppression in Adult Higher Education Classes." *Adult Education Quarterly*, 1993, 3(4), 203–226.

Tisdell, E. *Creating Inclusive Adult Learning Environments: Insights from Multicultural and Feminist Pedagogy*. Columbus, Ohio: ERIC Clearinghouse on Adult, Career, and Vocational Education, 1995.

Tisdell, E. J. "Using Life Experience to Teach Feminist Theory." In D. Boud and N. Miller (eds.), *Working with Experience: Animating Learning*. New York: Routledge, 1996.

Tisdell, E. "Poststructural Feminist Pedagogies: The Possibilities and Limitations of a Feminist Emancipatory Adult Learning Theory and Practice." *Adult Education Quarterly*, 1998, 48(3), 139–156.

T'Kenye, C. "The Nurturing Perspective: Facilitating Self-Efficacy." In D. D. Pratt and Associates, *Five Perspectives on Teaching in Adult and Higher Education*. Malabar, Fla.: Krieger, 1998.

Treichler, P. A. and Kramarae, C. "Women's Talk in the Ivory Tower." *Communication Quarterly*, 1983, 31(2), 118–132.

Turner, C. W. "Clinical Applications of the Stone Center Theoretical Approach to Minority Women." In J. Jordan (ed.), *Women's Growth in Diversity: More Writings from the Stone Center*. New York: Guilford Press, 1997.

Valenzuela, A. "Liberal Gender Role Attitudes and Academic Achievement Among Mexican-Origin Adolescents in Two Houston Inner-City Catholic Schools." *Hispanic Journal of Behavioral Sciences*, 1993, 15(3), 310–323.

Van Velsor, E., and Hughes, M. W. *Gender Differences in the Development of Managers: How Women Managers Learn from Experience*. Report no. 145. Greensboro, N.C.: Center for Creative Leadership, 1990.

Vila, P. "Narrative Identities: The Employment of the Mexican on the U.S.–Mexican Border." *Sociological Quarterly*, 1997, 38(1), 147–183.

Voices Group. "Weaving Our Quilts: The Silent Stories of Women in Academia." Presentation at the annual meeting of the American Educational Research Association, New York, 1996.

Walker, A. *In Search of Our Mothers' Gardens*. New York: Harcourt Brace Jovanovich, 1983.

Walters, S., and Manicom, L. (eds.). *Gender in Popular Education*. London: Zed Books, 1996.

Weiler, K. *Women Teaching for Change: Gender, Class and Power*. Wilton, Conn.: Bergin & Garvey, 1988.

Wells, S. J. "Learning and leadership of women entrepreneurs: An exploratory study." Unpublished doctoral dissertation, North Carolina State University, 1994.

White, M., and Epston, D. *Narrative Means to Therapeutic Ends*. New York: Norton, 1990.

Wingfield, L., and Haste, H. "Connectedness and Separateness: Cognitive Style or Moral Orientation?" *Journal of Moral Education*, 1987, 16(3), 123–139.

Wink, J. *Critical Pedagogy: Notes from the Real World*. White Plains, N.Y.: Longman, 1997.

Witherell, C., and Noddings, N. (eds.). *Stories Lives Tell: Narrative and Dialogue in Education*. New York: Teachers College Press, 1991.

Witkin, H. A., Moore, C. A., Goodenough, D. R., and Cox, P. "Field-Dependent and Field-Independent Cognitive Styles and Their Educational Implications." *Review of Educational Research*, 1977, 47, 1–64.

Zimmerman, M. K. "The Women's Health Movement: A Critique of Medical Enterprise and the Position of Women." In B. B. Hess and M. M. Ferree (eds.), *Analyzing Gender: A Handbook of Social Science Research*. Thousand Oaks, Calif.: Sage, 1987.

Index